641.5631
Updike
JUL 29 2010

D0172444

LACTOSE FREE AND AS ~~GOOD AS~~ THE ORIGINAL? EVEN BETTER!

LEMON SWIRL CHEESECAKE . . .

Rich, sinfully creamy sweetness contrasting with an exquisite taste of lemon, this beauty won a ribbon against "real" cheese-cakes at the Malibu Annual Pie Contest. The judges didn't know it was lactose free. Your guests won't either!

VEAL PARMIGIANA . . .

Spicy tomato sauce, tender veal, irresistible melted cheese—that's Italian! But this "parmigiana" is 100% lactose free, and so simple, you can create it in minutes!

CHICKEN À LA KING . . .

An old-fashioned favorite, this dish is wonderfully warming on a frosty day, but families love it anytime. And now no one has to say no to this truly elegant adaptation . . .

ALL-AMERICAN WHIPPED MASHED POTATOES . . .

Fluffy, white, buttery, these are genuine, from-scratch mashed, and absolutely the best you've ever tasted!

LACTOSE-FREE CRAB QUICHE . . .

A hint of Chablis, chunks of mouthwatering crab, and quiche so authentic-tasting, not even a chef would know it uses lactose-free substitutes. Serve this to the ladies who lunch . . . or to everybody!

THE LACTOSE-FREE COOKBOOK

Powell Branch Library Powell WY

THE LACTOSE-FREE COOKBOOK

SHERI UPDIKE

Powell Branch Library
217 East Third
Powell, Wyoming 82435

WARNER BOOKS

A Time Warner Company

If you purchase this book without a cover you should be aware that this book may have been stolen property and reported as "unsold and destroyed" to the publisher. In such case neither the author nor the publisher has received any payment for this "stripped book."

Copyright © 1998 by Sheri Updike
All rights reserved.

Warner Books, Inc., 1271 Avenue of the Americas, New York, NY 10020
Visit our Web site at http://warnerbooks.com

 A Time Warner Company

Printed in the United States of America

First Printing: September 1998

10 9 8 7 6 5 4 3 2

Library of Congress Cataloging-in-Publication Data

Updike, Sheri.
   The lactose-free cookbook / Sheri Updike.
      p. cm.
   Includes index.
   ISBN 0-446-67393-5
   1. Lactose intolerance—Diet therapy—Recipes. 2. Milk-free diet—
Recipes. I. Title.
   RC632.L33U94   1998
   616.3'998—dc21   97-51214
                                                CIP

Book design and composition by L&G McRee
Cover design by David Bamford
Cover photographs by Reed Kaestner/Zephyr Images

ATTENTION: SCHOOLS AND CORPORATIONS
WARNER books are available at quantity discounts with bulk purchase for educational, business, or sales promotional use. For information, please write to: SPECIAL SALES DEPARTMENT, WARNER BOOKS, 1271 AVENUE OF THE AMERICAS, NEW YORK, NY 10020

Dedication

Without the love and support of my family, I never could have realized my dream. For this, a simple thank you is just not enough. I believe in the family, and ours has always been very close, so I want to dedicate this book to my family.

To the love of my life, my husband Zip (and they said it wouldn't last!) . . . thirty years of love, through good and bad times, you are my best friend, my life. Without you this book would never have been written. Thank you for enduring those "taste-testing" sessions . . . never spitting anything out, and always tactfully explaining how it needed a little more work—with a smile!

To my beautiful daughter Christina, whose creativity and independence I greatly admire. You never stop reaching for your star, no matter how hard the stretch gets. Thank you for turning my own words around on me in our many discussions, and making me believe in myself. I am very proud of the woman you have become and the friends we have found in each other.

And finally, to my wonderful son, David, whose business sense and humor astound me. I am very proud of the man you have become. I thank you for the words of wisdom you share and the way you can always make me laugh, even when I don't feel like it. Also for having so-o-o many friends willing to taste-test, even when I didn't want them to.

Family is the foundation I have built my life on. Without the love and support of my husband, and our two precious gifts, Christina and David, my dream would never have become a reality. For this I am forever grateful.

Acknowledgments

Everyone should have a fairy godmother . . . mine is Amy Einhorn! With a whisk of her magical wand, she made my dream an exciting reality. For this I will be eternally grateful. Thank you, Amy, for having the faith in me I wasn't sure I had. You are a wonderful friend, aside from being the *best* editor!

To my "special friend" Sandy Hoevel, thank you for your never-ending words of wisdom and encouragement, for knowing me better than I know myself, and for the hours of laughter that we continue to find in ourselves. A friend like you is one in a million . . . and I'm glad you're mine.

In memory of my dad, Hugh Rawdon, who taught me that the impossible wasn't. His love lives in the faces of my children, and he'll always be in my heart.

And finally, to the two women in my life I couldn't have lived without: my mother-in-law, Elaine Updike, who taught me everything she knows about cooking with patience and love. You never laughed when I measured your dashes, pinches, and sprinkles; you gave me wonderful memories of frantic holiday baking late into the nights, laughing ourselves silly. And of course to my mom, Eileen Duffy, who raised me to believe in myself, to make a difference and be proud of who I am. Thank you, Mom, for encouraging my creativity, for teaching me the importance of family and for being there. I love you.

If this book helps one person, I know I've made a difference . . . one I couldn't have made without these people. Thank you all.

Contents

Introduction 1

About Lactose-Free Substitutes 7

The "Safe" List of Lactose-Free Substitutions 13

Off-the-Shelf "Safe" List 23

Quick Fixin' List 31

Author's Note 33

Appetizers 35

Soups 45

Breakfast 53

Breads 65

Side Dishes 89

Beef 117

Poultry 127

Pork 143

Seafood 147

Main-Dish Casseroles and Hearty Dishes 159

Pastas and Italian Dishes 171

Cakes 191
Cheesecakes 211
Pies 223
Pastries and Special Treats 233
Cookies 257
Candies 295
"Ice Cream" and Creamy Desserts 305
Special Drinks 325
Sauces and Frostings 333
Index 355
About the Author 369

THE
LACTOSE-
FREE
COOKBOOK

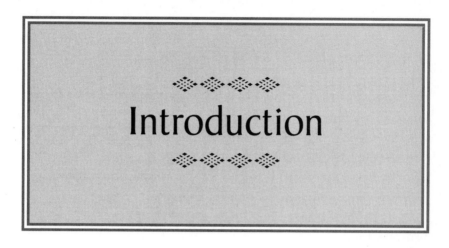

Introduction

Milk. How could it be *bad* for you? Didn't your mother drill it into your head to drink your milk? Television, magazines, billboards . . . everywhere you look, there are "white mustaches" reciting the virtues of milk. Milk and cookies are part of the American image. After all, how could you eat a cookie without . . . MILK?

Well, hold on to your cookies . . . approximately 80% of the world's population can *not* drink milk without experiencing some digestive problems. And some accounts state that one in five Americans have these problems. What those commercials and wonderful ad campaigns should say is, "Got Lactose Intolerance?" because that is the *norm*—those "white mustaches" aren't. You need to realize that you *do* have choices, and you *can* enjoy your favorite foods without experiencing the embarrassing discomfort and pain.

"What's the big deal? So I'll give up drinking milk," you may say. Unfortunately, it's not that easy. While lactose exists in foods that are easy to identify—like ice cream, cottage cheese, and margarine—it also exists in many foods you never dreamed of—like cold cuts, breads, and chips.

WHAT IS LACTOSE INTOLERANCE?

To be Lactose Intolerant is to lack the enzyme necessary to properly digest the lactose, or milk sugar, in a simple glass of milk. This enzyme is called the lactase enzyme, and it exists in the cells on the surface of the small intestine. Sufficient amounts of this enzyme change the lactose into two sugars: galactose and glucose. Then the lactose enzyme moves through your body, fueling your cells with energy. But if you lack sufficient levels of lactase to break down the lactose, then it remains in your small intestine for an extended period of time. Eventually it will be carried to your colon, where bacteria will cause it to ferment. This fermentation is what causes you to have diarrhea, cramping, bloating, excessive gas, stomach distension, etc. The degree of severity of these symptoms is as individual as people are. It all depends on the level of the lactase enzyme you possess. You can just experience mild discomfort or you can suffer severe diarrhea or pain. But one thing is very clear: for people who have Lactose Intolerance the problem is as traumatic as most diseases, because it changes your life.

Lactose Intolerance is a difficult problem to diagnose. The reason is its symptoms are very embarrassing, and the patient can find a million reasons to attribute his discomfort to—the "flu," a "virus going around," "stress" (these days when aren't people stressed!), and so forth—rather than seek a medical diagnosis for his or her excessive diarrhea, gas, or bloating.

There are tests that can be done by your physician to make sure that Lactose Intolerance is actually the problem. Doctors often tend to look in other areas for the cause of distress at first examination, but it's good to rule out other more critical problems first. If you know your body, keep track of what you're eating and its effects, then you'll be able to narrow it down yourself. Remember, everyone's level of tolerance is different . . . it's up to you to find yours. You may feel fine after eating fettuccine Alfredo but double over with stomach cramps after a scoop of ice cream.

Sounds pretty ominous, huh? Well, it doesn't have to be. That's what I want you to understand. Being Lactose Intolerant is *normal,* not abnormal. Simply explained, the lactase enzyme is meant to diminish naturally through our aging process. At birth, the lactase level is high because mother's milk contains twice the lactose that cow's milk has. As we grow, the need for this enzyme is reduced or completely eliminated. We were never meant to continue consuming milk or dairy products! But throughout history, cultures have created "dairy societies," finding new ways to use milk and milk by-products. Which brings us to today . . . where we have been raised to believe that milk is good for you, the healthy American way. The truth is, there are millions of people who are Lactose Intolerant.

Okay, so where does all this leave you, if you are Lactose Intolerant? The easy answer and the most obvious one is, "Just give it up." Yes, that works, if you think just giving up a glass of milk will do it. But it won't. You won't believe the list of foods lactose is included in. While lactose is found in ice cream, butter, and cheeses, did you know it's also in dairy-free foods prepared in restaurants when you dine out, and in prescription and over-the-counter medicines? Lactose is a great filler and anticaking agent used by many manufacturers in many items. Check birth control pills . . . it's in those, too, and in simple things such as seasonings: Lawry's Salt, Accent, Bon Appetit Seasoned Salt! If a product contains monosodium glutamate (MSG), it also contains lactose because lactose is a filler used in MSG. And the list goes on. If you keep eliminating foods from your diet that contain lactose, pretty soon you'll feel as if there aren't any choices left! Life gets very boring. Mealtime becomes "meaningless" time. There's little enjoyment or anticipation left in *any* meal.

So far I have given you nothing but bad news. And I'll bet you're asking yourself, "Who is this 'Grim Reaper,' and what makes her an expert?" Well, my "official title" is not "Grim Reaper," or physician, dietitian, nutritionist, or even chef. I am a wife of over twenty-eight years, and a working mother of two great kids. I love to cook . . . it's my passion. For over ten years, my husband has been affected by Lactose Intolerance, severely. His solution to this problem was the obvious—"just give it up." For a person who was raised on good, wholesome farm cooking, eating was an event, not a necessity! Discovering he was Lactose Intolerant turned my husband's world upside down. He began cutting out milk, then butter, cream, cakes, cookies, and so on. My journeys to the grocery store became "pilgrimages," because I was reading every label that went into my cart. Two hours later, I'd arrive home, excited about a new addition to his limited list. For our growing family, dinnertime and Sunday brunch were very big. Slowly, my husband began losing interest in these meals because it meant watching us enjoy his favorite dishes while he had to abstain. Sometimes the temptation was too much, and he'd have a slice of my famous cheesecake, but then the suffering I watched him endure afterward was too much for me. I wouldn't accept the fact that he *couldn't* have his favorites, let alone so many everyday staples. So, over ten years ago, I embarked on my mission to adjust my recipes, to search for store foods without lactose, and to show my husband that his love for food was *not* over! He has choices, and so do you. No, I'm definitely not an expert. What I am is a wife who loves her husband and has expanded his food horizon so much that I want to share it with everyone who desperately wants a "choice" of good, real food that happens to be lactose free. I don't have all the answers, but I do have a few good ones.

If you have searched the bookstores or specialty cookstores, you know there isn't a "lactose-free cookbook." For over ten years, I've been looking for one. Even though Lactose Intolerance is so prominent, no one has yet written a book to help the millions of people who deal with this problem. But this book isn't a restricted dietary format just for those who are

Lactose Intolerant. It contains "real food" recipes that you can make and serve to everyone without them ever knowing they are lactose free! No one will feel deprived, I assure you! And for the person who is Lactose Intolerant, the feeling of being different won't be there, since they'll be reaching for the same serving dishes as everyone else.

I wish I could tell you that all the lactose recipes I tried to duplicate were a smashing success. But the man who ate my mistakes wouldn't be so generous. He wouldn't let the opportunity go by to tell you about my first attempts to make "real" ice cream. I had read that you could substitute margarine and lactose-free milk for cream. . . . Don't try it. As I was anxiously waiting for my husband's remarks after his first, *big* bite . . . the expression on his face was priceless, and he couldn't answer me because he had greasy slime coating his lips! But I continued to experiment and I scoured the stores for the right substitutions. In the end, he did forgive me because now he enjoys **real vanilla ice cream**. And so can you!

In these pages you'll find recipes that even the most inexperienced cook can prepare with confidence and pride. But more important, these pages contain *choices*, something you haven't had a lot of lately. You will also find the practical experience *without* the mistakes as you benefit from my husband's courageous assessments! The recipes have been tested. My panel was composed of unsuspecting "victims" (my children, their friends, our friends). And the raves were unanimous! No one knew they were eating lactose-free foods. That is the real test. In fact, I entered the annual Malibu Pie Festival (it's an annual event for me, too) in October 1996, and won third place for a lemon cheesecake, third place for a peach melba cobbler pie, and second place for a chocolate raspberry tart—all lactose free . . . all *unknown* to the judges! I have cooked on holidays for my husband's business associates, sometimes for as many as a hundred people. Everything was homemade, taking me three days of constant cooking to prepare three picnic tables full of food—

all lactose free. And year after year, all those people have looked forward to these barbecues, raving about the food.

My book isn't a complete "know-it-all" book about Lactose Intolerance. All it does is take traditional recipes and make them lactose free. The information that I'm passing on to you is what I have learned over ten years. For Christmas a friend gave me *Milk Is Not for Every Body,* by Steve Carper. This wonderful book covers all the technical, everyday questions as well as giving clear explanations. I highly recommend this book for a more comprehensive, easy-to-read understanding of Lactose Intolerance.

For our twenty-fifth wedding anniversary, my husband and I went on a little cruise. One day at lunch, we were seated with two elderly ladies and I noticed one of them had very little on her plate. I commented that she ate like a bird, and she told me she had a dairy problem . . . Lactose Intolerance. Well, two hours later we finished our conversation and I had filled her head with all of the choices that she had. From that day on, whenever I passed her table, her plate was full and there was a big smile on her face! The joy that this brought me was incredible. That's why I want to share my searching and experimenting, my knowledge, trials, and tribulations with all the millions of people who are affected by lactose, because I care about you and the look in that little old lady's eyes could be in *yours*.

About Lactose-Free Substitutes . . .

I guess you could say this list of lactose-free substitutes is a "winning lottery ticket" for the Lactose Intolerant. This list gives you choices and lets you have just about all the food you love back in your life. When I was frantically scouring the bookstores and libraries for something that would help me cook lactose free, the tidbits of information I found were not rewarding. A common substitute for milk in a recipe is water . . . or juice. Common sense tells you this will change the taste and texture of the dish. After having to serve my husband "gray" mashed potatoes, using a manufactured store-brand substitution, I decided there must be something better out there! No one should have to be limited to such things.

My search is ongoing. Yours should be, too. Never stop looking for new products. Thanks to the little bit of awareness that the food industries are developing, more manufacturers are presenting better-quality lactose-free alternatives. Try them; some will work or taste better than others . . . find your favorites. The best places to seek out specialty items (as these are sometimes categorized) are health food stores, the more exclusive food store chains, and even bulk suppliers (such as Smart N Final or Price Costco) that supply restaurants. Always keep your eyes open, you never know where you'll run across a useful ingredient. If you find an item at one of the more expensive food stores, approach your local grocery store's manager, request the item . . . and keep hounding him to order it. Remember, you aren't the only one with Lactose Intolerance, just the most informed one.

As you experiment with substituting an ingredient in a recipe, take into consideration that you may need to adjust the other ingredients to compensate for the specific taste of that substitution. If a substitution is very sweet by itself, you may want to cut the amount of sugar called for in the original recipe to compensate. Choose a good cream cheese alternative, one with body and creamier texture. I once used a cheap alternative for a cheesecake and found disaster waiting for me. It was a gray, liquid substitute that had no body, so after blending and whipping, it was more soupy than creamy. My cheesecake did not hold up firm; it looked as if it was going to slide off the plate. But don't get frustrated. Just be patient—it may take a few times to get your recipe "right."

Another area to explore is "the little pill." Pharmaceutical companies have produced lactase enzyme products, available over the counter, to be taken in conjunction with meals containing lactose. You can choose chewable tablets, caplets, liquid drops, or a powder. Taking these products within five minutes of consuming your meal has shown a 70 to 90% reduction of the lactose content. This is because the lactase goes right to the intestine and starts working on the lactose as it is being digested. Taking the pills at the end of the meal proves less effective, with only minimum relief because the food is already involved in the digestive process. In my husband's case, his tolerance was so sensitive in the beginning that the pills could not help him. After staying on a strict lactose-free diet, he enjoys the luxury of taking a few "pills" before eating in a restaurant, in case the bread or another ingredient has lactose in it. It provides a little added insurance of a pain-free evening.

Now, the most important information I can give you is what to stay away from. Memorize the following ingredients . . . and associate them with discomfort and pain. I call them "Lactose and Its Tricky Little Friends" because without knowing what they are you might think you were "safe" after reading a label. Dairy free does not necessarily mean lactose free. You need to watch out for:

- lactose—the sugar found in milk
- whey—combination milk sugar and milk protein
- milk and milk products
- butter
- cream
- curds
- milk solids
- dry milk
- Simplesse—an artificial fat substitute made of skim milk and egg whites

These are the worst and most common offenders. If lactic acid is listed in the ingredients, this is not a "bad" thing. Lactic acid is lactose free because it is the end result of what the bacteria does to lactose in cultured milks. It is "safe" by itself.

If you have a sensitivity to milk protein as well, you'll be adding to your list:

- sodium caseinate
- casein
- lactalbumin
- lactoglobulin

Lactose is quite valuable to large food producers because, used as a filler, it maintains a long shelf life for many items. Whether bagged, boxed, or wrapped, in the end lactose makes the item taste "homemade" longer. Lactose can add volume, texture, taste, tenderness, and shelf life to a variety of foods. Remember, you are not just limited to giving up a glass of milk . . . but anything creamy, au gratin, batter dipped, powdered, gravied, mashed, or casseroled! Also watch out for chocolates (no more white chocolate), cold cuts, dips, appetizers, salad dressings, sauces, cakes, cookies, breads, candies, chips, pastries, pies, spaghetti sauces . . . and the list goes on.

Another area that is easily overlooked is the pharmacy. Yes, just as the food producers love to use lactose as a filler, so do the pharmaceutical companies. Lactose is great as an anticaking agent and for coating pills. Lactose is also tasteless. Over-the-counter drugs at least list their inactive ingredients, but prescription drugs pose another problem. You don't receive the original packaging to verify the inactive ingredients. The amount of lactose used as a filler or anticaking agent may be minimal, but accumulated doses of it, as well as the lactose in other foods you have that day, can pose a problem. Once my husband had diarrhea so badly he became dehydrated. We couldn't pin down what the culprit was until we found out that the doctor had given him a new prescription medicine that contained lactose. Once that was completely out of his system, he was fine. From then on I always check medications. Did you know that G. D. Searle's Demulen is the *only* lactose-free oral contraceptive that can be found? Geritol contains no lactose. In *Milk Is Not for Every Body,* Steve Carper provides the reader with an excellent list of medications, prescription, and over-the-counter drugs that contain lactose. He also advises you on forms of these medications that do not have any lactose in them. It is an invaluable resource.

LABELING

This may be a good place to vent my opinion! I guess I'm naive. I assumed that our government, in its infinite wisdom, had set up stringent regulations for our system of production of foods, medicines, etc. And of course everyone follows the rules. I mean if something says, "nondairy" or "lactose free," it is, right? You'd be surprised when you start reading the labels! A while ago, a friend gave my husband a protein drink mix. He was so excited because it said "lactose free." Well, right under that it said, whey peptides. According to this label, "peptides" are the "preferred mechanism for the human metabolism to absorb amino acids from digested protein." All over the can of drink mix was the word "whey." Lucky for me the can also had an 800 number to call if you had questions . . . boy, did I have questions! This "lactose-free" protein drink mix contained 360 mg of lactose! I was told by the representative of the company that according to the FDA, any item containing less than 1/2 gram of lactose per serving can be labeled "lactose free." I was furious! It seems that under the FDA's rules, revised in 1994, what you read is not always what you get. The simple word "free" only has to mean extremely low, not zero.

"No added" is another phrase used. This means if any form of lactose is part of the *original* ingredients, the manufacturer did not add any more lactose, compounding the problem. Anyone who is highly sensitive to lactose has a good chance of having reactions because of this type of labeling. I believe that someone this sensitive, as my husband is, has a right to know that there is a possibility of side effects from using these products. Although changes have occurred with some "nondairy" products, the FDA regulators do not seem to be paying attention to products claiming to be Lactose Free. The squeaky-wheel-gets-the-oil syndrome may work in this case. The more lactose-intolerant people band together and speak up to have labeling changes made, the more government agencies will realize how many people there are who have a vested interest in "lactose . . . *totally free*" products. They say there is safety in numbers; maybe there is the power of persuasion, too.

Kosher dietary laws require that *pareve* (or *parve*) be labeled on all foods containing absolutely no dairy (therefore, lactose free). These foods, including kosher meats, are all safe. If you see a kosher food package with a "D," that means it contains some milk or milk by-product. If you come across any other product marked "dairy free," *read the label carefully* . . . you'll be surprised how many of these do have some milk product used in them.

Life without lactose isn't easy. But it also isn't impossible. Once you familiarize yourself with the basics, it isn't that difficult. You can still enjoy a glass of cold milk (Lactaid 100) with your Oreos (just make them Hydrox chocolate cookies; real Oreos are on the no-no list).

The following pages have the "winning lottery numbers" for you! Here you will find a list of substitutions for key ingredients—milk, cream, butter, and cheeses—followed by recipes that I know are foolproof. Remember, this can't be a complete list of substitutes, because new items pop up all the time. Plus the area you live in makes a difference—a small rural area is not as likely to have a variety of substitutions as a metropolitan area. But you can request items from your store manager, mail-order some, and call companies to find local carriers.

You will be adding to this list of substitutions yourself. *You are the one that is going to take charge of your life by reading those labels, learning what your alternatives are, and remembering that the *choice is yours!*

One last reminder: Products sometimes change, so while the original version may have been lactose free, the "new and improved" version may have lactose added. *Read the labels!*

The "Safe" List of Lactose-Free Substitutions

ALTERNATIVE BUTTERS

Hollywood Safflower Oil Margarine—my particular favorite. I like the way it melts and blends in cooking. My husband loves the way it tastes (so does my daughter and she isn't Lactose Intolerant). I served it to my mom, who has to watch her cholesterol and she loved it (it contains 0 cholesterol).

Others are:

Weight Watchers light margarine
Shedd's Willow Run soybean margarine
Shedd's Spread Country Crock (tub only) Margarine
Promise Ultra Margarine
Mazola Sweet Unsalted Margarine
Diet Imperial Margarine
Blue Bonnet Diet Margarine
Purity Margarine
Parkay Light Margarine
Marv-Parv
Nucoa Smart Beat Super Light Margarine
Mother's Soft Margarine

Fleischmann's Lower Fat Margarine (tub only)
Fleischmann's Sweet Unsalted Margarine
Spectrum Naturals
Spectrum Spread

Kosher, *pareve* margarines are also free of any milk products. Be aware that you may not be able to fry with some of these because they are totally milk free, made with a base of soybean oil or canola oil that is nonhydrogenated (this means without hydrogen, which is necessary to turn the oil into a fat).

ALTERNATIVE CREAMS AND WHIPPED TOPPINGS

Pastry Pride Nondairy Whipped Topping—my favorite, used in my recipes. You can find it at restaurant supply stores or bulk-purchase stores. In my area, Smart N Final carries it. I place extras in the freezer, so I'm always prepared. I use it in making "ice cream," and any dish that calls for cream, or whipping cream.

Top Hat Whipped Topping, or Squeeze Pro Nondairy Whipped Topping, ready to use—they come already in a pastry tube. I freeze it and defrost it in the refrigerator when I'm ready to use it. If I have leftovers, it has a replacement cap for storing. I have used the topping on the Black Forest Tower cake, where the whipping topping actually holds up the cake layers. It has proved to retain its solid density and does not reduce to a liquid. This means it will hold up very well during a party or whenever you want to leave your desserts out for a while. It also gives a professional touch to your desserts because of the decorator tip.

Cool Whip (original only)
Rich's Richwhip

ALTERNATIVE MILKS

Lactaid 100 Lactose-Free Milk—my particular favorite because it is "real" milk without the lactose. I use the 2% variety in all of my recipes because it is richer and heavier. It is also sweeter, so you will have to take this into consideration by cutting down on the sugar in your individual recipes. My husband prefers the nonfat version to drink or in cereal. It is less sweet-tasting. Any way you use it, because it is "real" milk, no one will taste anything different! And that's important when you are striving to cook for a family or group. It is also easy to find, since it's now being stocked at many local grocery stores.

Knudsen Dairies Lactose-Free and Reduced Milks—new to the markets and, at the time of this writing, difficult to find in all supermarkets. It is available in the Western United States. Knudsen has not only duplicated Lactaid milk's quality, but they have reduced the sweetness, so making adjustments to recipes is not as vital. There is a big price difference, making this one a good value.

JerseyMaid Lactose-Free and Reduced Milks—again, new to the markets, and less expensive than Lactaid. Same good quality and taste. JerseyMaid has also reduced the sweetness of their lactose-free line, making this a good choice for value and taste.

EdenSoy Organic Soy Beverages
WestSoy Organic Beverages
Vitasoy
Rice Dream Beverages
Carnation Coffee-mate Non-Dairy Creamer, liquid form also
Mocha Mix Non-Dairy Creamer
Coffee Rich Non-Dairy Creamer
Vitamite Non-Dairy Milk Substitute

Eden Foods Soymilks
Perx Frozen Non-Dairy milk substitute
Soyamel
Soy Moo by Health Valley
Solait Beverage Powder
Acidophilus Milk (fermented, not sweet or SAM)*
Miscellaneous rice milks at health food stores
Miscellaneous soy milks at health food stores

Of all of these substitute milks, I found Lactaid, Knudsen, and JerseyMaid to be superior. Their taste is closest to the real thing, just a little sweeter, and with a little adjustment, they won't alter your recipes. Make the test yourself, and find the one right for you. Remember to *read* those labels. Manufacturers change ingredients without warning, so foods you are used to buying can suddenly turn out to be "off your list"! (At the time of this writing, JerseyMaid and Knudsen had just introduced their lines of lactose-free milk. Look for other dairies to follow suit.)

Additionally, "soured milks," such as acidophilus, yogurt, kumiss or kefir, have cultures of bacteria that form their own type of lactase enzyme. This breaks down almost 40% of the lactose into lactic acid, lowering the lactose to below the level of intolerance for many people. The secret of reducing the lactose content is in the fermentation period . . . how long it's fermented . . . the longer the better for the Lactose Intolerant. The only problem is that as it sours it becomes harder to acquire a taste for it. As I said before, the levels of intolerance are as varied as people are. You will be the only person who knows for sure. Remember, you can try the lactase enzyme pills that are available in conjunction with any of these suggestions. You may find the right combinations for you.

*Acidophilus cultured or fermented milk is made by adding *Lactobacillus acidophilus* bacteria to skim or lowfat milk, souring it. Fermentation is the key to the reduction of the lactose content. Depending on the length of fermentation, lactose can be reduced by as much as half the content in lowfat milk. This can make it tolerable to some Lactose-Intolerant people.

In recipes that call for buttermilk or sour milk, you can achieve a similar flavor with the substitution of 100% lactose-free milk and vinegar. Into a measuring cup, place 1 tablespoon vinegar. Fill the rest of the cup with 100% lactose-free 2% milk to equal 1 level cup. Allow it to set together (it will appear curdly) for about 5 minutes.

ALTERNATIVE CHEESES

TofuRella Cheeses—these tofu-based cheeses are my favorites. They are easier to locate; most times you can find them in your local grocery store. They melt very well if you shred them finely. My husband enjoys the "cheddar" on a Ritz cracker! They do well frozen, both shredded and in block form.

Soya Kaas Cheeses—are soymilk and tofu–based cheeses. I use them a lot. They shred and melt well, and keep well in the refrigerator. They also freeze very well.

Formagg—this was one of the first cheeses I found in my quest. It comes shredded and sliced. It is a canola oil–based cheese. It is available in the cheese section of some grocery stores.

Soymage cheese alternative
Veggie Cheese alternatives
White Wave

These are the most available brands I've found. Most of them are made from tofu or soy products. But there is another side to the "cheese issue." Through the processing and aging of most cheeses, the lactose content is lowered considerably, and in most cases just about completely removed. Firm cheeses are achieved by removing the liquid (or whey) from the curds during processing. By eliminating the whey, you are eliminating the lactose, so obviously these are the best kinds of "real" cheese to choose.

Rule of thumb: The longer a cheese is aged, the lower the lactose. The firmer the cheese, the lower the lactose. As always, check those labels! Look for imported cheeses, because many times they are aged longer than their American counterparts, which means that they're lower in lactose. My husband has been able to enjoy a few slices of imported, aged cheddar or imported aged Swiss without symptoms. Just don't go crazy, or you'll be experiencing the discomfort you are trying to avoid.

Another cheese to enjoy is fresh mozzarella. This ball form of mozzarella is packaged in liquid and comes lactose free, so look for that on the label to make sure you choose the right one. When using this mozzarella, dry the ball with a paper towel, eliminating as much liquid as possible before attempting to grate it. If you don't, you will find a lot of water escaping from it during cooking. Do not freeze it. It is sold in markets, especially Italian markets.

ALTERNATIVE SOUR CREAM AND CREAM CHEESES

Tofutti Sour Supreme Better Than Sour Cream—I prefer this brand because it is 100% lactose free. So you can enjoy it without *any* consequences. It is pure white in color and solid in density, which means a lot when incorporating it in a recipe.

IMO Sour Cream Substitute—this is not as "pure" as the Tofutti brand. You believe you are buying a substitute for the real thing . . . but read the label! It contains whey. The redeeming factor is the added *S. lactis* culture. Depending on your tolerance level, you may be able to handle a little of this substitute with few consequences. My husband cannot conceive the concept of "sparingly" . . . to him, a baked potato is not edible unless it is smothered in sour cream! So, he does experience some discomfort from this alternative.

Tofutti Better Than Cream Cheese—my preference because I usually blend it in a recipe, and its color is white . . . like real cream cheese. It is more of a solid, so it holds up well in a recipe. If you like this cream cheese and wish to spread it on a bagel or such, simply add 3 to 4 tablespoons 100% lactose-free 2% milk with 8 ounces cream cheese alternative in a mixing bowl. Beat the ingredients until light and fluffy. For fun, replace lactose-free milk with 1/4 cup honey or with 3 to 4 tablespoons maple syrup.

Soya Kaas, Cream Cheese Style—this is good also, but the color is a little darker and the texture is more watery. This is because it is made from tofu. However, depending on your recipe, it does the job.

Whatever the brand name, these soft cheeses should not be frozen. As with real cream cheese and sour cream, they just do not hold up well. I have tried freezing them and in a pinch they will work . . . but it's a mess. Don't gamble and end up ruining your recipe, wasting your time and money.

ALTERNATIVE COTTAGE CHEESES

"Nancy's" Lowfat Cottage Cheese, cultured with *L. acidophilus*, contains live cultures, as well as lactic cultures, all lowering the lactose content considerably but not completely. The actual lactose content is very minimal. My husband tolerates this very well (in moderate proportion), but you will need to determine your individual tolerance level.

Lactose-Free Cottage Cheeses, made by the Soyco and Galaxy food companies, are very difficult to purchase in some areas. I haven't been successful finding them in my area of southern California.

Your Own Special Blend—when you can't find any of the above, and until there is lactose-free ricotta—blend until smooth with a hand mixer 1 package firm tofu with 8 ounces lactose-free cream cheese. Use this substitute to fill lasagna, ravioli, shells. Remember that tofu takes on the taste of incorporated ingredients, so add some mushrooms and spices . . . you will be surprised at the tasty result.

ALTERNATIVE FROZEN DESSERTS (ICE CREAM, SORBETS, ETC.)

Mocha Mix
Rice Dream
Tofutti
Tuscan Tofu Bars
Tofulicious
Ice Bean
Dole Fruit Sorbet
Jell-O Gelatin Pops
Häagen-Dazs Le Sorbet
Penguino's
Baskin-Robbins sorbets and ices

Remember to always choose fruit *sorbets*, not sherbets, which are traditionally made with milk. Any frozen juice bar or ice should be fine.

LACTASE ENZYME PRODUCTS

Lactaid
Dairy Ease
Lactrase
Lacteeze Drops
Nature's Way Lactase Enzyme
Nature's Plus Say Yes to Dairy
Solgar Lactase
Schiff Natural Milk Digest-Aid

I have included this list of lactase enzyme products for your convenience. You will recognize Lactaid and Dairy Ease because of the advertising campaigns you have seen. They are good choices and can be found in just about any pharmacy. This means you are always within reach of relief. But this book is about life without having to worry about taking "the pill." Unfortunately, eating out in restaurants or at friends' homes poses different problems and this little pill may very well see you through the evening without pain or discomfort.

These substitutions are the most critical in creating a dish that is lactose free. Without being able to provide alternatives for milk, cream, butter, and cheeses, so many recipes would be out of reach of the Lactose Intolerant. With these key options, the sky's the limit. Experiment, be creative! And I can't stress enough the importance of **reading labels**. Know your food and what is in it.

Off-the-Shelf "Safe" List of Lactose-Free Brand Name Products

The search for lactose-free products is never ending. I have spent countless hours reading labels with tiny print in every super-market I go into, hoping to find a new "safe" food. I want you to benefit from my efforts by having this list of "Sheri approved" brand name products that are available at your local supermarket. This can be an excellent beginning for your own list. However, products change, so while the following brands contain no lactose as of this writing, checking labels *is* a way of life.

APPETIZERS AND CRACKERS

> Mrs. T's Potato and Onion Filled Pierogies
> Ling Ling Chicken Potstickers
> Moore's Breaded Mushrooms
> Kosher Meats and Products
> Chinese Egg Rolls: Chicken, Shrimp, Lobster, Pork
> Ritz Crackers, Sociables Crackers, and Zesta and
>   Nabisco Saltines
> Triscuit Whole Wheat Wafers
> Potato'n Sesame Snack Thins
> Oysterette Soup and Oyster Crackers

Keebler Town House Oval Crackers
Wheatsworth Stone Ground Wheat Crackers
Plain Ry-Krisp

SOUPS

Progresso Ready-to-Serve Chicken Pasta
Healthy Choice Chili Beef
Lipton Chicken Noodle
Lipton Noodle
Campbell's Condensed Golden Mushroom
  (not plain Mushroom)
Campbell's Vegetable
Campbell's Condensed Manhattan Clam Chowder
Campbell's Condensed New England Clam Chowder

BREAKFAST FOODS

Quaker Instant Oatmeal—Apple & Cinnamon
  (not Maple & Brown Sugar)
Cream of Wheat
Cream of Rice
Post Fruity Pebbles
Kellogg's Corn Pops
Trix, Cheerios, Froot Loops
Post and Nabisco Shredded Wheat, Frosted Mini-Wheats
Quaker Puffed Rice and Puffed Wheat
  (no Honey Bunches of Oats)
Quaker Instant Grits, Team Flakes
Aunt Jemima Original, Whole Wheat and Buckwheat
  Pancake & Waffle Mixes
Hungry Jack Original and Light Pancake Mixes
Kellogg's Strawberry, Frosted Strawberry, or Frosted
  Blueberry Pop Tarts
**(No Bisquick or Jiffy Baking Mix . . . and forget
  Carnation Instant Breakfast.)**

BREADS

Old Country French Bread

Bohemian Hearth Old-Fashioned White, Sweet Hawaiian, Hot Dog and Hamburger Buns

Di Carlo Italian Sliced Bread, French, Sourdough, Vienna

Pepperidge Farm Club Rolls, Frozen Pastry Sheets and Puffs

Stella D'Oro Breadsticks, Breakfast Treats, Chocolate Breakfast Treats

Sunbeam White Bread, Pioneer Brown 'n' Serve Rolls and Breads

Raisin Bread, Pumpernickel, Rye, Pitas

Western Bagels, Jiffy Cornbread Mix

Melba Toast, plain or garlic

Shake 'n' Bake, only Original Pork and Original Chicken

Kellogg's Corn Flake Crumbs

Nabisco Cracker Meal

Honey Maid Graham Cracker Crumbs

Pioneer Plain Croutons, Brown 'n' Serve Sourdough Breads, Regular Sourdough

Musso's Old-Fashioned Italian Garlic Croutons

"THE MEAT AND POTATOES"

Canned Tuna, Crab, Shrimp, Canned Chicken, Turkey

Hormel Canned Spam, Sloppy Joes, Deviled Ham, Ham Patties, Dinty Moore Beef Stew, Dinty Moore Corned Beef

Libby Corned Beef

Carnation Sandwich Spreads: Chicken, Ham, Tuna, or Turkey Salads

Canned Sardines in Mustard or Tomato Sauces

Pillsbury Boil-in-Bag Entrees: Shrimp Creole, Chicken with Garden Vegetables, Szechwan Beef

Chun King Products: Beef, Chicken, Pork, or Shrimp Chow Meins; Stir-Fry Vegetables and Sauce Mix; Beef

Pepper Oriental; Boil-in-Bag Sweet & Sour Pork; Boil-in-Bag Fried Rice with Pork

La Choy Products: Shrimp, Chicken, Lobster, or Meat and Shrimp Egg Rolls; Shrimp or Chicken Chow Meins; Sweet & Sour Pork or Chicken; Beef Pepper Oriental Dinner; Fried Rice with Meat; Chicken Won Ton

Lean Cuisine Products: Beef Teriyaki Dinner Supreme, Baked Chicken Breast Dinner Supreme, Linguini with Clam Sauce Entree, Chicken Chow Mein with Rice Entree, Chicken a l'Orange with Almond Rice, Chicken Cacciatore with Vermicelli, Oriental Beef with Vegetables and Rice, Meatball Stew, Stuffed Cabbage with Meat in Tomato Sauce, Oriental Scallops and Vegetables with Rice

Swanson Products: Take-Out-Style Fried Chicken, Chicken Nibbles with French Fries, Salisbury Steak with Mushroom Gravy, Fried Chicken, Nibbles, Thighs & Drumsticks or Breast Portions, Fish 'n' Chips

Armour Products: Lite Veal or Beef Pepper Steaks, Sliced Beef with Broccoli Classic Lite, Sweet & Sour Pork or Chicken, Stuffed Green Peppers, Cod Almondine, Boneless Short Ribs with BBQ Sauce, Beef Burgundy, Chicken Teriyaki

Ore Ida Snackin' Fries

Marquez Supreme Taquitos Beef or Chicken

Banquet Frozen Beef Pot Pie

Butterball turkeys or turkey parts

Kosher Meats, Cold Cuts, and Hot Dogs

Ball Park Bun-Size Beef Hot Dogs

Some Store-Brand Hot Dogs

Francisco Canned Turkey Gravy

Prego Tomato & Basil Sauce

Barilla Marinara or Tomato & Basil Sauce

Prego Summer Tomato Sauce

Hunt's Tomato Sauce and Paste

Tone's Poultry Gravy Mix, Tone's Au Jus Gravy Mix
Kraft Barbecue Sauces
Worcestershire Sauce
Soy Sauce

Canned vegetables are usually safe, even cream-style corn, butter beans, butternut or buttercup squash. With canned tuna, watch for the ingredient "hydrolyzed casein protein."

Ketchups, mustards, relishes, mayonnaise, salsas, horseradish, tartar sauce, and clam sauce are just about always lactose free. Barbecue sauces and most marinades are lactose free also, but watch those gourmet types. Pasta sauces are a little more difficult. Cheese and butter are used in a lot of them. I have listed the common ones that are lactose free. In the gravy department, chicken gravies are usually no-nos, while the same producer can give you a turkey gravy that's fine. I prefer the Tone's brand found in bulk or restaurant supply stores, as it produces a rich, creamy gravy in quantities I need because it is a dry mix.

Most casseroles, frozen or gourmet packaged, are out. As for the packaged salads, unless they provide a vinegar and oil dressing and do not contain croutons or cheese in the salad, they, too, are out.

CAKES, COOKIES, PASTRIES

Packaged Angel Food Cake
Packaged Lady Fingers
Pepperidge Farm Pastry Sheets and Puffs
Kosher Bakery Cakes, Cookies, and Pastries
Ghirardelli Double Chocolate Brownie Mix
Duncan Hines Mixes: Moist Devil's Food, Lemon, Yellow,
    or Marble Cake; Cinnamon Crumbcake; Chewy
    Brownie; Angel Food Cake (not the fat-free version);
    Butter Golden Cake

Dromedary Pound Cake

Betty Crocker "Golden" Pound Cake Mix (not the new version; Betty Crocker is now marking packages that contain milk products)

Pillsbury Mixes: Fudge and Walnut Brownie, Gingerbread

Ghirardelli Semi Sweet and Double Chocolate Chocolate Chips, Dark Chocolate, Sweet Ground Chocolate, Non Pareils, Dark Chocolate Bar

Hershey's Reduced Fat Baking Chips (not Nestlé or Hershey's Regular Semi Sweet Chocolate Chips), Cocoa for Baking, Dark Chocolate Bar

Baker's Semi Sweet or Unsweetened Baking Chocolate Squares

Ambrosia Semi Sweet Chocolate Chips

Droste Imported Cocoa

Duncan Hines Homestyle Dark Chocolate Frosting

SnackWell Chocolate Fudge Frosting

Pillsbury Creamy Chocolate Fudge Frosting

Pepperidge Farms Santa Fe Cookies, Old Fashion Ginger Man Cookies

Keebler Pecan Sandies, Almond Sandies

Hydrox (not Oreo), Vienna Fingers

Cinnamon Teddy Grahams and Honey Teddy Grahams

Stella D'Oro Swiss Fudge, Anisette Sponge, Anginetti, Margherite Combination

Honey Maid, Keebler, and Nabisco Honey Graham Crackers

Honey Maid Cinnamon Grahams (not Keebler)

Keebler Chocolate Grahams (not Honey Maid)

Mother's Iced Oatmeal, Striped Shortbread, Double Fudge Cookies

FROZEN OR CREAMY DESSERT TREATS

MaMa's Italian Ices

Dole Fruit Sorbets

Baskin-Robbins Sorbets and Ices

Jell-O Gelatin Pops
Häagen-Dazs Sorbets (even Chocolate)
Any Plain True Frozen Fruit Bars; Any True Sorbets
Jell-O Chocolate, Pistachio, Banana Cream *Instant* Puddings
Jell-O Vanilla, Butterscotch Cook 'n' Serve Puddings (not Instant)
Royal Vanilla, Chocolate Instant Puddings
Minute Tapioca
All Jell-O Gelatin
Mocha Mix
Scoopy's Cake Ice Cream Cones
Colosso Cake Ice Cream Cones (not Keebler)

BEVERAGES

Plain Tea and Coffee (hot or iced)
Ghirardelli Sweet Ground Chocolate & Cocoa
Ghirardelli Old Fashioned Hot Cocoas: White Mocha, Chocolate Mocha, Double Chocolate, Pralines & Cream
Tang Breakfast Beverage, Kool-Aid
Hawaiian Punch, Fruit Juices
Cream Soda, Soft Drinks
Crème de Menthe or Crème de Cacao
TGI Friday's Frozen Drink Mixes are Nondairy
Heublein Frozen Drink Mixes

Obviously, the "International" coffees have some lactose; so do many hot cocoa mixes. Be careful of the mixes that state they are "lactose free." I've found that the labeling can be misrepresented, and in many cases you will find lactose in them. Homemade hot cocoa will satisfy that craving—use lactose-free milk and cocoa powder.

There are a lot of frozen drink mixes that do not contain lactose, but I would be wary ordering a creamy mixed drink in a bar. Remember, coconut milk, the liquid that is extracted from the center of a fresh coconut, does not have lactose. As long as it is not "soaked" in cow's milk, it is true coconut milk. Specialty or Asian grocery stores are excellent places to find real coconut milk.

SALAD DRESSINGS

Hidden Valley Honey Bacon, Red Wine, and Herb
Best Foods Fat Free French, Fat Free Ranch, and Regular
  Thousand Island
Newman's Own Balsamic Vinaigrette

LITTLE EXTRAS

Always check the house brand or generic brands in any of these categories. You will be surprised at what you find.

Apple butter, peanut and almond butters, and even true fruit butters are all lactose free. Prebasted turkeys are now using vegetable oil, as are packaged hams.

In the health food stores, substitutions and new products are available in the cheese category. Supermarkets are beginning to supply these choices and are slowly stocking them. Let your store manager know what you need; let's make choice available for everyone.

Quick Fixin' List

This is a list of recipes that are perfect for quick solutions to panic situations: unexpected company, fast dinner on a busy night, a special treat for that "A" paper, or "just because . . ." These recipes are time-savers, using items you have on hand for a result you'll be praised for.

Throw-together dinners are sometimes the best. I love to do the "just because" treats for family and friends. Their big smiles make my day.

Although the treat may look like it took all day to create, no one has to know it was a "quickie." The best part is they are all lactose free, so you don't have to think about them or stress about the ingredients . . . the worry is all gone!

APPETIZERS

Herb-Garlic Bread 37
Parmesan Eggplant Slices 40

Powell Branch Library Powell WY

MAIN MEALS

Creamy Chicken Soup 48
Dad's Famous Pancakes 55
Lactose-Free Omelet 56
Poached Eggs 59
Scrambled Eggs 60
Waffles 62
Creamed Dried Beef 119
Paprika Chicken 140
Quick Flounder au Gratin 151
Baked Cheesy Egg Casseroles 160
Egg Salad 162
Stuffed Potatoes 165
The Grilled BLT Comeback 166
Creamy Asparagus Pasta 177
Lactose-Free Fettuccine Alfredo 180
Linguine with Garlic and Olive Oil 184

TREATS

Quick Pudding Surprise 317
A Cool Peach Drink 326
Brandy Alexander 329
Strawberry Smoothie 330
The Float 330
The Ultimate Milk Shake 331

Author's Note

All the following recipes do not contain lactose unless noted in small amounts (for example when using aged cheese). While at first glance some traditional recipes may seem lactose free, you can be guaranteed that *my* recipes truly are. I've discovered all the hidden places lactose can insert itself into a seemingly "safe" dish, and found alternative ingredients. Remember, always *read labels carefully.*

Appetizers

What is an appetizer? Some people say it's an hors d'oeuvre, an antipasto or canapé. But, for the Lactose Intolerant, an appetizer is . . . skipped. You just don't know what's in them, so they're the first to go. You bypass this part of the meal and just hope you can find "something" to eat at dinner!

This section comprises appetizers that you can eat . . . no skipping. Using these recipes as a base, you can create your own versions of the "appetizer world." Remember, Lactose Intolerant doesn't mean "plain, bland, and boring!"

Baked Potato Skins

Allow your guests to add their favorite toppings, by serving these treats on a tray along with small bowls of sour cream alternative, special sauces, olives, etc. Let everyone have a hand in the appetizers!

Makes 6 servings
Preparation time: 30 minutes

6 small baking potatoes, scrubbed and dried
1/4 cup safflower oil margarine, Hollywood, melted
1 cup shredded cheddar cheese alternative, TofuRella
1/4 cup real bacon pieces, Hormel
1/4 cup diced green onions
Freshly ground pepper

Pierce the potatoes several times with a fork. Place in the microwave on high for 18 minutes. (If you don't have a carousel, turn the potatoes at least once during cooking.) The potatoes are done when they're tender to piercing. Remove from the microwave and cool.

When cool enough to handle, cut the potatoes in half lengthwise. Scoop out the potato, leaving a thin coating along the skin. (Reserve the cooked potato, you can use most of it for other potato dishes, such as hash browns.)

Place the potato skins, cut side up, on a baking sheet. Brush the melted safflower margarine completely over the inside of the potato skins. Take a little of the reserved potato (about 1 tablespoon, mashed) and put in the bottom of each skin. Sprinkle with the cheddar cheese alternative, bacon pieces, or desired toppings. Finish by sprinkling green onions and pepper on top.

Return to the microwave, cooking long enough to melt the cheese and to warm the potatoes.

Per Serving: Calories: 203 Cholesterol: 7mg Dietary Fiber: 2g Protein: 7g
Sodium: 321mg Carbohydrate: 21g Total Fat: 11g Saturated Fat: 2g
Calories from Fat: 48%, Calories from Carbohydrates: 40%, Calories from Protein: 12%

Herb-Garlic Bread

For a stronger oregano flavor, use 1 1/2 teaspoons finely chopped fresh oregano. In place of the Parmesan cheese alternative, you can use imported, aged Parmesan cheese and grate it. Try a little first to test the level of tolerance in your system.

Makes 24 servings
Preparation time: 15 minutes

1/4 cup safflower oil margarine, Hollywood
1 garlic clove, minced
1/2 teaspoon dried oregano
1 1-pound loaf The French Connection bread (page 81),
   or any lactose-free French bread (see page 25)
1 tablespoon grated Parmesan cheese alternative, Soyco

Preheat the oven to broil. In a mixing bowl, blend together the safflower margarine, garlic, and oregano. Spread on slices of French bread and then sprinkle generously with the Parmesan cheese alternative.

Place on a rack in the preheated broiler. Broil until the tops are light brown and bubbly, approximately 3 minutes.

*Makes a great addition to any Italian dinner
or served as an appetizer.*

Per Serving: Calories: 70 Cholesterol: 0mg Dietary Fiber: 1g Protein: 2g
Sodium: 139mg Carbohydrate: 10g Total Fat: 3g Saturated Fat: .5g
Calories from Fat: 33%, Calories from Carbohydrates: 57%, Calories from Protein: 10%

Roasted Garlic on French Bread

By cooking these garlic heads slowly, they become very mellow, soft, and creamy. This makes them easier to digest, so you can enjoy the garlic without the aftereffects! Serve them along with an Italian dish, roast lamb, or seafood, or as an appetizer. For added appeal, serve with a chunky tomato basil sauce.

Makes 12 servings
Preparation time: 1 hour

4 heads garlic
2 tablespoons olive oil
1/2 teaspoon dried oregano
1/2 teaspoon salt
Dash freshly ground pepper
1 1-pound loaf The French Connection bread (page 81),
    or any lactose-free French bread (see page 25)
3 tablespoons safflower oil margarine, Hollywood, melted
1 teaspoon chopped parsley
Grated Parmesan cheese alternative, Soyco, or imported
    aged Parmesan cheese, for seasoning

Prepare the garlic by chopping off the top quarter inch of the heads. Remove any loose, papery skin, but leave the heads whole. Start your barbecue grill according to the manufacturer's instructions. Position the rack 4 to 6 inches above the flame or heat.

In a bowl, mix the olive oil, oregano, salt, and pepper with a fork until well blended. Toss in the garlic heads and coat with the mixture evenly. Slice the French bread; brush with melted safflower margarine. Set aside.

Put the coated garlic heads in the center of the grilling rack on the barbecue. Grill for 30 to 40 minutes, turning several times with tongs. (The cloves should feel very soft when done.) During the last few minutes, place the French bread slices on heavy-duty foil and place alongside the garlic heads. Lightly toast both sides of the slices, then remove from the grill and keep warm.

Remove the garlic heads when they are very soft. Squeeze the whole cloves and they will separate from their skins. Place the soft garlic pieces on top of the warm French bread slices and sprinkle with parsley and the Parmesan cheese alternative or freshly grated aged Parmesan. Serve warm.

Appetizer or side dish, this makes a great accompaniment!

Per Serving (without cheese): Calories: 150 Cholesterol: 0mg Dietary Fiber: 1g
Protein: 3g Sodium: 348mg Carbohydrate: 20g Total Fat: 6g Saturated Fat: 1g
Calories from Fat: 38%, Calories from Carbohydrates: 53%, Calories from Protein: 9%

Parmesan Eggplant Slices

To serve an appetizer, place the eggplant on a platter with a small bowl of warmed jarred tomato sauce or homemade marinara sauce (page 181) for dipping. You can serve them as a side dish with any meal. Quick, different, and basic. Just add your own imagination and create!

Makes 4 servings
Preparation time: 15 minutes

1 large eggplant
4 tablespoons olive oil
3 tablespoons grated Parmesan cheese alternative, Soyco

Preheat the oven to the broil setting. Wash and pat dry the eggplant. Trim off the stem end, slice it in half lengthwise, and then slice each half into half-moon slices about 1/4 inch thick. Place in a single layer on a rack in the broiler pan. Brush each slice with olive oil and sprinkle with the cheese alternative. Broil in the oven 3 to 4 inches from the heat until tender and browned, about 5 minutes each side. When turning the slices over, repeat brushing with oil and sprinkling with cheese. Remove from the oven and serve.

Per Serving: Calories: 166 Cholesterol: 0mg Dietary Fiber: 3g Protein: 3g
Sodium: 93mg Carbohydrate: 7g Total Fat: 14g Saturated Fat: 2g
Calories from Fat: 76%, Calories from Carbohydrates: 16%, Calories from Protein: 8%

Spinach Triangles

*T*hese appetizers can be placed in the freezer on a baking sheet until firm, then placed in a freezer bag and kept frozen until ready to use. Then put them on an ungreased baking sheet, brush with melted safflower margarine, and bake a minute or two longer than the recipe below. This is a great appetizer to have on hand for unexpected company!

Makes 20 servings
Preparation time: 2 hours 20 minutes

10 ounces frozen chopped spinach
2 tablespoons virgin olive oil, light
1 medium shallot, minced
1 large egg, slightly beaten
1/3 cup grated Parmesan cheese alternative, Soyco
Dash freshly ground pepper
1/3 pound phyllo dough sheets, cut into strips
1/2 cup safflower oil margarine, Hollywood, melted

Preheat the oven to 425° F. Thaw the frozen spinach and squeeze dry.

Heat the olive oil in a saucepan over medium heat. Add the shallot and cook until tender. Remove the saucepan from the heat and stir in the egg, spinach, Parmesan cheese alternative, and pepper. Stir until blended. Set aside.

Unwrap the phyllo dough and, with a serrated-edge knife, cut strips lengthwise about 2 inches wide. Place on wax paper, covering with a lightly damp towel (to prevent drying out). Working with one strip at a time, brush one side with melted safflower margarine. Place 1 teaspoonful of the spinach mixture at the end of the strip. Fold one corner diagonally over the mixture, making a right angle . . . continue in this manner until the complete strip forms a finished triangle. Repeat the process with the remaining strips until all the spinach filling is used.

Place the filled triangles on ungreased baking sheets, brush the tops with the melted margarine. Bake in the preheated oven for about 15 minutes until golden brown. Serve immediately.

Wonderful make-ahead appetizers!

Per Serving: Calories: 87 Cholesterol: 11mg Dietary Fiber: .4g Protein: 2g
Sodium: 119mg Carbohydrate: 6g Total Fat: 7g Saturated Fat: 1g
Calories from Fat: 66%, Calories from Carbohydrates: 24%, Calories from Protein: 10%

Stuffed Mushrooms

In this recipe, you are using real fresh mozzarella, substituting with store brands that are lactose free, so no one will know there is a difference. You can change the fresh mozzarella to cheddar cheese or any other favorite cheese alternative you like. This will only make these appetizers better.

Makes 24 servings
Preparation time: 30 minutes

24 large fresh button mushrooms
1/4 cup safflower oil margarine, Hollywood
1/4 cup diced shallots
1 garlic clove, minced
2/3 cup bread crumbs, Pioneer, very fine
1/2 cup shredded fresh mozzarella, Del Pastore

Clean the mushrooms by washing and patting them dry or brushing. Remove the stems and chop finely (reserving the caps to be filled later), making approximately 1 cup of mushroom-stem pieces.

Using a medium saucepan, melt the safflower margarine. Add the chopped mushroom stems, shallots, and garlic; sauté until tender. Add the bread crumbs and mozzarella and toss until mixed. Remove from the heat and fill the reserved mushroom caps with the mixture.

Preheat the oven to 425° F. and arrange the caps, filled side up, on a baking sheet. If desired, sprinkle additional shredded cheese on the tops. Bake 8 to 10 minutes until thoroughly warm.

Per Serving: Calories: 42 Cholesterol: 2mg Dietary Fiber: .3g Protein: 2g
Sodium: 44mg Carbohydrate: 3g Total Fat: 3g Saturated Fat: .8g
Calories from Fat: 57%, Calories from Carbohydrates: 27%, Calories from Protein: 16%

Soups

Creamy soups? Impossible, you say? Not when you know the right substitutes. Enjoy the wonderful world of rich, creamy soups . . . without the consequences!

Chilled Strawberry Soup

Here's a delicious way to enjoy fresh strawberries! You can freeze the soup and enjoy it year round. It's also perfect as a dessert: Allow the sliced strawberries to float on top and add some nondairy whipping cream.

Makes 4 servings
Preparation time: 30 minutes
Chill time: 1 to 2 hours

1 pint fresh strawberries
1/2 cup sugar
1 teaspoon grated lemon peel
2 tablespoons lemon juice
1/2 cup white wine

Reserve 3 strawberries for garnishing. Rinse and hull remaining berries. In a covered blender, place the hulled strawberries and all other ingredients. Blend together at medium speed until smooth. Refrigerate, covered, until chilled (at least 1 hour).

To serve, chill soup or dessert bowls. Take the reserved whole strawberries and slice. Place the chilled soup into bowls and top with the sliced berries.

A wonderful first-course soup for a summer meal!

Per Serving: Calories: 141 Cholesterol: 0mg Dietary Fiber: 2g Protein: 1g
Sodium: 3mg Carbohydrate: 31g Total Fat: .3g Saturated Fat: 0g
Calories from Fat: 2%, Calories from Carbohydrates: 96%, Calories from Protein: 2%

Creamy Celery Soup

*T*his soup can be made ahead. Simply follow the recipe below, but omit adding the whipping cream alternative. Cool the soup and place in a covered freezer container. To serve, remove and thaw in a saucepan, stirring over low heat. When completely heated, add the whipping cream alternative, stir, and serve.

Makes 6 servings
Preparation time: 30 minutes

1/4 cup safflower oil margarine, Hollywood
2 large shallots, quartered
1 cup chopped potato
2 cups chopped celery
1 cup water
1 small bay leaf
1 teaspoon salt
1/4 teaspoon white pepper
2 cups 100% lactose-free 2% lowfat milk
8 sprigs fresh parsley
1/2 cup whipping cream alternative, Pastry Pride

In a large skillet, melt the safflower margarine. Add the chopped shallots and cook until browned and tender. Add the chopped potato, celery, water, bay leaf, salt, and pepper, and cook until vegetables are soft. Remove the bay leaf and discard.

In a blender, pour 1 cup of the lactose-free milk, ladle in about half the hot cooked celery mixture. Cover and process on BLEND until smooth. Remove from the blender and place in a large saucepan. Repeat the process with the remaining cup of milk and cooked celery mixture and place in the saucepan when smooth. Chop the parsley sprigs and add to the saucepan. Heat thoroughly. Stir in the whipping cream alternative just before ready to serve.

Serve with a salad and you've got an entire
light dinner!

Per Serving: Calories: 208 Cholesterol: 7mg Dietary Fiber: 1g Protein: 4g
Sodium: 539mg Carbohydrate: 14g Total Fat: 16g Saturated Fat: 7g
Calories from Fat: 66%, Calories from Carbohydrates: 27%, Calories from Protein: 7%

Creamy Chicken Soup

Creamy soups are a problem if you're Lactose Intolerant, unless they're homemade! This recipe is an easy, quick solution. To save time, you can use leftover chicken or canned chicken.

Makes 12 servings
Preparation time: 20 minutes

4 tablespoons safflower oil margarine, Hollywood
6 tablespoons all-purpose flour
6 cups chicken broth
2 cups whipping cream alternative, Pastry Pride
3 cups cooked and chopped chicken
Dash freshly ground pepper, to taste
Fresh snipped parsley, for garnish

In a large saucepan on low heat, melt the safflower margarine and stir in the flour. Raise the heat to medium low, and add the chicken broth and the whipping cream alternative a little at a time, blending completely after each addition. When all the broth and cream are added, allow the mixture to cook until bubbly. Be careful not to burn. Continue to cook, stirring for another minute or two. Stir in the cooked chicken, and heat thoroughly.

Ladle into soup bowls, pepper to taste, and garnish with parsley.

Per Serving: Calories: 301 Cholesterol: 33mg Dietary Fiber: 0g Protein: 16g
Sodium: 892mg Carbohydrate: 13g Total Fat: 21g Saturated Fat: 12g
Calories from Fat: 61%, Calories from Carbohydrates: 17%, Calories from Protein: 22%

Creamy Mushroom Soup

For this easy, delicious soup, my husband loves button mushrooms, which are mild in flavor, but you can choose your favorite. Both the substitution of safflower margarine and the whipping cream alternative will go undetected because of the consistency and taste of the soup. Plus choose a shallot instead of an onion to add the mild, gentle flavor of onion. If you want canned soup, remember to read the labels. Campbell's Mushroom Soup is out, but Campbell's Golden Mushroom soup is lactose free. So, when shopping, read those labels carefully.

Makes 8 servings
Preparation time: 45 minutes

1 pound mushrooms
1/2 cup safflower oil margarine, Hollywood
1 teaspoon lemon juice
1 small shallot, minced
1/3 cup all-purpose flour
31/2 cups chicken broth
1 cup whipping cream alternative, Pastry Pride
Dash freshly ground pepper

Clean and trim the mushrooms, removing the stems and setting aside. Next, thinly slice the mushroom caps. In a large pot, heat the safflower margarine over high heat until melted. Add the sliced mushroom caps and lemon juice, cooking until tender. Carefully remove the mushrooms, leaving the juices in the pot, and place the mushrooms in a bowl for later.

Reduce the heat to low and place the mushroom stems and shallot into the pot. Stir several times, cooking the shallot until tender, about 5 minutes. Slowly add the flour, stirring constantly to blend completely. Continue to cook an additional minute, while stirring. Slowly add the chicken broth, blending with the flour. Allow the mixture to thicken, stirring to avoid burning.

Remove the pot from the heat and, using a Braun or similar handheld blender, beat the mixture until smooth, 2 to 3 minutes. Return to the heat, stir in the whipping cream alternative, pepper, and sliced mushroom caps. Bring the soup to a boil, and simmer for a few minutes.

Ladle into warm soup bowls, garnish with bacon bits, toasted croutons, or even some Parmesan cheese alternative!

A great winter dinner, or first course!

Per Serving (without garnish): Calories: 275 Cholesterol: lmg Dietary Fiber: .7g
Protein: 7g Sodium: 832mg Carbohydrate: 14g Total Fat: 22g Saturated Fat: 10g
Calories from Fat: 71%, Calories from Carbohydrates: 20%, Calories from Protein: 9%

French Onion Soup

*S*erve this classic as a quick dinner or as a first course. Remember, if you're using store-bought French bread, check the ingredients for lactose.

Makes 6 servings
Preparation time: 40 minutes

1/4 cup safflower oil margarine, Hollywood
3 large onions, sliced
1 teaspoon sugar
1 tablespoon all-purpose flour
21/2 cups water
1/2 cup port wine
2 101/2-ounce cans condensed beef broth (bouillon),
   Campbell's
1 loaf The French Connection bread (page 81), or any
   lactose-free French bread (see page 25)
6 slices Swiss cheese alternative, Soyco

Preheat the oven to 325° F. In a large Dutch oven (a large saucepan with ear handles and a cover, great for slow-cooking large quantities), melt the safflower margarine over medium heat. Add the onions and sugar; cook for about 10 minutes, stirring occasionally. Blend in the flour with the pan juices. Next add the water, wine, and undiluted beef broth until the mixture boils. Reduce the heat to low, cover the pot, and simmer for another 10 minutes.

Cut the French bread into 1-inch slices. Hold aside 6 slices to place in the soup; the rest can be served with the soup. Take the 6 slices and toast lightly in the oven until light brown.

Ladle the soup into oven-safe bowls, top each bowl with a toasted French bread slice and drape a slice of Swiss cheese alternative over the bread and soup. Raise the oven heat to 425° F. Place the bowls on a cookie sheet and put in the oven for about 8 minutes. You just want to melt the cheese.

Serve with a salad and the rest of the French bread.

Per Serving: Calories: 223 Cholesterol: 3mg Dietary Fiber: 2g Protein: 8g
Sodium: 1273mg Carbohydrate: 19g Total Fat: 11g Saturated Fat: 2g
Calories from Fat: 47%, Calories from Carbohydrates: 37%, Calories from Protein: 16%

Breakfast

If you are Lactose Intolerant, even a bowl of cereal can cause a devastating reaction. Check the cereal boxes; it's surprising what you will find. Milk isn't the only lactose culprit.

At our house Sunday brunch is a special time. So, I began to find ways to change simple recipes to include my husband. Now we can really enjoy a wonderful meal *together*. This section contains many of these recipes.

Brunch Baked Potato Skins

This recipe adds a little variety to brunch. You can prepare the skins the day before, arrange them on a tray, cover them, and place in your refrigerator. At time of serving, make the scrambled eggs, fill the potato skins, microwave them to melt the cheese, and serve! You can use the reserved potatoes to make hash browns or other potato side dishes.

Makes 12 servings
Preparation time: 30 minutes

6 small baking potatoes, scrubbed and dried
1/4 cup safflower oil margarine, Hollywood, melted
3 servings cooked Scrambled Eggs (page 60)
1 cup shredded cheddar cheese alternative, TofuRella
1/4 cup real bacon bits, Hormel
1/4 cup diced green onions
Freshly ground pepper

Pierce the potatoes several times with a fork. Place in the microwave on high for 18 minutes. Potatoes are done when they are tender to piercing. Remove from the microwave and cool.

When cool enough to handle, cut the potatoes in half lengthwise. Scoop out the potato, leaving a thin coating of potato along the skin. Reserve the cooked potato to make hash browns.

Place the potato skins, cut side up, in a shallow baking pan. Brush the melted safflower margarine completely over the inside of the potato skins. Spoon in the scrambled eggs, top with the cheddar cheese alternative, bacon pieces, and green onions.

Finish by sprinkling freshly ground pepper over the completed potatoes. Return to the microwave, cooking long enough to melt the cheese and to warm the potatoes.

*A great make-ahead dish for
a family brunch!*

Per Serving: Calories: 170 Cholesterol: 111 mg Dietary Fiber: 1g Protein: 7g
Sodium: 226mg Carbohydrate: 12g Total Fat: 11g Saturated Fat: 2g
Calories from Fat: 58%, Calories from Carbohydrates: 27%, Calories from Protein: 15%

Dad's Famous Pancakes

These pancakes are light and fluffy, so make plenty! Serve with flavored fruit "butters" and syrups for variety . . . or microwave homemade preserves until melted and pour over the pancakes.

Makes 10 pancakes
Preparation time: 10 minutes

1 cup pancake mix, Aunt Jemima
1 1/8 cups 100% lactose-free 2% lowfat milk
1 tablespoon vegetable oil
1 large egg, slightly beaten

Lightly grease a skillet or electric fry pan (or a nonstick fry pan), then preheat the skillet to 375° F. Test for readiness by sprinkling drops of water on the pan . . . if the water sizzles and disappears, the pan's ready.

Meanwhile, combine all the ingredients in a medium mixing bowl, whisking together until blended smooth (breaking down all lumps).

Pour a small amount of batter (1/4 cup) onto the heated skillet. When bubbles form over the top of the batter and the bottom edges start browning, gently flip the pancakes over and finish cooking until the undersides are golden. Place on a warmed plate and keep warm until ready to serve. (If necessary, lightly brush the skillet with additional oil for multiple batches.)

Microwave leftovers for next morning's breakfast.

Per Serving: Calories: 38 Cholesterol: 23mg Dietary Fiber: 0g Protein: 2g
Sodium: 37mg Carbohydrate: 2g Total Fat: 2g Saturated Fat: .7g
Calories from Fat: 58%, Calories from Carbohydrates: 25%, Calories from Protein: 17%

Lactose-Free Omelet

Add fresh sliced mushrooms, diced tomatoes, peppers, onions, veggies, and cheese alternatives. This is a meal in itself!

Makes 2 servings
Preparation time: 15 minutes

4 medium eggs, slightly beaten
1/3 cup 100% lactose-free 2% lowfat milk
2 tablespoons safflower oil margarine, Hollywood
Dash salt
Dash freshly ground pepper

In a small mixing bowl, place the eggs and lactose-free milk. With a whisk, blend until light and fluffy.

In a 9-inch skillet or omelet pan, melt the safflower margarine, coating the entire pan, over medium heat. Pour the egg mixture into the pan (if using an omelet pan, divide the mixture, placing approximately half in each side of the pan). Reduce the heat slightly and allow the eggs to cook slowly. Run a spatula along the set edges; this will allow the uncooked eggs to flow to the bottom. (If you desire a filling in your omelet, add it now.)

Allow the omelet to cook until all but a small area on top is moist, sprinkle with salt and pepper, flip the omelet in half for a few seconds, then turn it onto a plate. If using an omelet pan, flip the omelet onto both sides for a few minutes each before turning it onto the plate.

Per Serving: Calories: 271 Cholesterol: 428mg Dietary Fiber: 0g Protein: 14g
Sodium: 262mg Carbohydrate: 3g Total Fat: 23g Saturated Fat: 6g
Calories from Fat: 75%, Calories from Carbohydrates: 5%, Calories from Protein: 20%

Old Country French Toast

For a wonderfully elegant breakfast, warm ready-to-use blueberry or cherry pie filling in the microwave, then stir and pour across the center of the French toast. You can also serve it with warmed fruit syrups or homemade jams.

Makes 6 servings; approximately 2½ slices per person
Preparation time: 30 minutes

**2 tablespoons safflower oil margarine, Hollywood, for
    coating the pan
7 medium eggs, slightly beaten
3/4 cup 100% lactose-free 2% lowfat milk
1 package French bread, Old Country, thick sliced
Dash ground cinnamon
Sprinkle powdered sugar**

Heat a griddle or electric fry pan to medium heat (350° F.). Coat the pan with the safflower margarine.

In a large, wide bowl, whisk the eggs and lactose-free milk together until blended. Dip thick-sliced bread into the egg mixture, coating both sides. Allow the excess to drain before placing the bread in the pan. Cook approximately 3 minutes, or until a golden brown, flip the slices over, and repeat on the other side.

Line a large platter with the cooked French toast. Dust with cinnamon and powdered sugar, and serve.

Per Serving: Calories: 340 Cholesterol: 250mg Dietary Fiber: 2g Protein: 16g
Sodium: 748mg Carbohydrate: 44g Total Fat: 11g Saturated Fat: 3g
Calories from Fat: 28%, Calories from Carbohydrates: 53%, Calories from Protein: 19%

Poached Eggs

I realize there is no lactose in these simple ingredients, but it's what you do with them. This recipe can stand alone, or be the beginning of so many things, for example, eggs Benedict. Often in our frustration to find "something different" to eat, we forget that the simplest may sometimes be the best! This is truly the easiest, fastest way to prepare a light dinner, breakfast, or brunch. (Watch your breads for lactose content.)

Makes 1 serving
Preparation time: 5 minutes

Egg poacher insert
PAM cooking spray
2 large eggs

Lightly coat the egg poacher insert with PAM cooking spray. Carefully break the eggs into individual cups of the insert. Place the entire insert into a fry pan filled with 1/2 cup water. Do not allow the water to touch the bottom of the insert cups. Cover the fry pan and cook on low to medium heat. Watch carefully; it takes only a few minutes for the eggs to reach the desired doneness. According to personal taste, as the eggs cook the whites will become opaque and the yolks will harden.

Turn out onto toast, English muffins, or a plate. Serve with hash browns and fresh fruit. This is the easiest way I have found to poach an egg, successfully!

Makes a great late dinner or brunch dish.

Per Serving: Calories: 149 Cholesterol: 425mg Dietary Fiber: 0g Protein: 13g
Sodium: 126mg Carbohydrate: 1g Total Fat: 10g Saturated Fat: 3g
Calories from Fat: 62%, Calories from Carbohydrates: 3%, Calories from Protein: 35%

Scrambled Eggs

T his basic scrambled egg recipe can be used as a basis for omelets. For variety, prior to completing cooking, top with ¹/₄ cup shredded cheddar cheese alternative and/or mozzarella alternative and bacon pieces for an "open omelet" effect.

Makes 1 serving
Preparation time: 8 minutes

2 large eggs, slightly beaten
3 tablespoons 100% lactose-free 2% lowfat milk
1 tablespoon safflower oil margarine, Hollywood
Dash freshly ground pepper
Dash salt (optional)

In a small mixing bowl, whisk the eggs with the lactose-free milk until light and fluffy. Melt the safflower margarine in a fry pan over medium heat, coating the entire bottom of the pan. Add the egg mixture all at once, and cook until the eggs begin to set. With a whisk or spatula, gently fluff the cooked eggs to allow the uncooked portion to flow to the heat source. About halfway through cooking, grind some fresh pepper over the eggs. (You may add salt if desired.) Be careful not to dry the eggs out; they should be removed from the heat while they have a "moist" look. Serve on a warm plate with your choice of toast, English muffin, etc.

Per Serving (without bread or salt): Calories: 273 Cholesterol: 429mg
Dietary Fiber: 0g Protein: 14g Sodium: 264mg Carbohydrate: 4g Total Fat: 23g
Saturated Fat: 6g Calories from Fat: 75%, Calories from Carbohydrates: 5%,
Calories from Protein: 20%

Eggs in a Mushroom Cup

*A*n easy, elegant brunch idea that brings two favorites together. It is important to use jumbo mushrooms and medium eggs in order to allow the eggs to cook properly.

Makes 4 servings
Preparation time: 20 minutes

8 very large fresh mushrooms
1 tablespoon lemon juice
1 garlic clove, finely chopped
2 tablespoons finely chopped shallots
1 1/2 teaspoons dried tarragon
1/8 teaspoon salt
Dash freshly ground pepper
3 tablespoons safflower oil margarine, Hollywood
8 medium eggs
1/2 cup whipping cream alternative, Pastry Pride

Preheat the oven to 400° F.

Remove the stems from the mushrooms, brush clean, and gently rub with the lemon juice to prevent discoloration.

Generously grease a shallow, heatproof baking dish with safflower margarine. Sprinkle the bottom of the baking dish with the finely chopped garlic and shallots and place the mushrooms, stem side down, in the dish. Place the baking dish on a stove burner and sauté over medium heat for 2 to 3 minutes.

Remove from the heat, turn the mushrooms over, and season with tarragon, salt, and pepper. Also place a small piece of the safflower margarine in each mushroom cap.

Place the baking dish with the mushrooms in the oven for about 3 minutes. After about 1¹/₂ minutes, baste the mushroom caps with the juices from the pan (this prevents drying).

Remove the baking dish from the oven. Break 1 egg into each mushroom cap. Then spoon the whipping cream alternative over the top of each egg. Cover the baking dish loosely with a piece of aluminum foil and return the dish to the oven. Bake for another 3 to 5 minutes, depending on your desired taste.

Remove the dish from the oven and carefully place on a serving dish. Serve immediately.

Per Serving: Calories: 345 Cholesterol: 425mg Dietary Fiber: 0g Protein: 14g
Sodium: 311mg Carbohydrate: 11g Total Fat: 28g Saturated Fat: 12g
Calories from Fat: 72%, Calories from Carbohydrates: 12%, Calories from Protein: 16%

Waffles

These waffles are light and airy but filling. For a special idea, use leftover breakfast waffles as dessert. Microwave until warm, pour canned pie filling (flavor of your choice) over the waffles, and top with homemade lactose-free ice cream. Or just wrap leftovers for a quick breakfast the next morning.

Makes 8 servings
Preparation time: 15 minutes

PAM cooking spray
13/4 cups all-purpose flour
2 teaspoons baking powder
1 tablespoon sugar
1/2 teaspoon salt
3 large eggs
11/2 cups 100% lactose-free 2% lowfat milk
1/3 cup vegetable oil

Follow the manufacturer's instructions for operating your Teflon waffle iron. Spray the waffle iron with PAM cooking spray and preheat to the instructed temperature.

Combine all the dry ingredients into a medium mixing bowl, whisking together. In a separate small mixing bowl, whisk together the eggs and lactose-free milk. When light and fluffy, add to the dry ingredients and blend. Next add the vegetable oil, just until blended. Pour the manufacturer's recommended amount of batter into the waffle iron and close to bake. Repeat until all the batter is used, keeping the baked waffles warm until ready to serve.

Top with fruit-flavored syrups or fresh fruit.

Per Serving (without topping): Calories: 239 Cholesterol: 83mg Dietary Fiber: 0g
Protein: 7g Sodium: 272mg Carbohydrate: 25g Total Fat: 12g Saturated Fat: 2g
Calories from Fat: 46%, Calories from Carbohydrates: 43%, Calories from Protein: 11%

Breads

Breads without lactose are difficult to find. Lactose is a great "filler" that provides texture, volume, taste, and shelf life to many foods. Investigate store brands or fresh bakery breads to find lactose-free candidates. Sourdough, French, or Italian breads are good choices.

This section contains homemade breads . . . where the sky is the limit! The art of breadmaking was revolutionized by the bread machine. Just adding ingredients and pushing a button lets the smell of homemade bread fill the air, beckoning everyone into the kitchen. I love the convenience of the bread machine, but in case you don't have one, I have included a few recipes that don't require it.

What's your pleasure? Oatmeal buttermilk bread? Corn bread? Date-nut bread? Well, here's your beginning collection of recipes. Enjoy the new choices.

Apple Bread

(Bread Machine Recipe)

Apples and cinnamon are always a wonderful combination, but this bread is extra-delicious. It won't last long!

Makes one 1½-pound loaf; 16 servings
Preparation time: 10 minutes

4 teaspoons safflower oil margarine, Hollywood
1/3 cup applesauce
3/4 cup apple juice
2 cups bread flour
1 cup wheat flour, whole grain
1 tablespoon honey
3/4 teaspoon sea salt
1½ teaspoons ground cinnamon
1 teaspoon bread machine yeast

Follow your bread machine manufacturer's directions, adding all ingredients as listed.

Wonderful served warm for breakfast.

Per Serving (1 slice): Calories: 98 Cholesterol: 0mg Dietary Fiber: 2g Protein: 3g
Sodium: 99mg Carbohydrate: 20g Total Fat: 1g Saturated Fat: 0g
Calories from Fat: 10%, Calories from Carbohydrates: 78%, Calories from Protein: 12%

Banana-Nut Bread

*T*hese freeze great, so they're always ready to serve. Thaw the breads at room temperature for 30 minutes. The small loaves make wonderful gifts—put them in holiday gift bags with decorative bows.

Makes 3 small loaves; 12 servings
Preparation time: 20 minutes

11/2 teaspoons white vinegar
1/2 cup 100% lactose-free 2% lowfat milk
1/2 cup walnuts
1/2 cup safflower oil margarine, Hollywood, softened
2 cups all-purpose flour, dip and sweep method
1 teaspoon baking powder
1 teaspoon baking soda
3/4 teaspoon salt
12/3 cups sugar
3 bananas, very ripe, mashed
1 teaspoon vanilla extract
2 large eggs, slightly beaten
solid vegetable shortening, Crisco, for greasing the pan

Preheat the oven to 350° F. Place the vinegar into a glass measuring cup. Fill the rest of the cup up to the 1/2-cup mark with the lactose-free milk. This makes 1/2 cup sour-milk substitute. Set aside while you prepare the rest of the recipe.

Place the walnuts in a nut chopper and chop finely. Cream the safflower margarine and dry ingredients. Add half the sour milk, half the mashed bananas, and the vanilla, and blend. Beat in the eggs, nuts, and the remaining milk and bananas, about 2 minutes until completely blended.

Generously grease a 5 × 9-inch loaf pan (for gift giving, use small 3 × 6-inch aluminum loaf pans) with the shortening. Fill the pan with batter approximately two thirds full.

Bake in the oven for at least 25 minutes; watch carefully during the last 10 minutes. Test for doneness by inserting a toothpick in the center of the loaf. Allow it to cool on a wire rack. Then remove from the pan and package as desired.

*Serve as a breakfast bread or a
nutritious snack.*

Per Serving (1 slice): Calories: 326 Cholesterol: 36mg Dietary Fiber: 1g Protein: 5g
Sodium: 362mg Carbohydrate: 52g Total Fat: 12g Saturated Fat: 2g
Calories from Fat: 33%, Calories from Carbohydrates: 61%, Calories from Protein: 6%

Blueberry Muffins

These muffins taste wonderful and are easy to make. They make a family breakfast or brunch very special. I have even served them with dinner instead of rolls. When buying bakery or grocery muffins, read the labels first! The best place to look for muffins is the bakery department of your grocery store. Fresh-baked muffins often do not contain lactose, while packaged ones do.

Makes 12 muffins
Preparation time: 20 minutes

1³/4 cups all-purpose flour, sifted
¹/2 cup sugar
2 teaspoons baking powder
¹/2 teaspoon salt
1 teaspoon ground cinnamon
1 large egg, slightly beaten
¹/4 cup vegetable oil, Crisco
³/4 cup 100% lactose-free 2% lowfat milk
³/4 cup blueberries, rinsed and drained

Preheat the oven to 400° F. Lightly grease the cups in a muffin pan or line them with paper bake cups. Set aside.

Combine the flour, sugar, baking powder, salt, and cinnamon. In a separate bowl, mix the egg, oil, and lactose-free milk. Once blended, combine with the dry ingredients, using a wooden spoon, until just blended. Batter will be lumpy. Fold in the blueberries.

Spoon the batter into the prepared muffin pan. Place in the oven for approximately 20 minutes. The muffins will be light brown and a toothpick will come out clean when inserted in the center. Pop the muffins out of the pan and serve warm.

Per Serving (1 muffin): Calories: 127 Cholesterol: 19mg Dietary Fiber: 0g Protein: 3g
Sodium: 75mg Carbohydrate: 16g Total Fat: 6g Saturated Fat: 1g
Calories from Fat: 39%, Calories from Carbohydrates: 52%, Calories from Protein: 9%

Sweet Biscuits

These "baby biscuits" are a special treat for breakfast or dinner. The addition of whipping cream alternative makes them rich and sweet.

Makes 5 to 6 dozen
Preparation time: 30 minutes

13/4 cups all-purpose flour
1/2 teaspoon salt
1 tablespoon sugar
1 tablespoon baking powder
6 tablespoons safflower oil margarine, Hollywood, cut
   into pieces
3/4 cup whipping cream alternative, Pastry Pride

Preheat the oven to 450° F. Sift the flour twice. Combine the flour with the salt, sugar, and baking powder in a large bowl. Stir to blend well. Using a pastry blender (or a fork), cut the safflower margarine into the dry ingredients until it forms crumbs. Slowly add the whipping cream alternative, cutting in just to blend. Try not to overblend; too much handling will make the dough tough.

On a floured surface, knead the mixture until it forms a soft dough. Flatten the dough into 1/4-inch thickness, and use a 1-inch round, floured cutter to cut out shapes. Place the round dough shapes on an ungreased baking sheet. Return to the remaining dough and mold the scraps into 1/4-inch thickness, cutting additional rounds until all the dough is used.

Bake in the oven 8 to 10 minutes. Biscuits will be golden brown. Serve warm.

Freeze the extras for a quick addition to any meal.

Per Serving (I biscuit): Calories: 29 Cholesterol: 0mg Dietary Fiber: 0g Protein: .3g
Sodium: 42mg Carbohydrate: 3g Total Fat: 2g Saturated Fat: .8g
Calories from Fat: 55%, Calories from Carbohydrates: 41%, Calories from Protein: 4%

Glazed Cinnamon Rolls

(Bread Machine Used to Mix and Rise Dough)

These rolls, fragrant with cinnamon, are very special. You can let them rise overnight and finish them in the morning. For variety, add raisins, or chopped apples, or both to the filling.

Makes 8 rolls
Preparation time: 2½ hours

1 cup water
2 tablespoons safflower oil margarine, Hollywood,
   softened
3 cups bread flour
1/4 cup granulated sugar
1 teaspoon salt
2½ teaspoons bread machine yeast
1/3 cup granulated sugar
2 teaspoons ground cinnamon
2 tablespoons safflower oil margarine, Hollywood, melted

For the glaze
1 cup confectioners' sugar
1/2 teaspoon vanilla extract
2 tablespoons 100% lactose-free 2% lowfat milk

Using a bread machine, place the water, safflower margarine, flour, 1/4 cup sugar, salt, and yeast in that order. Choose the dough cycle and follow the manufacturer's instructions. The bread machine is only used for the mixing and the initial rising of the dough in this recipe.

Meanwhile, grease a 9 × 9 × 2-inch baking pan and set aside. In a small mixing bowl, combine 1/3 cup sugar and the cinnamon. Also set aside.

Preheat the oven to 375° F. When the dough is ready, flatten it into a 9-inch square on a lightly floured surface. Brush with the melted safflower margarine. Generously sprinkle the cinnamon and sugar mixture over the entire 9-inch square. Roll the dough up as you would a jelly roll, pinching the edges to seal. Slice the roll into 1-inch slices, placing in the greased baking pan, cut side down. Cover with a tea towel and allow to double in size. This should take 1 to 1 1/2 hours.

Place the dough slices into the oven and bake for 25 to 30 minutes. The buns should be golden brown.

During the last few minutes of baking, assemble the glaze topping. In a small bowl, combine the confectioners' sugar, vanilla, and lactose-free milk. Stir until smooth and drizzly.

Remove the buns from the oven. Gently remove the buns from the pan onto a wire rack to cool. Immediately drizzle the glaze over the hot rolls. Serve warm.

These rolls turn any breakfast into something special!

Per Serving (1 roll): Calories: 319 Cholesterol: 0mg Dietary Fiber: 2g Protein: 6g
Sodium: 327mg Carbohydrate: 63g Total Fat: 6g Saturated Fat: 1g
Calories from Fat: 17%, Calories from Carbohydrates: 76%, Calories from Protein: 7%

Granna's Date-Nut Bread

*T*his wonderful old-time breakfast bread is a family hand-me-down from my husband's Granna Hadley. It was a regular every Christmas along with homemade elderberry jelly. It freezes great, and defrosts in 30 minutes.

Makes 16 servings
Preparation time: 20 minutes

1 cup dates, pitted and chopped
2 teaspoons baking soda
2 cups boiling water
2 tablespoons solid all-vegetable shortening, Crisco
2 cups sugar
4 cups all-purpose flour
1 teaspoon salt
1 cup finely chopped walnuts
2 teaspoons vanilla extract

Preheat the oven to 350° F. Wash out 1-pound tin cans to use for baking pans. (Or you can use loaf, bundt, or decorative bread pans.)

Place the first 5 ingredients together in a large bowl, mixing well. Gradually add the rest of the ingredients and blend well.

Pour the batter into the washed baking tins, and bake for 55 minutes, or until the batter stops sizzling. Cool on a wire rack. Remove from the tins by running a butter knife carefully around the inside edge and turning upside down. Wrap in plastic wrap.

Serve with safflower margarine for a breakfast treat.

Per Serving (1 slice): Calories: 303 Cholesterol: 0mg Dietary Fiber: 1g Protein: 5g
Sodium: 293mg Carbohydrate: 58g Total Fat: 6g Saturated Fat: .7g
Calories from Fat: 18%, Calories from Carbohydrates: 75%, Calories from Protein: 7%

Light Rye Bread

(Bread Machine Recipe)

This recipe makes a light and airy loaf. Store-bought bread labels have to be read very carefully. It is very difficult to find a loaf without lactose or its tricky little friends! With a bread machine, you can try making your favorite kinds with no work at all.

Makes one 1½-pound loaf; 16 servings
Preparation time: 10 minutes

1½ cups water
2 tablespoons safflower oil margarine, Hollywood
1 tablespoon sugar
1 teaspoon sea salt
2 teaspoons caraway seeds
3¼ cups bread flour
⅓ cup rye flour
2 teaspoons bread machine yeast

Place all the ingredients into the bread machine, in order. Follow the manufacturer's instructions for a medium-crust bread or white bread.

Makes a great companion for any meal.

Per Serving (1 slice): Calories: 107 Cholesterol: 0mg Dietary Fiber: 1g Protein: 4g
Sodium: 133mg Carbohydrate: 21g Total Fat: 2g Saturated Fat: .3g
Calories from Fat: 13%, Calories from Carbohydrates: 74%, Calories from Protein: 13%

Wheat Bread

Very simple pleasures, such as this bread, fall by the wayside with Lactose Intolerance. But knowledge of the substitutes you can use can bring them back. Try this delicious homemade bread.

Makes two 22-ounce loaves
Preparation time: 3 hours

41/2 cups whole wheat flour
21/2 to 3 cups bread flour
1 cup 100% lactose-free 2% lowfat milk
1 cup water
1/4 cup safflower oil margarine, Hollywood
1/4 cup dark molasses
1 package quick-rise yeast
2 teaspoons salt

For the glaze
1 medium egg yolk
1 teaspoon water

Premix the whole wheat flour with only 21/2 cups of the bread flour in a medium bowl. Stir to blend.

In a saucepan over low heat, warm the lactose-free milk, water, safflower margarine, and molasses. As this is warming up to a temperature of 110° F., place 2 cups of the flour mixture into the bowl of a standing mixer. To this add the yeast and salt, stirring to blend. Now slowly add the warmed milk mixture, stirring to combine, then beating until smooth. Gradually add the remaining flour mixture, stirring to blend well. (For this step, if you are not using a standing mixer bowl, a large bowl will work well.)

Using the dough hook on the standing mixer, knead the dough, adding additional bread flour as necessary until the dough pulls cleanly from the sides of the bowl and is no longer sticky. This should take about 6 to 7 minutes. (If you are not using a standing mixer, knead by hand, adding additional bread flour until the dough is smooth and elastic. This should take about 10 minutes.)

Grease a large bowl with additional margarine or solid shortening. Gather the dough up into a ball, placing it into the greased bowl. Roll the dough around the sides of the bowl, greasing all sides of the dough. Cover the bowl with plastic wrap and allow the dough to rise in a warm place until it has doubled. This should take about 1 to 1 1/2 hours.

After the dough has risen, generously grease two 8 1/2 × 4 1/2-inch loaf pans. Set aside. Using a flat workspace, lightly flour it and a rolling pin. Remove the risen dough from the bowl and turn out onto the floured workspace. Flatten the dough and cut it in half. Now, using the floured rolling pin, roll each half into a rectangle about 12 × 7 inches. From the 7-inch side, roll the dough up like a jelly roll, pinching the seams together to seal. Lay, seam side down, in the prepared loaf pans. Generously grease 2 pieces of plastic wrap large enough to cover each loaf-pan top. Cover and place in a warm place to rise. The dough should double in size, taking about 1 hour.

Preheat the oven to 375° F. Place the rack in the middle of the oven.

In a small bowl, beat the egg yolk slightly, add the water, and mix. Brush this mixture on the tops of the loaves before placing them in the oven. Bake in the oven for about 30 to 40 minutes. The tops of the loaves will be a golden brown, and there will be a hollow sound if you tap the bottoms. Allow the loaves to cool on a wire rack.

Per Serving (1 slice): Calories: 195 Cholesterol: 12mg Dietary Fiber: 4g Protein: 7g
Sodium: 245mg Carbohydrate: 36g Total Fat: 4g Saturated Fat: 1g
Calories from Fat: 17%, Calories from Carbohydrates: 70%, Calories from Protein: 13%

Oatmeal Buttermilk Bread

(Bread Machine Recipe)

Old-time flavor makes this bread so special. It's so delicious on its own, you won't be able to keep it around for long!

Makes one 1½-pound loaf; 16 servings
Preparation time: 10 minutes

1 cup rolled oats
1¼ tablespoons vinegar
1¼ cups 100% lactose-free 2% lowfat milk
1 tablespoon safflower oil margarine, Hollywood
2 tablespoons honey
2¾ cups bread flour
¾ teaspoon sea salt
1 teaspoon bread machine yeast

Preheat the oven to 350° F. In a shallow baking pan, place the rolled oats. Place in the oven for 15 to 20 minutes until lightly browned. Cool.

In a 2-cup glass measuring cup, place the vinegar and fill with lactose-free milk to make 1¼ cups. Allow to stand a few minutes. This is your substitute for buttermilk.

Follow your bread machine manufacturer's directions, placing all the remaining ingredients into the machine.

A wonderful morning bread, but great at any time.

Per Serving (1 slice): Calories: 113 Cholesterol: 2mg Dietary Fiber: 1g Protein: 4g
Sodium: 105mg Carbohydrate: 22g Total Fat: 2g Saturated Fat: .4g
Calories from Fat: 11%, Calories from Carbohydrates: 74%, Calories from Protein: 15%

Quick Corn Bread

*J*iffy *brand corn muffin mix contains no lactose and provides a great, quick alternative to rolls or bread. Following the directions on the box, you can turn this recipe into muffins, if you prefer.*

Makes 8 servings
Preparation time: 10 minutes

2 8 1/2-ounce packages corn muffin mix, Jiffy
2 large eggs
2/3 cup 100% lactose-free 2% lowfat milk

Preheat the oven to 400° F. Generously grease a 9 × 13-inch glass baking pan. Empty both packages of mix into a medium mixing bowl, add the eggs and lactose-free milk. Stir together until just blended, eliminating large lumps. Turn into the prepared pan and bake for 20 to 25 minutes. Serve warm.

Great with soups, breakfast, or dinner!

Per Serving: Calories: 73 Cholesterol: 62mg Dietary Fiber: 0g Protein: 3g
Sodium: 100mg Carbohydrate: 8g Total Fat: 3g Saturated Fat: .9g
Calories from Fat: 36%, Calories from Carbohydrates: 47%, Calories from Protein: 17%

Raisin Sticky Buns

(Bread Machine Recipe)

These buns won't last long! If you don't care for raisins, you can use walnuts or pecans or both raisins and nuts. Try not to handle the dough too much; it will make it tough.

Makes 8 servings
Preparation time: 1 hour

1 cup water
2 tablespoons safflower oil margarine, Hollywood
2 1/2 cups bread flour
1/4 cup granulated sugar
1 teaspoon sea salt
2 1/2 teaspoons bread machine yeast
1/3 cup granulated sugar
1/2 cup raisins
1 1/2 teaspoons ground cinnamon
1/4 cup safflower oil margarine, Hollywood, melted
1/3 cup light brown sugar, packed
1 tablespoon light corn syrup
1 cup raisins
2 tablespoons safflower oil margarine, Hollywood,
   softened

Into a bread machine, place the water, 2 tablespoons safflower margarine, bread flour, 1/4 cup granulated sugar, sea salt, and yeast, in that order. Select the dough cycle and follow the manufacturer's instructions.

Meanwhile, in a small mixing bowl, blend together 1/3 cup granulated sugar, 1/2 cup raisins, and the cinnamon. Set aside; this is the filling.

Preheat the oven to 375° F. Into an ungreased 9 × 9 × 2-inch baking dish, place the melted safflower margarine, brown sugar, and corn syrup. Stir together until completely mixed. Sprinkle 1 cup raisins over the mixture. Set aside.

Return to the dough when it is finished in the bread machine. On a lightly floured surface, flatten the dough and roll it out to about a 9-inch square. Brush with 2 tablespoons softened safflower margarine. Generously spread the cinnamon-sugar raisin mixture over the entire area. Now, roll dough up tightly like a jelly roll, pinching the edges to seal.

Slice the roll into 1-inch pieces, placing them in the baking dish over the brown sugar topping. Cover with a damp tea towel and allow to double in size in a warm place (about 1 hour).

Bake in the oven for about 25 minutes, or until golden brown. Remove from the oven, invert on a plate, leaving the buns in the pan. Let stand for 2 to 3 minutes, making sure all the topping drizzles down through the buns. Serve warm.

A great addition to brunch!

Per Serving (1 bun): Calories: 369 Cholesterol: 0mg Dietary Fiber: 3g Protein: 6g
Sodium: 331 mg Carbohydrate: 72g Total Fat: 9g Saturated Fat: 1g
Calories from Fat: 21%, Calories from Carbohydrates: 73%, Calories from Protein: 6%

The French Connection

(Bread Machine Used to Mix and Rise Dough)

Some store-bought and bakery French breads are made with lactose; so read the labels carefully. Not only will these homemade loaves fill your kitchen with wonderful smells, but they will complement any dish.

Makes 2 loaves; 24 servings
Preparation time: 2 hours

1 cup water
2 3/4 cups bread flour
1 1/2 teaspoons bread machine yeast
1 tablespoon sugar
1 teaspoon sea salt

For the glaze
1 large egg yolk, slightly beaten
1 tablespoon water

Measure the ingredients and begin placing them in your bread machine, liquids first (unless otherwise recommended by the manufacturer). Place the 1 cup of water, cover with the flour, yeast, sugar, and salt, being very careful that the yeast doesn't come in contact with the water. Do not add the egg yolk or the tablespoon of water yet.

Press the bread machine's setting for dough, and follow the manufacturer's instructions. Generously grease a large mixing bowl. Remove the finished dough from the machine and coat the dough with grease by rolling it around the sides of the greased bowl. Now, cover the dough and allow it to double in size in a warm place. If an indentation is left when testing the dough, it is done.

Grease 2 baking sheets and preheat the oven to 375° F. On a lightly floured surface, knead the dough and roll into a 16 × 12-inch rectangle. Cutting the dough in half, take each half and roll up tightly, like a jelly roll. Taper the ends by gently rolling back and forth.

Place the loaves on the baking sheets, and slash lengthwise down the middle of each loaf. Cover and again let them rise for about 30 to 45 minutes in a warm place.

Mix the egg yolk and the tablespoon of water together and brush the tops of each loaf. Bake in the oven for 20 to 25 minutes, checking for light browning on the tops.

Great served with any meal.

Per Serving (1 slice): Calories: 50 Cholesterol: 9mg Dietary Fiber: .5g Protein: 2g
Sodium: 79mg Carbohydrate: 11g Total Fat: .2g Saturated Fat: .1g
Calories from Fat: 4%, Calories from Carbohydrates: 81%, Calories from Protein: 15%

Plain White Bread

(Bread Machine Recipe)

*W*hite bread seems to be the hardest to find lactose free. Therefore, it is wonderful to be able to serve a plain, white bread slice. Remember, you can make a loaf, slice it, and freeze it (wrap it well). Then you have it on hand to serve anytime.

Makes one 1½-pound loaf; 16 servings
Preparation time: 10 minutes

1¼ cups 100% lactose-free 2% lowfat milk
2 teaspoons safflower oil margarine, Hollywood
3 cups bread flour
1 tablespoon sugar
½ teaspoon sea salt
1 teaspoon bread machine yeast

Using a bread machine, follow your manufacturer's directions. Start at the top of the list and add all the ingredients in order, making sure to keep the yeast on top away from the liquids.

Great for sandwiches, toast, or anything.

Per Serving (1 slice): Calories: 92 Cholesterol: 2mg Dietary Fiber: .8g Protein: 4g
Sodium: 73mg Carbohydrate: 18g Total Fat: .9g Saturated Fat: .3g
Calories from Fat: 8%, Calories from Carbohydrates: 77%, Calories from Protein: 15%

Basic White Bread

If you don't have a bread machine, use this recipe to make wonderful lactose-free sandwiches, stuffing, toast, bread crumbs, or even croutons.

Makes two 1¼-pound large loaves
Preparation time: 2 hours

6 cups bread flour
1 package quick-rise yeast
2 teaspoons salt
1 cup water
1 cup 100% lactose-free 2% lowfat milk
3 tablespoons safflower oil margarine, Hollywood

For the glaze
1 large egg yolk
1 teaspoon water

Into a standing mixer bowl (or a large mixing bowl), place 4 cups of the bread flour, the yeast, and salt. Combine the water, lactose-free milk, and safflower margarine in a medium saucepan, heating to 110° F. (about lukewarm). Add the lukewarm mixture slowly to the flour, salt, and yeast mixture. Stir in additional bread flour with a wooden spoon, forming a soft dough that holds its shape.

Knead with the dough hook on a standing mixer, adding additional flour as needed. After about 6 to 7 minutes, the dough should no longer be sticky and should pull cleanly from the sides of the workbowl. If kneading by hand, allow 10 minutes for the dough to become smooth and elastic.

Generously grease all sides of a large bowl with a little extra margarine. Gather up the dough into a ball and roll around the greased bowl, coating all sides of the dough. Place plastic wrap over the bowl, set in a warm area, and allow to rise until dough doubles in size. This will take about 45 to 60 minutes.

Generously grease two loaf pans (8½ × 4½ inches). Set aside. Lightly flour a work surface and a rolling pin. Take the bread dough from the bowl and place it on the floured surface. Flatten the dough, divide it in half, and make two balls. Working with one ball at a time, roll out, using the floured rolling pin to form a 12 × 7-inch rectangle. Roll up like a jelly roll, beginning at the shorter side, and seal the seams by pinching them together. Lift the roll and place in the greased loaf pan, seam side down. Lay a piece of greased plastic wrap over the loaf pan and allow the dough to rise again in a warm place (about 45 minutes).

Preheat the oven to 400° F. In a small bowl, whisk together the egg yolk and teaspoon of water. This will make a glaze for the top crust of the bread. Before placing the loaf pans into the oven, brush the loaves with this glaze.

Bake for 30 to 40 minutes. Bread is done when golden brown and a hollow sound can be heard when tapping the bottoms. Remove from the pans and allow to cool on a wire rack.

Per Serving (1 slice): Calories: 175 Cholesterol: 12mg Dietary Fiber: 1g Protein: 6g
Sodium: 239mg Carbohydrate: 31g Total Fat: 3g Saturated Fat: .6g
Calories from Fat: 16%, Calories from Carbohydrates: 71%, Calories from Protein: 13%

The Ultimate Egg Bread

(Bread Machine Recipe)

This recipe is simple and easy. A wonderful bread to eat alone or with meals. By substituting the milk and margarine, the consistency will be the same as regular egg bread, but the lactose content won't be!

Makes one 1½-pound loaf; 16 servings
Preparation time: 10 minutes

3/4 cup 100% lactose-free 2% lowfat milk
2 large eggs, slightly beaten
3 tablespoons safflower oil margarine, Hollywood
1½ teaspoons sea salt
3 cups bread flour
1/2 cup sugar
1½ teaspoons bread machine yeast

Start with the top of the ingredient list and add all the ingredients in order to the bread machine. (Don't allow the yeast to come in contact with any liquid.)

Follow manufacturer's instructions for a light bread.

Per Serving (1 slice): Calories: 133 Cholesterol: 28mg Dietary Fiber: .8g Protein: 4g
Sodium: 212mg Carbohydrate: 23g Total Fat: 3g Saturated Fat: .7g
Calories from Fat: 20%, Calories from Carbohydrates: 68%, Calories from Protein: 12%

Potato Scones

For a very different lunch or accompaniment, try these scones made with leftover mashed potatoes. You'll see how fast they disappear.

Makes 24 to 28 scones
Preparation time: 30 minutes

2 tablespoons sugar
2 tablespoons baking powder
3 cups all-purpose flour
1 teaspoon salt
3/4 cup safflower oil margarine, Hollywood
2 cups All-American Whipped Mashed Potatoes, cold
　(page 90)
1/4 cup 100% lactose-free 2% lowfat milk
2 large eggs, slightly beaten

For the glaze
1 large egg yolk
1 teaspoon water
1 tablespoon poppy or sesame seeds

Preheat the oven to 425° F. and lightly grease 2 large cookie sheets.

Place the sugar, baking powder, flour, and salt in a large bowl. Stir to combine. Cut the safflower margarine into the dry ingredients using a pastry blender or a fork. The dough will resemble crumbs after a few minutes.

Add the cold potatoes, lactose-free milk, and eggs, stirring with a wooden spoon to combine. Continue blending until the dough pulls away from the sides of the bowl.

On a floured surface, gently knead the soft dough about 30 seconds. Using a floured rolling pin, flatten the dough to 1/2-inch thickness. Use a diamond-shaped cutter about 2 × 3 inches; lightly flour it and cut out shapes. Gather up scraps, flatten them, and continue cutting out shapes until all the dough is used.

Place the diamond-shaped pieces of dough on the prepared cookie sheets, leaving about 1 inch between them for expansion. In a small bowl, whisk the egg yolk and water together, then brush over the tops of the shapes. Finish by sprinkling the poppy or sesame seeds over the tops.

Bake in the oven 20 to 25 minutes, just until the scones are a golden brown.

Here's an inventive way to use those leftover mashed potatoes.

Per Serving (1 scone): Calories: 120 Cholesterol: 23mg Dietary Fiber: 0g Protein: 3g
Sodium: 248mg Carbohydrate: 14g Total Fat: 6g Saturated Fat: 1g
Calories from Fat: 45%, Calories from Carbohydrates: 47%, Calories from Protein: 8%

Side Dishes

Let's see, what side-dish options do you have when you eliminate lactose? Lots! The ones here are just starters . . . once you get used to substituting and changing recipes, your choices are limitless! Remember to use fresh vegetables and herbs whenever possible. Fresh ingredients always make any dish better.

All-American Whipped Mashed Potatoes

This is a simple recipe and oh, what a crowd pleaser! My daughter, Chrissy, makes it the best. By whipping the potatoes with an electric mixer, they become light and airy. You can sprinkle parsley on top or celery flakes. If you prefer, leave the skins on and continue with the recipe.

Before using Lactaid, Knudsen, or JerseyMaid lactose-free milks, I tried other nondairy brands only to have gray-looking lumpy potatoes. The 2% lactose-free milk gives the potatoes a creamier body. And they are so fluffy and white no one will guess they are not made with regular milk. I allow my guests to add their own salt and freshly ground pepper, so I don't add them to the recipe.

Makes 6 servings
Preparation time: 30 minutes

4 large baking potatoes
3/4 cup 100% lactose-free 2% lowfat milk, warmed
2 tablespoons safflower oil margarine, Hollywood

Peel the potatoes and chop them into medium pieces. Immediately place them in a large pot, covering with water. Bring to a boil over high heat, uncovered, reduce to medium low, and continue to cook for about 20 minutes, or until the potatoes are tender when pierced with a fork.

Drain the potatoes and place in a warm, large mixing bowl. With an electric hand mixer (or a stationary one) on low speed, begin to mash the potatoes. When you have eliminated all large lumps, begin to slowly add the warmed lactose-free milk. Blend after each addition until you have light, fluffy mashed potatoes. You may add the safflower margarine while blending in the milk, or simply top the finished potatoes with pats of margarine. Serve immediately, or cover and reheat in the microwave (1 minute on high) if necessary.

Mashed potatoes complement any meal.

Per Serving: Calories: 109 Cholesterol: 3mg Dietary Fiber: 1g Protein: 3g
Sodium: 58mg Carbohydrate: 15g Total Fat: 5g Saturated Fat: 1g
Calories from Fat: 38%, Calories from Carbohydrates: 53%, Calories from Protein: 9%

Baked Garlic Tomatoes

*W*hen preparing this dish, remember to select your bread crumbs carefully. No dried whey! Pioneer is the one I choose most often, but I have found several store brands that are lactose free. Choose a strong-flavored tomato—fresh tomatoes from your garden, or from the local farmers' market are your best bet.

Makes 4 servings
Preparation time: 15 minutes

2 large red ripe tomatoes, cut in half
3 tablespoons bread crumbs, Pioneer
2 garlic cloves, minced
2 tablespoons chopped fresh parsley
Freshly ground pepper, optional
3 tablespoons virgin olive oil, light

Preheat the oven to 425° F. Arrange halved tomatoes, cut side up, on foil-covered cookie sheets.

In a small bowl, mix together the bread crumbs, garlic, parsley, and pepper (as desired). Spoon over the tomato halves, then generously drizzle the olive oil over the tops of the tomatoes. Bake in the oven on the top rack for 8 to 10 minutes only until lightly browned. Serve at once.

Makes a fine appetizer or simple side dish.

Per Serving: Calories: 125 Cholesterol: 0mg Dietary Fiber: 1g Protein: 2g
Sodium: 42mg Carbohydrate: 7g Total Fat: 10g Saturated Fat: 1g
Calories from Fat: 72%, Calories from Carbohydrates: 23%, Calories from Protein: 5%

Baked Tomato-Zucchini Dish

This recipe is easy to make. Whether the vegetables are home-grown or from the local farmers' market, they are a welcome side dish at any outdoor meal. You can experiment with different combinations of your favorite herbs. Remember the rule about using "real" Parmesan: It must be aged and imported—that lowers the lactose content—and first make sure that your system can handle a little of the real stuff.

Makes 6 servings
Preparation time: 1 hour

2 tablespoons virgin olive oil, light
2 large shallots, sliced
1 large garlic clove, minced
1 pound red ripe tomatoes, sliced 1/4 inch thick
1 pound zucchini, sliced 1/2 inch thick
1/2 teaspoon dried oregano
1/2 teaspoon fresh parsley, chopped
1/8 teaspoon dried basil
2 tablespoons grated Parmesan cheese alternative, Soyco
Freshly ground pepper, to taste

Preheat the oven to 350° F. In a medium fry pan, heat 1 tablespoon of the olive oil. Add the shallots and garlic; sauté for about 20 minutes on low heat. They should be soft and golden when done.

Spread the cooked shallots and garlic over the bottom of a gratin or baking dish about 12 inches in size.

Slice the tomatoes into 1/4-inch slices and set aside. Slice the zucchini into 1/2-inch slices and set aside. Arrange the tomato slices down the center of the gratin dish, and layer the zucchini slices in rows on both sides. If you are using a baking dish, just alternate rows of tomato slices and zucchini slices.

In a small bowl, mix the oregano, parsley, and basil. Sprinkle on top of the slices, followed by Parmesan cheese alternative and pepper. Take the remaining olive oil and drizzle over the entire top of the tomato and zucchini slices.

Bake in the oven for about 25 minutes. Vegetables should be tender when cooked. Serve hot or warm.

A great summer lunch or supper dish with fresh garden vegetables.

Per Serving: Calories: 81 Cholesterol: 0mg Dietary Fiber: 2g Protein: 3g
Sodium: 51mg Carbohydrate: 8g Total Fat: 5g Saturated Fat: 1g
Calories from Fat: 53%, Calories from Carbohydrates: 34%, Calories from Protein: 13%

Broccoli Cheddar Casserole

*V*ery little preparation is needed for this quick casserole. Remember to use Campbell's Golden Mushroom soup because regular canned mushroom soup is not lactose free.

Makes 8 servings
Preparation time: 15 minutes

1 tablespoon safflower oil margarine, Hollywood
10 ounces frozen broccoli, thawed and drained
2 large eggs, slightly beaten
1 10^{1}/2-ounce can Campbell's Golden Mushroom soup, undiluted
1 cup shredded cheddar cheese alternative, TofuRella
1 cup mayonnaise, Best Foods or Hellmann's
1/2 teaspoon minced garlic
1 cup sourdough croutons, Pioneer, coarsely chopped
1 tablespoon finely chopped parsley
1/2 teaspoon paprika

Preheat the oven to 350° F., and lightly grease a 2-quart casserole dish with the safflower margarine.

In a large mixing bowl, combine the broccoli, eggs, undiluted soup, cheddar cheese alternative, mayonnaise, and garlic. Toss together until mixed.

Place in the greased casserole dish. In a small mixing bowl, combine the croutons, parsley, and paprika. Sprinkle over the top of the casserole. You can add additional seasonings if desired to the crouton topping. Bake for 30 minutes. Serve immediately.

Per Serving: Calories: 340 Cholesterol: 64mg Dietary Fiber: 1g Protein: 9g
Sodium: 656mg Carbohydrate: 9g Total Fat: 30g Saturated Fat: 4g
Calories from Fat: 80%, Calories from Carbohydrates: 10%, Calories from Protein: 10%

Cherry Tomato Sauté

This quick summer dish is a great addition to a barbecue. Using olive oil and Parmesan cheese alternative turns this crowd pleaser into a lactose-free pleaser!

Makes 6 servings
Preparation time: 15 minutes

1 tablespoon virgin olive oil, light
1 pint cherry tomatoes, rinsed and drained
1 tablespoon finely chopped fresh parsley
1 teaspoon dried oregano
1 teaspoon dried basil
1/4 cup grated Parmesan cheese alternative, Soyco
Freshly ground pepper, to taste

In a large skillet, heat the olive oil over medium heat. Add the tomatoes to the hot oil and sauté, stirring several times, for about 3 minutes. Tomatoes should be soft but not broken. Sprinkle with the herbs and three quarters of the Parmesan cheese alternative, toss tomatoes to coat, and season with pepper.

Remove from the skillet and place in a warmed serving dish. Sprinkle the remaining cheese alternative as the finale.

A great summer side dish for any meal.

Per Serving: Calories: 50 Cholesterol: 0mg Dietary Fiber: .8g Protein: 3g
Sodium: 87mg Carbohydrate: 3g Total Fat: 3g Saturated Fat: .3g
Calories from Fat: 54%, Calories from Carbohydrates: 25%, Calories from Protein: 21%

Creamed Onions

*U*sing *100% lactose-free 2% lowfat milk and safflower margarine in this recipe matches the taste and consistency of the real thing.*

Makes 8 servings
Preparation time: 30 minutes

1/2 teaspoon salt
2 pounds small white onions, whole
6 tablespoons safflower oil margarine, Hollywood
3 tablespoons all-purpose flour
11/2 cups 100% lactose-free 2% lowfat milk
Dash paprika

Fill a 2-quart saucepan with 1 inch of water. Add 1/4 teaspoon of the salt and bring to a boil over medium heat. Add the onions and return to a boil. Turn the heat down to low, cover, and simmer for 10 to 15 minutes until onions are tender.

While the onions are cooking, melt the safflower margarine in a 1-quart saucepan. Into the melted margarine add the flour, stirring constantly until smooth. Very slowly add the lactose-free milk and the remaining 1/4 teaspoon salt. Continue to cook, stirring constantly until mixture thickens.

Returning to the onions, drain and place in serving dish. Slowly pour the thickened sauce over the onions. Sprinkle the paprika just before serving.

An extra-special side dish for onion lovers.

Per Serving: Calories: 132 Cholesterol: 4mg Dietary Fiber: 2g Protein: 3g
Sodium: 664mg Carbohydrate: 9g Total Fat: 10g Saturated Fat: 2g
Calories from Fat: 66%, Calories from Carbohydrates: 26%, Calories from Protein: 8%

The Carrot Soufflé

Simple and easy, this soufflé is very versatile . . . it can be served as a light lunch or supper, or as an elegant side dish.

Makes 6 to 8 servings
Preparation time: 30 minutes

4 large carrots
1/2 cup safflower oil margarine, Hollywood
1/2 cup all-purpose flour
11/2 cups whipping cream alternative,
　　Pastry Pride
6 large eggs, separated
1/2 teaspoon ground nutmeg
1/2 teaspoon salt
1/4 teaspoon freshly ground pepper

Begin by peeling and slicing the carrots. Place them in a saucepan, covering them with water. Bring to a boil and cook for about 10 minutes. They should be tender. Remove from the saucepan, drain, and set aside to cool slightly.

Using a food processor with the blade attachment, puree the cooled, drained carrots until they are smooth. Remove 1 cup of the carrot puree, set it aside, and scrape the remaining carrot mixture into a bowl.

In a saucepan over low heat, melt the safflower margarine. Stir in the flour, breaking up the lumps until smooth. Continue to heat and stir another minute before adding the whipping cream alternative slowly. Once this is well blended, add the 1 cup reserved carrot puree; stir constantly over medium heat until the sauce thickens and bubbles.

In a small bowl, whisk just the egg yolks until they are thick and a pale yellow. Take a small portion of the hot carrot puree sauce and add it to the yolks slowly. Blend together (this will introduce the hot sauce to the yolks without "cooking" the yolks and clumping), then fold yolks into the saucepan with the carrot puree sauce, constantly stirring gently. Once blended, add the nutmeg, salt, and pepper. Set this aside and allow to cool.

Preheat the oven to 350° F. and lightly grease a 1 1/2-quart soufflé dish.

In a medium chilled bowl, beat the egg whites until stiff peaks form. Be careful not to dry out the mixture. Gently fold the stiff egg whites into the cooled carrot sauce. Slowly pour the mixture into the prepared soufflé dish and place in the oven.

Bake for about 1 hour. The soufflé should be puffed up high and set. Serve immediately.

Per Serving: Calories: 358 Cholesterol: 159mg Dietary Fiber: 1g Protein: 6g
Sodium: 353mg Carbohydrate: 19g Total Fat: 30g Saturated Fat: 15g
Calories from Fat: 73%, Calories from Carbohydrates: 21%, Calories from Protein: 6%

Deviled Eggs

Always a crowd pleaser, deviled eggs can also be lactose free.

Makes 12 servings
Preparation time: 30 minutes

6 medium eggs
1/4 cup mayonnaise, Best Foods or Hellmann's
1 teaspoon mustard powder
1/8 teaspoon salt
Pepper, to taste
Dash paprika

Place the eggs into a pot; cover with water. Bring to a boil over high heat. Continue to boil, reducing heat just slightly (to prevent spilling over) for 10 minutes.

Remove the pot from the heat and immediately submerge it into cool water. Tap one eggshell to crack gently; peel under cool running water. Repeat with the other eggs.

Slice the eggs in half lengthwise, spooning out the yolks. Place the white "cradles" on a tray and the yolks into a bowl. Break the yolks up with a fork until crumby. Add the mayonnaise, mustard powder, salt, and pepper, mixing well with the fork.

The mixture may now be put into a pastry tube or just spooned into the "cradles." Before serving, sprinkle paprika on top of each egg for a finishing touch.

Per Serving: Calories: 71 Cholesterol: 108mg Dietary Fiber: 0g Protein: 3g
Sodium: 84mg Carbohydrate: .3g Total Fat: 6g Saturated Fat: 1g
Calories from Fat: 80%, Calories from Carbohydrates: 2%, Calories from Protein: 18%

French-fried Onion Rings

With the substitution of the lactose-free milk, no one will notice anything different about these onion rings. As a side dish, they go great with barbecues. Just watch them disappear!

Makes 6 servings
Preparation time: 15 minutes

Vegetable oil, for deep-frying
1/2 cup 100% lactose-free 2% lowfat milk
1 cup all-purpose flour
1/2 teaspoon salt
1/2 teaspoon seasoned pepper
3 Bermuda or other large onions, sliced 1/4 inch thick

Using a deep-fryer or an electric skillet, follow the manufacturer's instructions. If you are using a 2-quart saucepan, fill to at least 1 inch with the vegetable oil and heat to about 370° F.

Prepare two separate bowls for dipping—one with the lactose-free milk and one with the flour, salt, and seasoned pepper. Place paper towels on a platter to drain the finished onion rings.

Take the onion slices and separate them into rings. Dip each ring into the milk, then into the flour mixture. Repeat again, so as to coat each ring twice.

Place the onion rings into the hot oil for about 3 minutes each. Rings should be lightly browned. Remove and drain them on the prepared platter with the paper towels.

Serve right away.

Make great appetizers or serve as a side dish.

Per Serving: Calories: 102 Cholesterol: 2mg Dietary Fiber: 1g Protein: 4g
Sodium: 463mg Carbohydrate: 20g Total Fat: .7g Saturated Fat: .3g
Calories from Fat: 6%, Calories from Carbohydrates: 80%, Calories from Protein: 14%

(**Note:** These nutritional values do not include the vegetable oil in which you deep-fry the onions.)

Grilled Stuffed Mushrooms

These little mouthfuls can be prepared ahead of time and tossed on the barbecue at dinner time. Remember to check your bread-crumb label. If you desire, you can use a Parmesan or cheddar cheese alternative instead of the mozzarella. Fresh lactose-free mozzarella can be used as well.

Makes 6 appetizer servings; 2 to 3 main-course servings
Preparation time: 40 minutes

12 large fresh white mushrooms
2 tablespoons virgin olive oil, light
1 small shallot, minced
1 garlic clove, minced
1/2 cup bread crumbs, Pioneer
1/4 cup finely shredded mozzarella alternative, TofuRella
1/2 teaspoon dried oregano
Dash freshly ground pepper, to taste
1 1/2 tablespoons whipping cream alternative,
  Pastry Pride

Prepare the mushrooms by gently brushing them clean. Pull the stems from the mushrooms, opening up a pocket to fill with the stuffing. Place the stems in a small bowl and chop.

In a sauté pan, heat 1 to 1½ tablespoons of the olive oil. Add the chopped stems, shallot, and garlic. Stir while cooking until tender and all liquid has evaporated, approximately 5 to 7 minutes. Empty into a medium bowl and combine with the bread crumbs, mozzarella cheese alternative, oregano, pepper, and cream. Toss until well coated and mixed.

Preheat the barbecue grill. With the remaining olive oil, carefully brush the outside of the mushroom caps. Spoon the prepared stuffing into each cap until it mounds out of the cap.

Place the prepared stuffed mushroom caps in the center of the grill rack, close the cover, and cook for about 20 minutes. Stuffing will be browned and mushrooms will be tender.

Serve these hot or at room temperature.

Great as appetizers, a side dish, or even
a vegetarian main course.

Per Serving: Calories: 95 Cholesterol: 0mg Dietary Fiber: .8g Protein: 2g
Sodium: 71mg Carbohydrate: 9g Total Fat: 6g Saturated Fat: 2g
Calories from Fat: 55%, Calories from Carbohydrates: 36%, Calories from Protein: 9%

Lactose-Free Potato Gratin

This recipe uses no milk, so its texture is cheesy rather than creamy. Again, no missing ingredients to detect, so no one will guess it's lactose free!

Makes 4 servings
Preparation time: 25 minutes

1 garlic clove, halved
3 tablespoons safflower oil margarine, Hollywood
1¹/₂ pounds potatoes, red skinned or waxy
Ground white pepper, salt, and ground nutmeg,
    for seasoning
2 ounces cheddar cheese alternative, TofuRella,
    shredded
1³/₄ cups chicken broth

Preheat the oven to 350° F. Split the garlic clove in half and using cut edges rub the sides and bottom of an 8 × 10-inch baking dish. Discard the garlic. Using 1 tablespoon of the safflower margarine, grease the baking dish and set aside.

Peel the potatoes and slice in a food processor, using the thin slicing disk. Take the sliced potatoes and place them in a medium bowl full of cold water for 5 minutes. This removes starch and prevents the slices from sticking together. Next, drain and pat dry the potato slices with paper towels.

Take about half the potato slices and arrange in the baking dish in overlapping rows. Sprinkle with white pepper and a dash of salt and nutmeg, then generously layer half the shredded cheese alternative over the potatoes. Take 1 tablespoon of the margarine, breaking it into small pieces, and dot over the cheese. Finish layering the remaining potato slices, same as the bottom layer, in overlapping rows. Pour the chicken broth over the top of the potato slices, and finish by layering with shredded cheese and dotting with the remaining table-spoon of margarine. Season with pepper, salt, and nutmeg.

Bake in the oven, uncovered, for about 1 hour. The potatoes should be tender and the top golden. Allow to cool slightly for easier serving.

*Create a different dish by changing
the cheese substitutes!*

Per Serving: Calories: 280 Cholesterol: lmg Dietary Fiber: 3g Protein: llg
Sodium: 92lmg Carbohydrate: 33g Total Fat: l3g Saturated Fat: 2g
Calories from Fat: 40%, Calories from Carbohydrates: 45%, Calories from Protein: l5%

Quick-Bake Veggies

These won't last long! Pick your favorite veggies—the choice is yours. To serve as an appetizer, place them around a small bowl of homemade buttermilk dressing (lactose free, of course!).

Makes 8 servings
Preparation time: 20 minutes

1 cup bread crumbs, Pioneer
1/3 cup grated Parmesan cheese alternative, Soyco
1 tablespoon dried parsley, crushed
1 teaspoon dried oregano, crushed
1 teaspoon seasoned pepper
2/3 cup mayonnaise, Best Foods or Hellmann's

1 cup broccoli flowerets
1/2 cup cauliflower flowerets
1/2 cup button mushrooms
1 cup baby carrots
1 cup zucchini, cut into strips
1 cup yellow squash, sliced 1/4 inch thick
1/2 cup bell pepper, cut into strips
1/2 cup asparagus, top half of spear

Preheat the oven to 425° F. Using two gallon-size resealable bags, fill one with the bread crumbs, Parmesan cheese alternative, and seasonings. Close and shake to mix completely. Fill the other bag with the mayonnaise and vegetables; zip closed, and gently shake to coat all the vegetables with the mayonnaise.

Carefully remove the mayonnaise-coated veggies, and place half at a time into the bag filled with the bread crumbs. Coat the veggies well with bread-crumb mixture by shaking the bag gently. In a single layer, place the coated veggies on an ungreased cookie sheet. Place the cookie sheet into the oven and bake until golden, approximately 10 minutes. Serve immediately.

Appetizers, snacks, or a side dish ... so easy and quick!

Per Serving: Calories: 221 Cholesterol: 7mg Dietary Fiber: 2g Protein: 5g
Sodium: 322mg Carbohydrate: 15g Total Fat: 16g Saturated Fat: 2g
Calories from Fat: 63%, Calories from Carbohydrates: 27%, Calories from Protein: 10%

Sautéed Garlic Mushrooms

You can vary the degree of garlic according to your taste, as well as your selection of mushrooms. When changing mushrooms, take into consideration the range of flavors as well as mildness and strength. There are Parmesan cheese alternatives on the market; remember, however, the longer a cheese ages, the lower its lactose content. American Parmesan cheeses have about a 3.7% lactose content because of their short aging process. However, a good imported Italian Parmesan cheese is aged for years, giving it a minuscule lactose content when you only use a sprinkle or two. Because of this you can often enjoy this cheese without any consequences.

Makes 8 servings
Preparation time: 25 minutes

3 tablespoons olive oil
4 garlic cloves, crushed
3 cups whole mushrooms, white or button
1 teaspoon grated Parmesan cheese alternative, Soyco,
   or imported aged Parmesan cheese
1 teaspoon fresh parsley, chopped
Dash freshly ground pepper

In a medium fry pan (with a lid), heat the olive oil and garlic until the garlic is tender. Add the mushrooms, stirring to coat with the hot oil. Cover, let simmer a few minutes. Continue to stir and allow all mushrooms to cook, absorbing the oil and garlic. Cover the pan after each stir. When all the mushrooms are tender, sprinkle with Parmesan cheese alternative, parsley, and pepper. Remove from the pan and serve.

As an appetizer or side dish, these are a hit!

Per Serving: Calories: 55 Cholesterol: 0mg Dietary Fiber: .4g Protein: .8g
Sodium: 7mg Carbohydrate: 2g Total Fat: 5g Saturated Fat: .7g
Calories from Fat: 82%, Calories from Carbohydrates: 13%, Calories from Protein: 5%

Scalloped French Potatoes

With the substitutions of 100% lactose-free 2% lowfat milk, safflower margarine, and whipping cream alternative, you don't lose any rich, creamy taste in this fantastic dish. A footnote to the cook with a hectic family schedule: this dish is a great "holdover." It will stay hot in a warm oven without drying out for about an hour. If necessary, you can always moisten it with a little extra cream on top.

Special little tricks can change this dish just enough to make it your specialty. Try adding freshly grated aged Parmesan cheese or Parmesan cheese alternative, or a sprinkle of fresh, chopped Italian parsley, on top before baking.

Makes 6 servings
Preparation time: 30 minutes

2 1/4 pounds potatoes
3 garlic cloves
3 2/3 cups 100% lactose-free 2% lowfat milk
1 medium whole bay leaf, Turkish
Dash ground nutmeg
Freshly ground pepper, to taste
2 tablespoons safflower oil margarine, Hollywood,
    softened
3 tablespoons whipping cream alternative, Pastry Pride

Preheat the oven to 350° F. while peeling and thinly slicing potatoes. Mince the garlic and set aside. In a large saucepan, place the potatoes and cover with the lactose-free milk (you can adjust this measurement if you need additional milk to completely cover the potatoes). Place the bay leaf, nutmeg, and pepper in the saucepan. Over medium heat, bring to a slow boil and simmer for about 15 minutes, stirring occasionally. You want the potatoes to just start getting soft . . . not get completely cooked. The milk will have thickened also.

With the softened safflower margarine, generously grease either an oval 14-inch gratin dish or an 8-cup baking dish that is shallow. Cover the bottom of your dish with the garlic.

Carefully remove the potatoes from the saucepan, using a slotted spoon, placing them in a layered fashion in the dish. Taste the milk in the saucepan and, if necessary, add more pepper or nutmeg. Remove the bay leaf and discard.

Spoon enough of the seasoned milk to come just even with the potatoes; you don't want to cover them. Now, spoon a thin layer of the whipping cream alternative over the top of your potatoes, covering them.

Bake in the oven for about 1 hour. The milk will be absorbed, and a golden-brown top will be the finished look.

Per Serving: Calories: 277 Cholesterol: 12mg Dietary Fiber: 3g Protein: 9g
Sodium: 133mg Carbohydrate: 40g Total Fat: 10g Saturated Fat: 4g
Calories from Fat: 31%, Calories from Carbohydrates: 57%, Calories from Protein: 12%

Broccoli Soufflé

Add your own creative ingredients to make this soufflé a personal specialty.

Makes 6 to 8 servings
Preparation time: 30 minutes

1 cup frozen chopped broccoli
1/2 cup safflower oil margarine, Hollywood
1/2 cup all-purpose flour
1 1/2 cups whipping cream alternative, Pastry Pride
4 tablespoons grated Parmesan cheese alternative, Soyco
6 large eggs, separated
1/2 teaspoon ground nutmeg
1/2 teaspoon salt
1/4 teaspoon freshly ground pepper

Thaw the broccoli and drain it well.

Over low heat, melt the safflower margarine. Stir in the flour, breaking up lumps until smooth. Continue to heat and stir another minute before adding the whipping cream alternative slowly. Once this is well blended, add the broccoli and 2 tablespoons of the Parmesan cheese alternative; stir constantly over medium heat until the sauce thickens and bubbles.

In a small bowl, whisk just the egg yolks until they are thick and a pale yellow. Take a small portion of the hot broccoli sauce and add to the yolks slowly. Blend together (this will introduce the hot sauce to the yolks without "cooking" the yolks and clumping), then fold the yolks into the saucepan with the broccoli sauce, constantly stirring gently. Once blended, add the nutmeg, salt, and pepper. Set this aside and allow to cool.

Preheat the oven to 350° F. and lightly grease a 1 1/2-quart soufflé dish.

In a medium chilled bowl, beat the egg whites until stiff peaks form. Be careful not to dry out the mixture. Gently fold the stiff whites into the cooled broccoli sauce. Slowly pour the mixture into the prepared soufflé dish and sprinkle the top with the remaining Parmesan cheese alternative; place in the oven.

Bake for about 1 hour and 10 minutes. Soufflé should be puffed up high and set. Serve immediately.

Per Serving: Calories: 360 Cholesterol: 159mg Dietary Fiber: 1g Protein: 8g
Sodium: 406mg Carbohydrate: 17g Total Fat: 30g Saturated Fat: 15g
Calories from Fat: 73%, Calories from Carbohydrates: 18%, Calories from Protein: 9%

Seasoned Cherry Tomatoes

This quick and easy summer vegetable dish has an Italian touch, drawing its flavor from the fresh herbs and sweet tomatoes. Serve it as an appetizer. Also makes a great side dish for a summer barbecue.

Makes 10 servings
Preparation time: 10 minutes

2 tablespoons finely chopped fresh parsley
1 teaspoon finely chopped fresh oregano
1 teaspoon finely chopped fresh basil
1 tablespoon olive oil
2 cups ripe cherry tomatoes
1/4 cup grated Parmesan cheese alternative, Soyco
Freshly ground pepper, to taste

In a small bowl, combine the herbs and the Parmesan cheese alternative. Set aside. In a large skillet, warm the oil over medium heat. Gently add the cherry tomatoes, stirring often for about 3 minutes. Tomatoes should be soft but not split. Sprinkle the herb mixture over tomatoes and toss gently to coat. Dust with pepper.

Per Serving: Calories: 30 Cholesterol: 0mg Dietary Fiber: .4g Protein: 2g
Sodium: 52mg Carbohydrate: 2g Total Fat: 2g Saturated Fat: .2g
Calories from Fat: 54%, Calories from Carbohydrates: 25%, Calories from Protein: 21%

Poultry Stuffing

Remember that simple is usually the best. This basic recipe has been handed down through our family. It adds just enough flavor to the turkey, and is very moist. I haven't met anyone who hasn't raved about it. Use only lactose-free bread for your stuffing. DiCarlo, Pioneer, or many bakery French breads are safe choices. If you have a difficult time finding one, you can always make your own.

Makes 16 servings
Preparation time: 30 minutes

2 1 1/4-pound loaves Basic White Bread (page 84),
    slightly stale, cubed, or any lactose-free bread
1 cup chopped celery
3/4 cup chopped onion
Poultry seasoning, Schilling, liberally sprinkled
1/2 cup safflower oil margarine, Hollywood, melted

Leave bread cubes in a roasting pan overnight to get stale, mixing up occasionally to expose fresh pieces.

Add the celery, onion, and poultry seasoning to the bread cubes in the roasting pan. Drip the melted safflower margarine over the mixture, covering all and making it moist. (You can adjust all the ingredients for personal taste.)

Stuff the turkey, packing it tight. Juices from the turkey will add to the moistness and flavor of the stuffing.

Per Serving: Calories: 166 Cholesterol: 0mg Dietary Fiber: 1g Protein: 4g
Sodium: 321mg Carbohydrate: 22g Total Fat: 8g Saturated Fat: 1g
Calories from Fat: 40%, Calories from Carbohydrates: 51%, Calories from Protein: 9%

Swiss Broccoli Casserole

Any way you prepare this dish, it turns broccoli into something very special. Substitute cheddar cheese alternative for a different flavor, or top the casserole with Pioneer bread crumbs for a crunchy topping.

Makes 8 servings
Preparation time: 25 minutes

1 pound fresh broccoli, coarsely chopped
2 teaspoons salt
3 tablespoons safflower oil margarine, Hollywood
2 tablespoons all-purpose flour

3 tablespoons minced shallots
11/4 cups 100% lactose-free 2% lowfat milk
2 cups shredded Swiss cheese alternative, Soyco
2 medium eggs, slightly beaten

Preheat the oven to 325° F. Generously grease a 10 × 6-inch baking dish and set aside.

Fill a 2-quart saucepan with 1 inch of water, and bring to a boil over high heat. Add the broccoli and 1/2 teaspoon of the salt. Return to a boil, cover, and continue to cook for about 8 to 10 minutes. Drain and allow to cool.

Melt the safflower margarine in another 2-quart saucepan over medium to low heat. Blend in the flour and the remaining 11/2 teaspoons salt, add the shallots, and cook only about 1 minute, or until tender. Stirring constantly, add the lactose-free milk very slowly for easier incorporation. Continue to cook until the mixture becomes smooth and thick and returns to a boil. At this point, remove the saucepan from the heat and stir in the Swiss cheese alternative and drained broccoli. As the cheese begins to melt, stir in the eggs. Pour the mixture into the prepared baking dish. Bake in the oven for 25 to 30 minutes. The casserole should be firm when touched.

An elegant side dish for any meal.

Per Serving: Calories: 215 Cholesterol: 56mg Dietary Fiber: 2g Protein: 16g
Sodium: 965mg Carbohydrate: 10g Total Fat: 12g Saturated Fat: 2g
Calories from Fat: 52%, Calories from Carbohydrates: 18%, Calories from Protein: 30%

Fry Pan Onions

If onions don't always agree with your stomach, the substitution of shallots can make a difference. The shallot is a milder member of the onion family and has a very gentle flavor. I tend to use a lot of shallots since my husband's system tolerates them much better than onions. I have found this is true with other Lactose-Intolerant people as well. Try them for yourself.

Makes 6 servings
Preparation time: 20 minutes

1/4 cup safflower oil margarine, Hollywood
5 medium white or yellow onions (or shallots), thinly
    sliced
1/4 teaspoon chopped fresh thyme leaves
1 teaspoon salt
1/8 teaspoon freshly ground pepper

Melt the safflower margarine in a large skillet, over medium heat. When the margarine is hot, add the sliced onions, cover, and cook for about 5 to 7 minutes. Add the thyme and seasonings, and continue to cook, uncovered, for about another 7 to 8 minutes. Stir several times, making sure the onion mixture is well blended and cooked. Turn out onto serving dish and serve.

Great for hamburgers at the barbecue.

Per Serving: Calories: 90 Cholesterol: 0mg Dietary Fiber: 2g Protein: 1g
Sodium: 890mg Carbohydrate: 5g Total Fat: 8g Saturated Fat: 1g
Calories from Fat: 75%, Calories from Carbohydrates: 21%, Calories from Protein: 4%

Walnut Green Bean Salad

In this bean salad the flavor of toasted walnuts is enhanced by garlic sautéed in olive oil, bringing a unique touch to a simple side dish. This salad will turn any meal into something special.

Makes 6 servings
Preparation time: 30 minutes

3/4 cup walnuts, chopped
4 slices crispy bacon, crumbled
3/4 pound green beans, sliced in halves
    crosswise
11/2 teaspoons virgin olive oil, light
2 garlic cloves, minced
Freshly ground pepper
1/4 cup grated imported Parmesan cheese,
    or Parmesan cheese alternative, Soyco

Preheat the oven to 350° F. Place the chopped walnuts in one layer on a cookie sheet. Bake for 8 to 10 minutes in the oven, tossing several times to ensure even toasting.

Cook the bacon, drain on paper towels, and set aside.

In a covered skillet, put 1/4 cup water and the green beans. Over medium heat, cook the beans until tender-crisp, about 4 to 5 minutes. Drain and place in a bowl. In the same skillet, place the olive oil and sauté the garlic. Gradually add the beans and walnuts, and crumble the bacon in. Flavor with pepper, and continue to cook for 3 to 4 minutes, uncovered. Stir often to coat and mix.

Turn out onto a warmed serving dish. Garnish with imported grated Parmesan cheese or Parmesan cheese alternative.

A unique bean salad for any meal, anytime.

Per Serving: Calories: 163 Cholesterol: 4mg Dietary Fiber: 3g Protein: 8g
Sodium: 151mg Carbohydrate: 6g Total Fat: 13g Saturated Fat: 2g
Calories from Fat: 66%, Calories from Carbohydrates: 15%, Calories from Protein: 19%

Beef

Beef . . . succulent, juicy, tender . . . those words make your mouth water! But you must watch what you use to tenderize the meat. Ac'cent, Lawry's salt, and other seasonings contain MSG . . . and lactose is present in MSG.

Beef Stroganoff

This is a fast and easy meal, and leftovers can be turned into an even quicker microwave lunch! The sour cream substitute makes the sauce creamy and rich.

Makes 8 servings
Preparation time: 45 minutes

1¹/2 pounds beef tenderloin, cut in thin strips
2 tablespoons all-purpose flour
Seasoned pepper
2 tablespoons safflower oil margarine, Hollywood
2 tablespoons olive oil
1¹/2 cups beef bouillon
1/4 cup sour cream alternative, Tofutti
2 tablespoons tomato paste
1/2 teaspoon paprika
Salt to taste

Dip the beef strips in flour and pepper. In a large skillet, melt the safflower margarine with oil, browning the beef for about 5 minutes. Slowly add the bouillon to the beef, stirring well and bringing to a boil. In a separate mixing bowl, combine the sour cream alternative, tomato paste, paprika, and salt with a whisk. Slowly stir the sour cream mixture into the beef mixture. Turn the heat to low and bring to a simmer. Cook 15 to 20 minutes, stirring frequently and never allowing the mixture to boil or burn. Remove from the heat and serve.

Serve on a bed of rice or egg noodles.

Per Serving: Calories: 312 Cholesterol: 60mg Dietary Fiber: 0g Protein: 16g
Sodium: 330mg Carbohydrate: 3g Total Fat: 26g Saturated Fat: 9g
Calories from Fat: 76%, Calories from Carbohydrates: 4%, Calories from Protein: 20%

Creamed Dried Beef

Who says you can't have "creamy" dishes if you're Lactose Intolerant? You just need the right substitutes!

Makes 3 servings
Preparation time: 20 minutes

2 tablespoons safflower oil margarine, Hollywood
4 ounces dried beef, coarsely chopped
2 tablespoons all-purpose flour
1 cup 100% lactose-free 2% lowfat milk
1/2 teaspoon Worcestershire sauce
Desired toast slices

In a skillet, melt the safflower margarine and cook the dried beef. Once the edges of the beef curl, push to the side of the pan and blend the flour into the melted margarine. Pour the lactose-free milk into the skillet, cooking over medium heat, and blend with the flour mixture, breaking up any lumps. Stir constantly as the mixture thickens and bubbles, slowly adding the dried beef back into the "milk" sauce. Add the Worcestershire sauce and stir well. Spoon the thick, rich beefy sauce over toast slices and serve.

Per Serving: Calories: 192 Cholesterol: 23mg Dietary Fiber: 0g Protein: 14g
Sodium: 1440mg Carbohydrate: 9g Total Fat: 11g Saturated Fat: 3g
Calories from Fat: 52%, Calories from Carbohydrates: 18%, Calories from Protein: 30%

(**Note:** Desired toast slices are not nutritionally calculated in recipe.)

Porterhouse Broiled Steaks

Seasoning can be a little tricky with Lactose Intolerance. Remember that MSG does contain lactose, so seasoned salts and spices must be checked thoroughly. This recipe is simple, lacking only in lactose.

Makes 8 servings
Preparation time: 45 minutes

1/3 cup safflower oil margarine, Hollywood
1/4 teaspoon seasoned pepper
1 teaspoon port wine
1/4 cup chopped fresh parsley
1 garlic clove, minced
PAM cooking spray
2 pounds porterhouse steak, 1 1/2 inches thick
2 tablespoons steak sauce, A.1

In a medium bowl, with an electric mixer beat the safflower margarine, seasoned pepper, port wine, parsley, and garlic together. Mold into a roll and place in clear plastic wrap. Refrigerate for 1 hour until firm. Preheat the oven to broil. Prepare the broiler pan by spraying PAM on the rack in the broiler pan. Place the steak on the rack and brush with the A.1 sauce. Slice the seasoned margarine and place around the top of the steak, reserving some for the other side.

Place the steak under the broiler about 4 inches from the heat source. Broil 6 to 8 minutes each side for rare or 8 to 10 minutes for medium to well done. As you flip the steak, repeat the brushing on of the A.1 sauce and pats of seasoned margarine.

Remove the steak to a carving board and cut around the T-bone. Always slice across the grain. Slice the steak and dot with seasoned margarine before serving, if desired. Serve on warmed plates.

Serve with lactose-free whipped potatoes and vegetables.

Per Serving: Calories: 322 Cholesterol: 63mg Dietary Fiber: .2g Protein: 17g
Sodium: 187mg Carbohydrate: 1g Total Fat: 28g Saturated Fat: 10g
Calories from Fat: 78%, Calories from Carbohydrates: 2%, Calories from Protein: 20%

Easy Beef Stew

You'll need a crockpot for this recipe—it's a great dinner that cooks itself. You can freeze leftovers in single containers for lunch or a fast dinner. Campbell's Golden Mushroom soup contains no lactose, unlike regular mushroom soup. Remember, *read the label.*

Makes 8 servings
Preparation time: 20 minutes
Cook time: 5 hours

1/3 **cup all-purpose flour**
1/2 **teaspoon seasoned pepper**
11/2 **pounds beef stew meat, cut into** 11/2**-inch chunks**
1/4 **cup olive oil**
2 103/4**-ounce cans Campbell's Golden Mushroom soup, undiluted**
2 10**-ounce packages frozen stewing mixed vegetables**
2 **large shallots, quartered**
1 10**-ounce package frozen baby carrots**
1 **cup port wine**

In a wide bowl, place the flour and seasoned pepper; stir. Roll the pieces of stew meat into the flour, shaking off any excess. Place on a plate and set aside. In a large fry pan, heat the olive oil over medium heat. Add the floured stew meat and brown on all sides. Remove the finished pieces and place in a separate bowl. Continue until all the meat is browned.

In a large crockpot, place 1 can of undiluted soup. Add 1 package of the stewing vegetables, 2 shallot quarters, and half the baby carrots. Now, layer all the stew meat (include any juices in the bowl) in the crockpot. Pour 1/2 cup of the port wine over the meat. Finish by adding the remaining vegetables and shallots, topping with the remaining 1/2 cup wine and the last undiluted can of soup. Follow the manufacturer's instructions for the crockpot, selecting the time frame you want. I allow at least 5 hours for slow cooking. Gently stir the stew from time to time to avoid burning the edges.

Per Serving: Calories: 434 Cholesterol: 86mg Dietary Fiber: 2g Protein: 26g
Sodium: 374mg Carbohydrate: 17g Total Fat: 25g Saturated Fat: 8g
Calories from Fat: 57%, Calories from Carbohydrates: 17%, Calories from Protein: 26%

Savory Meat Loaf

Meat loaf might seem like a "safe" food, but lactose can show up in any one of its ingredients. Make sure to read the labels of your bread crumbs and tomato sauce.

Makes 10 servings
Preparation time: 30 minutes

2 pounds lean ground beef, crumbled
2 medium eggs, slightly beaten
1 1/2 cups bread crumbs, Pioneer
1/2 cup warm water
1/4 cup port wine
1/3 cup canned tomato sauce, unseasoned
1 1-ounce envelope onion soup mix, Lipton

Preheat the oven to 350° F. In a very large bowl, combine all the ingredients, mixing very thoroughly. Place the mixture in a loaf pan (or shape into a loaf and place in a shallow pan). Bake for 1 hour, or until done.

This is a great make-ahead dinner for those on busy schedules.

Per Serving: Calories: 322 Cholesterol: 111mg Dietary Fiber: .9g Protein: 19g
Sodium: 471mg Carbohydrate: 13g Total Fat: 20g Saturated Fat: 8g
Calories from Fat: 58%, Calories from Carbohydrates: 17%, Calories from Protein: 25%

Stuffed Pepper Cups

Using ground turkey to stuff peppers is the nineties version of an old favorite! The pepper cups in this recipe are crispy. If you prefer softer peppers, after removing the seeds and membranes, precook them in salted, boiling water for about 5 minutes and drain.

Makes 6 servings
Preparation time: 30 minutes

6 medium green peppers
Salt, to taste
1 pound ground turkey (or beef)
1/3 cup chopped shallots
1 1-pound can diced tomatoes
1/2 cup water
1/2 cup long-grain rice
1 teaspoon Worcestershire sauce
1 cup shredded cheddar cheese alternative, TofuRella

Prepare the pepper cups by cutting the tops off and removing the seeds and membranes. Sprinkle the inside of the cups with salt.

Cook the ground turkey in a large skillet with the shallots until the meat is browned. Drain any juices from the pan. Then add the canned tomatoes, water, uncooked rice, and Worcestershire sauce. Cover the skillet and continue to cook until the rice is tender, approximately 15 minutes.

Preheat the oven to 350° F. Remove the skillet from the heat and stir in the cheddar cheese alternative. Stuff the prepared pepper cups with the meat mixture. Stand cups upright in a baking dish and bake, uncovered, for 20 to 25 minutes. Serve immediately.

Another easy make-ahead dinner for those busy days.

Per Serving: Calories: 309 Cholesterol: 60mg Dietary Fiber: 2g Protein: 23g
Sodium: 597mg Carbohydrate: 25g Total Fat: 14g Saturated Fat: 3g
Calories from Fat: 39%, Calories from Carbohydrates: 32%, Calories from Protein: 29%

Veal Parmigiana

At our favorite Italian restaurant, Rocco's, they prepare this meal especially for my husband except without the cheese. Remember, when you eat out in a restaurant, if there is a dish on the menu that is okay except for the cheese topping, ask them to leave it off. Or bring your own cheese alternative and have them top the dish with your special blend. Restaurants are very accommodating.

Makes 6 servings
Preparation time: 1 hour

1 1/2 cups Homemade Italian Sauce (page 181),
    or jarred
1 cup bread crumbs, Pioneer
Dash freshly ground pepper
1 teaspoon salt
2 large eggs, slightly beaten
6 4-ounce veal cutlets, sliced 1/4 inch thick
3 tablespoons virgin olive oil, light
6 ounces mozzarella alternative, TofuRella, sliced, or fresh
    mozzarella, dried and sliced
1/4 cup grated Parmesan cheese alternative, Soyco

Prepare Homemade Italian Sauce, or warm your favorite jarred marinara or spaghetti sauce (remember, read the ingredients).

Using two wide, shallow bowls, place the bread crumbs mixed with pepper and salt in one bowl and the lightly beaten eggs in the other. Dip the cutlets in the beaten egg, then in the bread crumbs, and repeat the process. Place on a platter until all the cutlets are coated.

In a large skillet place the olive oil and heat over medium-high heat. Put the cutlets into the skillet and brown on both sides, about 10 minutes. You may have to brown the cutlets in batches.

When all the cutlets are browned, arrange them in the skillet, spoon the sauce over the cutlets, and place a slice of mozzarella alternative on top of each. Sprinkle with grated Parmesan cheese alternative. Lower the heat, cover, and continue to cook until cheeses melt, approximately 5 minutes.

Serve immediately.

Per Serving (with TofuRella and Homemade Sauce): Calories: 302 Cholesterol: 166mg Dietary Fiber: 2g Protein: 30g Sodium: 1058mg Carbohydrate: 15g Total Fat: 12g Saturated Fat: 2g Calories from Fat: 38%, Calories from Carbohydrates: 21%, Calories from Protein: 41%

Poultry

Plain chicken dishes are always "safe." But why give up creamy sauces when a little knowledge will expand your choices? Enjoy these selections . . . then experiment, adding your own ideas.

Brandy Chicken

This dish is exciting to make for those dinner guests who like to stand around in the kitchen while you cook. It really makes them think you are quite the "gourmet"!

Makes 8 servings
Preparation time: 1 hour

1 whole frying chicken, cut up
1 cup brandy
Dash salt
Dash black pepper
1/4 cup all-purpose flour
1/2 cup safflower oil margarine, Hollywood
1 pound pearl onions
1/2 pound mushrooms, chopped
1 garlic clove, minced
1/2 teaspoon ground allspice
1 cup dry red wine
1/2 cup chicken stock
1 large egg yolk
2 tablespoons whipping cream alternative,
  Pastry Pride

Rinse the chicken pieces, dry, and marinate them in 1/2 cup of the brandy for 1/2 hour.

Add salt and pepper to the flour in a mixing bowl. Drain the chicken and dip in the seasoned flour, shaking off the excess. In a large heavy-gauge skillet, brown the chicken pieces in the safflower margarine. Add the onions, sprinkle with any remaining flour, and cook 1 minute. Pour the remaining 1/2 cup brandy over the chicken, ignite, and cook until the flames die out.

Then add the mushrooms, garlic, and allspice. Pour the wine and chicken stock over all the ingredients. Simmer, uncovered, for about 45 minutes to an hour.

Beat the egg yolk with the whipped cream alternative. Stir into the chicken mixture and cook until the sauce thickens slightly. Do not allow to boil. Serve immediately.

Steamed vegetables and fluffy rice are good companions to this dish.

Per Serving: Calories: 466 Cholesterol: 119mg Dietary Fiber: 1g Protein: 32g
Sodium: 397mg Carbohydrate: 11g Total Fat: 23g Saturated Fat: 6g
Calories from Fat: 54%, Calories from Carbohydrates: 12%, Calories from Protein: 34%

Cheesy Chicken Dinner

This is a fast, easy meal for hectic luncheons or evenings. For an Italian variation, replace the Swiss cheese alternative with slices of mozzarella alternative or fresh mozzarella, sprinkle with dried oregano, and serve over egg noodles. Tone's Poultry Gravy Mix, a powder mix, is wonderful for making a lactose-free quick gravy.

Makes 8 servings
Preparation time: 15 minutes

1/2 cup poultry gravy mix, Tone's (available at restaurant and bulk suppliers)
2 cups water
8 halves skinless and boneless chicken breasts
2 tablespoons safflower oil margarine, Hollywood, melted
1/2 cup bread crumbs, Pioneer
8 slices Swiss cheese alternative, Soyco
8 slices tomato, ripe and sliced 1/4 inch thick
4 cups cooked rice, hot
Fresh parsley or oregano, for garnish

Preheat the oven to 400° F. In a small saucepan, prepare the poultry gravy by adding the water to the mix. Slowly cook over medium-low heat, stirring often to ensure a smooth gravy. Lower the heat and simmer to thicken.

Rinse and pat dry the chicken breasts. In a small bowl, combine the melted safflower margarine and the bread crumbs until the mixture forms moist crumbs; set aside. Arrange the chicken breasts in a 3-quart casserole baking dish (single layer). Top each breast with a slice of Swiss cheese alternative. Pour the thickened poultry gravy over the cheese and chicken. Place a tomato slice on top of each breast, sprinkling moist bread crumbs over the tomato.

Place the casserole dish with the chicken breasts in the oven, and bake, uncovered, for about 20 to 25 minutes until the chicken is moist and no longer pink inside.

Make the rice following the manufacturer's instructions. Set aside.

Remove the casserole dish from the oven, carefully placing each chicken breast on a bed of rice on a serving platter. Pour excess poultry gravy over each chicken breast and rice.

Garnish with fresh parsley or fresh oregano.

Serve with a tossed salad and warm rolls.

Per Serving: Calories: 358 Cholesterol: 51mg Dietary Fiber: .8g Protein: 30g
Sodium: 676mg Carbohydrate: 42g Total Fat: 7g Saturated Fat: 1g
Calories from Fat: 18%, Calories from Carbohydrates: 48%, Calories from Protein: 34%

Chicken à la King

*T*his is a quick dinner that both looks and tastes so special! The rich and creamy sauce won't be detected as lactose free, so everyone can enjoy and no one will know.

Makes 8 servings
Preparation time: 45 minutes

8 single pastry dough shells, Pepperidge Farm
6 tablespoons safflower oil margarine, Hollywood
1/2 pound mushrooms, sliced
1/4 cup diced green pepper
6 tablespoons all-purpose flour
3 cups whipping cream alternative, Pastry Pride
4 cups canned, shredded chicken
2 large egg yolks
2 tablespoons sherry
1 teaspoon salt

Prepare and bake the pastry shells according to the directions on the package. Set aside, keeping warm.

In a large skillet over medium heat, melt the safflower margarine. Add the mushrooms and green pepper, and cook until tender, about 5 minutes. Stir in the flour, blending with the pan juices to thicken. Gradually add the whipping cream alternative, stirring constantly to thicken and blend completely. Add the chicken and bring to a boil, stirring often. Reduce the heat to low and cover. Cook for about 5 more minutes. Beat the egg yolks in a small bowl. Into the egg yolks add a small amount of the skillet mixture, whisking quickly so the eggs do not clump. Once blended well, add all the egg mixture back into the skillet and stir, blending completely. Continue cooking and thickening. Add the sherry and salt, stirring just to combine.

Remove from the heat and, using a large spoon, spoon into prepared pastry shells. Serve hot.

Makes fancy appetizers or a quick main dish.

Per Serving: Calories: 809 Cholesterol: 106mg Dietary Fiber: 2g Protein: 24g
Sodium: 1009mg Carbohydrate: 47g Total Fat: 58g Saturated Fat: 29g
Calories from Fat: 65%, Calories from Carbohydrates: 23%, Calories from Protein: 12%

Chicken Lasagna

I love this lasagna. It's very different from the traditional dish made with ground beef and cheese because you use ground chicken and brandy. You can use ground turkey if you prefer.

Makes 8 servings
Preparation time: 1 hour

1/2 pound lasagna noodles, cooked
1 tablespoon safflower oil margarine, Hollywood
3 tablespoons virgin olive oil, light
1 large carrot, peeled and chopped
1/2 cup minced celery
1 medium shallot, minced
1 large whole bay leaf
12 ounces ground chicken
3 tablespoons brandy
1 pound mushrooms, sliced
2 garlic cloves, minced
1/4 cup chopped fresh parsley

For the sauce
1 tablespoon safflower oil margarine, Hollywood
1 tablespoon all-purpose flour
3 cups 100% lactose-free 2% lowfat milk
2 tablespoons grated Parmesan cheese alternative, Soyco,
    or aged Parmesan cheese, grated
Pinch freshly grated nutmeg
Salt and pepper

Preheat the oven to 350° F. Cook the lasagna noodles according to the manufacturer's directions. Drain and set aside.

Using a large saucepan, place over low to medium heat. Melt the safflower margarine, then add 1 tablespoon of the olive oil, blending together. Place the carrot, celery, and shallot into the oil, and cook until golden brown. Add the bay leaf and ground chicken, breaking up the chicken meat; continue cooking for about 10 to 15 more minutes. When the meat is browned, add the brandy and continue to cook, stirring occasionally, until the brandy is evaporated. Remove from the stove and set aside.

In another skillet, heat the remaining 2 tablespoons olive oil over high heat, add the mushrooms, and sauté until browned. Add the garlic and parsley, and continue to cook for another 3 to 4 minutes. Set aside.

To make the sauce: In a large saucepan, melt the safflower margarine. Stir the flour into the melted safflower margarine and blend for 2 minutes. Removing the saucepan from the heat, slowly add the lactose-free milk, a little at a time, whisking into the flour mixture until completely blended. When the milk is completely blended, return the saucepan to low heat and cook for about 10 minutes, stirring occasionally. Lastly, add the Parmesan cheese alternative or aged, freshly grated Parmesan, the freshly grated nutmeg, and salt and pepper to taste. Remove from the heat.

In a large baking dish (or casserole dish), cover the bottom with a small coating of sauce (the milk mixture), then layer a row of the lasagna noodles, cover them with the chicken and mushroom mixture, then layers of sauce, noodles, chicken, and mushrooms, in order, ending with a layer of noodles, sprinkled with Parmesan cheese alternative or aged grated Parmesan.

Bake in the oven for about 25 minutes until the casserole is golden brown and bubbly.

Remove from the oven and allow to cool a few minutes before cutting.

Per Serving: Calories: 364 Cholesterol: 47mg Dietary Fiber: 2g Protein: 22g
Sodium: 162mg Carbohydrate: 32g Total Fat: 15g Saturated Fat: 4g
Calories from Fat: 38%, Calories from Carbohydrates: 37%, Calories from Protein: 25%

Chicken-Veggie Stew

Here, using a whipping cream alternative gives you the creamy sauce you would usually pass by in this dish. So, enjoy; it is lactose free!

Makes 8 servings
Preparation time: 1 hour 20 minutes

4 pounds boneless and skinless chicken breasts
1/4 teaspoon seasoned pepper
2 tablespoons virgin olive oil, light
3 tablespoons safflower oil margarine, Hollywood
3 large carrots, peeled and thinly sliced
1 pound baby potatoes, thickly sliced
3 stalks celery and leaves
1 large shallot, diced
3 medium leeks, pale green and white parts only, sliced
　lengthwise

4 medium parsnips, peeled and sliced
3 tablespoons all-purpose flour
3 cups chicken broth
1 medium bay leaf
2 teaspoons dried tarragon
1/4 cup whipping cream alternative, Pastry Pride

Rinse and pat dry the chicken breasts, then sprinkle with seasoned pepper. In a large pot, heat the olive oil over medium heat. Lightly brown the chicken pieces in the hot oil, approximately 5 minutes per side, being careful not to burn. If necessary, cook the chicken in batches, uncrowded, so as to completely brown all sides. As the chicken is done, remove from the pot and place in a large bowl. Skim the fat from the juices left in the pot and discard.

Add the safflower margarine to the pot. When the margarine is melted, add the veggies and stir to completely coat them with the melted margarine. Continue to cook for another 8 minutes, stirring to avoid burning. Sprinkle in the flour and stir, continuing to cook another 2 to 3 minutes. Slowly pour in the chicken broth, turning the heat up to high. When the broth boils, add the cooked chicken pieces, bay leaf, and 1 teaspoon of the dried tarragon. Stir to mix, reduce the heat to simmer, cover, and allow to cook approximately 30 minutes. During the cooking time, stir and flip the chicken pieces to ensure complete cooking.

Remove the chicken pieces from the pot and place in a deep serving dish; keep covered so chicken will remain warm while you finish the dish. Now, add the whipping cream alternative to the pot, stir to blend, and turn the heat to medium high. Continue to simmer the sauce, stirring and blending for about 10 minutes. The sauce will become thickened. Remove the bay leaf, and add the remaining teaspoon of tarragon. Stir to blend completely. Simmer another minute.

Ladle the veggies and sauce over the warm chicken pieces and serve immediately.

Serve with rice or noodles.

Per Serving: Calories: 534 Cholesterol: 133mg Dietary Fiber: 6g Protein: 60g
Sodium: 835mg Carbohydrate: 38g Total Fat: 15g Saturated Fat: 5g
Calories from Fat: 26%, Calories from Carbohydrates: 28%, Calories from Protein: 46%

Fusilli Chicken in Cream Sauce

*T*his delicious pasta dish features a creamy sauce, something that is hard to make lactose free. This is why good substitutions of equal consistency are so important. Fusilli is a corkscrew pasta; if you have another favorite pasta, of course you can use that.

Makes 8 servings
Preparation time: 45 minutes

5 cups broccoli flowerets
3/4 pound fusilli or other pasta shape
3 large skinless and boneless chicken breast halves
1/4 cup virgin olive oil, light
3 tablespoons chopped garlic cloves
1 cup dry white wine
1 cup whipping cream alternative, Pastry Pride
1 cup chicken broth
1/2 cup grated Parmesan cheese alternative, Soyco

Fill a large pot with salted water and bring to a boil. Add the broccoli and cook until crispy-tender, approximately 3 to 4 minutes. Remove with a slotted spoon and place in a large bowl. Using the same pot and water, add the fusilli pasta and cook only until firm and tender. Drain the pasta and set aside.

Slice the chicken breasts crosswise into 1/2-inch thick strips. In a large skillet, heat the olive oil over high heat. Into the hot oil, place the garlic and the chicken strips, and sauté until just cooked. This should take about 3 to 4 minutes. Using your slotted spoon, remove the chicken strips and place in the bowl with the broccoli.

Into the skillet juices add the wine, whipping cream alternative, and broth. Bring to a boil and stir constantly as the sauce thickens, about 8 minutes.

Spoon in the cooked pasta, broccoli, and chicken strips, stirring well. Sprinkle the Parmesan cheese alternative and toss to ensure all ingredients are covered. Heat thoroughly, stirring and tossing. Serve immediately.

Rolls and a salad complete this one-dish meal.

Per Serving: Calories: 446 Cholesterol: 19mg Dietary Fiber: 4g Protein: 21g
Sodium: 390mg Carbohydrate: 45g Total Fat: 18g Saturated Fat: 9g
Calories from Fat: 39%, Calories from Carbohydrates: 42%, Calories from Protein: 19%

Homemade Chicken Potpie

You may want to double this recipe because it is a crowd pleaser! A tip: Make a quick fruit pie with the leftover crust—use canned pie fillings and top with a strudel mix or crumb topping—and you have the makings of a sensational dinner.

Makes 8 servings
Preparation time: 45 minutes

For the crust
2 cups all-purpose flour, sifted
2/3 cup solid all-vegetable shortening, Crisco
1 teaspoon salt
Chilled water

For the filling
10 ounces frozen peas and carrots
1/4 cup safflower oil margarine, Hollywood
1/2 cup chopped shallots
1/3 cup all-purpose flour
1/2 teaspoon crushed marjoram
1/2 teaspoon salt
1/8 teaspoon freshly ground pepper
2 cups chicken broth
3/4 cup 100% lactose-free 2% lowfat milk
2 cans canned chicken, drained
1/4 cup dried parsley, crushed
Sugar, to dust

Prepare the pie crust by placing the flour, shortening, and salt in a large bowl. With a pastry blender, blend the dry ingredients until crumby. Slowly add the chilled water a little at a time until the dough starts to hold together. Set aside.

Place the frozen vegetables in a saucepan and follow the package directions for cooking. When done, drain and set aside.

In a large Dutch oven (a large saucepan with ear handles and a cover, great for slow-cooking large quantities), melt the safflower margarine over medium heat. Add the shallots, cooking until tender. Slowly stir in the flour, marjoram, salt, and pepper. The mixture will become thick and pasty. Add the chicken broth and lactose-free milk, stirring to blend, eliminating any lumps. Cook and stir occasionally until the mixture becomes thick and bubbly. Once it has thickened, add the cooked, drained vegetables, chicken, and parsley. Stir and continue cooking until the mixture reaches the bubbly stage again. Remove from the heat and pour into a 13 × 9-inch rectangular baking dish. Set aside. Preheat the oven to 450° F.

On a floured surface, roll out the pie crust. Handle the dough as little as possible for a flakier crust. Roll to a 10 × 13-inch rectangle to cover the top of your baking dish. Carefully place the dough on top of the chicken mixture in the dish. Crimp the edges all the way around. With a pastry brush or fingertips, coat the top of the crust with a little lactose-free milk. Sprinkle lightly with sugar. Use a knife to vent the crust top, as you would a pie. (Leftover pie crust can be saved in a plastic sandwich bag for a later use.)

Place the baking dish in the oven. Bake for approximately 15 to 20 minutes. The top should be golden brown.

Freeze individual servings for quick dinners or lunches.

Per Serving: Calories: 394 Cholesterol: 24mg Dietary Fiber: 2g Protein: 15g
Sodium: 1077mg Carbohydrate: 24g Total Fat: 26g Saturated Fat: 6g
Calories from Fat: 60%, Calories from Carbohydrates: 24%, Calories from Protein: 16%

Paprika Chicken

This dish has a creamy tomato taste. You can use onions instead of shallots; I prefer shallots because they are milder.

Makes 4 servings
Preparation time: 20 minutes

4 halves skinless and boneless chicken breasts
8 teaspoons paprika
Salt and pepper
2 large plum tomatoes
3 tablespoons safflower oil margarine, Hollywood
1 cup chopped shallots
2 cups chicken broth
1/2 cup sour cream alternative, Tofutti

Cut the chicken into strips about 1/2 inch wide and season with 2 teaspoons of the paprika, a dash of salt, and freshly ground pepper. Set aside. Chop the tomatoes and remove the seeds by straining. Set aside.

In a large skillet over medium heat, melt 2 tablespoons of the safflower margarine. Once melted and hot, add the chicken strips and sauté for about 4 minutes. Remove the cooked chicken and set aside.

Using the same skillet with the pan juices still hot, add the remaining 1 tablespoon margarine and sauté the shallots until tender. Stir in all the remaining paprika, add the tomatoes, and stir about 1 minute. Pour in the chicken broth, raise the heat to high, and bring the mixture to a boil. Continue to stir while boiling for about 5 minutes until the mixture becomes thickened. Place the chicken strips and any accumulated juices into the mixture; reduce the heat to low. Blend in the sour cream alternative, and simmer until the chicken is heated. Stir often. Add additional freshly ground pepper and salt to taste.

*Quick and easy! Serve over noodles
with a salad on the side.*

Per Serving: Calories: 274 Cholesterol: 52mg Dietary Fiber: 2g Protein: 28g
Sodium: 951mg Carbohydrate: 13g Total Fat: 13g Saturated Fat: 3g
Calories from Fat: 41%, Calories from Carbohydrates: 19%, Calories from Protein: 40%

Stuffed Turkey Rolls

Lactose free doesn't mean boring. You can experiment and whip up a gourmet delight just by selecting your substitutions carefully. Be creative! In this recipe, you can change things around: use boneless, skinless chicken breasts or even veal cutlets. The basic recipe remains the same . . . the stuffing ingredients can change to suit your preference.

Makes 5 servings
Preparation time: 40 minutes

1 cup bread crumbs, Pioneer
3/4 cup finely chopped celery
1/2 cup finely chopped shallots
1/2 cup coarsely chopped walnuts
1/4 cup raisins
1 large Red Delicious apple, peeled, cored, and cut
  into small pieces
1/4 cup safflower oil margarine, Hollywood, melted
1 pound turkey breast cutlets, ready for cooking
Dash salt
Dash seasoned pepper
2 tablespoons vegetable oil
1/2 cup port wine
1/4 cup apple cider

In a medium bowl, combine the bread crumbs, celery, shallots, walnuts, raisins, and apple pieces. Stir to mix. Add the melted safflower margarine and combine until moist. Set aside.

Prepare the turkey cutlets in the following way: cutting across the grain of a boned turkey breast half at a slight angle, slice the turkey into 3/8-inch slices. Place each slice between 2 sheets of plastic wrap and flatten to a thickness of 1/8 to 1/4 inch. Use a rolling pin to flatten the turkey breast because you do not want to make any holes in the cutlet. The cutlets are now ready to be stuffed and rolled.

Begin by seasoning the cutlets with a dash of salt and seasoned pepper. Taking the prepared stuffing, divide it evenly among the cutlets. Spread the stuffing almost to the edges. Now roll each cutlet up like a jelly roll, tucking in the ends, and secure each in 3 spots with string or even toothpicks.

In a large fry pan, heat the vegetable oil. Add the cutlet rolls, browning on all sides for about 5 to 7 minutes over medium heat. Add the port wine and apple cider, bringing them to a boil. Reduce the heat, cover the pan, and simmer for about 20 minutes, (turning once halfway through) until cutlets are completely cooked.

Remove the cooked turkey rolls to a cutting board. Remove the string or toothpicks, and slice the rolls. Place them on a serving platter and keep warm. Remove the juices from the pan and ladle over turkey roll slices. Serve.

Makes a great dish for a summer dinner!

Per Serving: Calories: 492 Cholesterol: 53mg Dietary Fiber: 3g Protein: 24g
Sodium: 296mg Carbohydrate: 32g Total Fat: 28g Saturated Fat: 4g
Calories from Fat: 53%, Calories from Carbohydrates: 27%, Calories from Protein: 20%

Pork

As they say, pork is the "other white meat." The following recipes use seasonings and sauces to make new twists on basic meals. Remember to cook pork thoroughly, no matter what the dish is.

Apple-Raisin Pork Chops

These pork chops are juicy and full of flavor. Using apple cider syrup, sautéing the sliced apples in the safflower margarine, and using simple seasoning, leaves out all chance of lactose. The MSG in seasonings and sauces can sneak up on you, so look for tasty alternatives. For a fancy barbecue dinner, to complete the meal add lactose-free hot rolls and salad.

Makes 5 servings
Preparation time: 30 minutes

5 4-ounce pork chops, 1 inch thick
Dash seasoned pepper
Dash salt
3 teaspoons apple cider syrup
3 tablespoons safflower oil margarine, Hollywood
2 tablespoons raisins
4 large apples
1 tablespoon ground cinnamon
1 tablespoon sugar

Rinse the pork chops, split them the width of the chop three fourths of the way through, and season lightly with salt and pepper. Baste with the apple cider syrup, inside as well as outside. Place the chops on a hot barbecue grill, and sear each side. Turn the heat down and continue cooking, basting as necessary until the chops are plump, juicy, and no longer pink inside, or about 30 minutes.

While grilling the chops, melt 1 tablespoon of the safflower margarine in a large fry pan (don't burn!). Add the raisins, stirring to coat with margarine. Cover the fry pan and simmer a few minutes until raisins are plump. Remove from the fry pan, placing the raisins and any remaining margarine into a bowl. Set aside.

Peel the apples, core, and thinly slice. Place 2 tablespoons margarine in the same fry pan and melt over medium heat. Place the apple slices into the melted margarine and cover the pan. Lightly brown and soften the apples for about 15 minutes, turning them occasionally. When the apples are just about ready, sprinkle with cinnamon and sugar (you can adjust the amounts according to individual taste). Return the raisins to the browning apple slices, tossing gently to mix. Cover and continue to brown a few more minutes. Remove from the heat.

Place the apple mixture inside the cooked pork chops. Arrange on a platter and pour the remaining apple mixture over the stuffed chops. Ready to serve!

Serve this dish with mashed potatoes, vegetables, and applesauce.

Per Serving: Calories: 389 Cholesterol: 74mg Dietary Fiber: 4g Protein: 24g
Sodium: 128mg Carbohydrate: 24g Total Fat: 22g Saturated Fat: 7g
Calories from Fat: 51%, Calories from Carbohydrates: 25%, Calories from Protein: 24%

Barbecued Baby Back Ribs

These ribs are juicy and mild. The ingredients you choose when making any dish can be lactose free, depending on the brands. Remember to read the labels, as manufacturers change ingredients from time to time without warning. For example, one barbecue sauce is not the same as another; so find one that leaves lactose out of the ingredients.

Makes 8 servings
Preparation time: 1 hour
Chill time: 2 hours

3 pounds pork back ribs
1/2 cup hickory smoke barbecue sauce, Kraft
1/2 cup port wine
Seasoned pepper, to taste

Rinse and pat dry slabs of pork ribs (baby back ribs); slice in half for easier handling. Mix the barbecue sauce and port wine in a bowl. Place the rib slabs in a shallow baking pan, and brush with the barbecue mix and sprinkle with seasoned pepper. Cover and marinate in the refrigerator for at least 2 hours.

Remove the ribs from the pan and coat with more barbecue sauce. Double-wrap in heavy-duty foil.

Ready the barbecue and place the foil packets on the grill. After about 5 minutes (the first initial turning), turn packets and lower the heat. Continue to turn packets every 15 minutes for the next hour. Watch carefully so as not to burn.

At the end of the cooking time, carefully remove the foil wrapping from each packet. Brush with additional barbecue sauce, return to the grill, and allow to cook an additional 5 to 7 minutes per side. Serve immediately, slicing into smaller portions (3 to 4 ribs each).

A great barbecue main dish.

Per Serving: Calories: 430 Cholesterol: 123mg Dietary Fiber: 0g Protein: 25g
Sodium: 310mg Carbohydrate: 6g Total Fat: 30g Saturated Fat: 11g
Calories from Fat: 69%, Calories from Carbohydrates: 6%, Calories from Protein: 25%

Seafood

This section gives you a few choices with basic fish dishes. The important thing to remember is once you have a working knowledge of what substitutions to use, the sky's the limit! Be creative.

Grilled Shrimp-Mushroom Kabobs

This is an elegant dinner offering for a warm summer evening. There's no lactose to worry about because only olive oil is used. Layer the finished kabobs on a bed of rice, surrounded by sprigs of parsley or thyme, for a dramatic presentation, or serve them with foil-wrapped baked potatoes.

Makes 6 servings
Preparation time: 1 hour
Chill time: 45 minutes

2 large lemons
18 large shrimp
18 large fresh white mushrooms
1/2 cup virgin olive oil, light
1 tablespoon chopped fresh thyme
1/4 cup dry white wine
1/4 teaspoon freshly ground pepper
6 skewers, to thread ingredients for grilling

Slice the lemons into 18 slices about 1/8 inch thick. Remove the seeds and set aside.

Clean and devein the shrimp. Brush the mushrooms clean and remove the stems, leaving them whole.

In a large glass mixing bowl, place the olive oil, thyme, wine, and pepper, whisking until well blended. Toss in the lemon slices and shrimp, coating evenly. Cover and place in the refrigerator for about 45 minutes. During the marinating time, toss a few times to ensure coating.

Start the barbecue grill, making sure to use a rack that is 4 to

6 inches away from the fire. Return to the marinade and toss in the mushrooms, coating them evenly as you did the shrimp and lemon slices. Let the mixture stand in the bowl on the counter for 10 more minutes.

To assemble the skewers, fold a lemon slice inside the curve of the shrimp, pinch together and pierce with the skewer, catching both ends of the shrimp. Follow with a mushroom cap. Continue this process until all the ingredients are threaded among the 6 skewers. Set the remaining marinade by the barbecue.

Place the skewers on the hot barbecue rack. Brush with the remaining marinade. A total of 8 to 10 minutes should complete the cooking, but you will need to stay with this, as frequent turning of the skewers is necessary. As you turn the skewers, brush on more marinade until all of it is gone. The shrimp will be pink and the mushrooms tender upon completion of cooking.

Per Serving: Calories: 229 Cholesterol: 59mg Dietary Fiber: .8g Protein: 10g
Sodium: 62mg Carbohydrate: 7g Total Fat: 19g Saturated Fat: 3g
Calories from Fat: 72%, Calories from Carbohydrates: 12%, Calories from Protein: 16%

Lactose-Free Crab Quiche

*W*hen using fresh mozzarella, carefully dry the ball of cheese with a paper towel as much as possible to absorb the fluid it comes in. This will make the mozzarella easier to shred and produces less watery results. This quiche freezes great. Cut it into individual portions and freeze in containers to have on hand for quick lunches or dinners.

Makes 8 servings
Preparation time: 1 hour 30 minutes

1/2 recipe Homemade Pie Crust (page 224)
4 tablespoons safflower oil margarine, Hollywood, softened
4 medium eggs, slightly beaten
2 cups whipping cream alternative, Pastry Pride
3/4 teaspoon salt
1/8 teaspoon ground nutmeg
1/4 pound fresh mozzarella, Del Pastore, shredded
2 tablespoons minced shallots
12 ounces crabmeat, shredded
2 tablespoons Chablis
1/4 teaspoon salt
1/8 teaspoon cayenne pepper
1/4 cup real bacon pieces, Hormel

Prepare the pie shell, lining a quiche dish or pie plate and coating it with 1 tablespoon of the safflower margarine. Place in the refrigerator until ready to fill. In a large bowl, using a wire whisk, beat the eggs, whipping cream alternative, salt, nutmeg, and shredded mozzarella. Set aside. Preheat the oven to 425° F.

In a small saucepan, melt the remaining 3 tablespoons margarine. Add the shallots and cook until tender, being careful not to burn. Add the cooked shallots to the creamed mixture, fold in the crabmeat, Chablis, salt, cayenne pepper, and bacon pieces.

Remove the pie shell from the refrigerator and fill with the creamed mixture. Bake in the oven for 15 minutes, then turn down the temperature to 325° F. and bake for another 35 minutes. The quiche is done when a knife comes out clean after being inserted in the center. Allow to stand 10 minutes before serving.

Per Serving: Calories: 514 Cholesterol: 149mg Dietary Fiber: 0g Protein: 17g
Sodium: 779mg Carbohydrate: 25g Total Fat: 28g Saturated Fat: 21g
Calories from Fat: 68%, Calories from Carbohydrates: 19%, Calories from Protein: 13%

Quick Flounder au Gratin

This dish is something you always have time to make on a busy weeknight. With minimum preparation, a full dinner will be on the table before you know it. Pick quick, easy-to-make side dishes to complete the meal.

Makes 8 servings
Preparation time: 20 minutes

1/4 cup bread crumbs, Pioneer
1/4 cup grated Parmesan cheese alternative, Soyco
2 tablespoons chopped parsley
1 pound flounder fillets
1/4 cup mayonnaise, Best Foods or Hellmann's

In a wide, shallow dish, place the bread crumbs, Parmesan cheese alternative, and parsley; stir to blend. Brush both sides of the fillets with the mayonnaise, then coat in the bread-crumb mixture. Place the coated fillets in a large, shallow baking dish (make sure it is microwave-proof) in a single layer. Cover the fillets with a sheet of wax paper. Place in the microwave on high for about 6 minutes, or until the fish is firm and moist. If you need to, rotate the dish halfway through cooking.

Per Serving: Calories: 112 Cholesterol: 3mg Dietary Fiber: .2g Protein: 11g
Sodium: 162mg Carbohydrate: 3g Total Fat: 6g Saturated Fat: .8g
Calories from Fat: 52%, Calories from Carbohydrates: 9%, Calories from Protein: 39%

Sautéed Scallops

The shallots give a gentle, milder onion flavor to this dish. I prefer to use shallots in as many dishes as possible because they are gentler than onions on Lactose-Intolerant stomachs. The use of fresh grated Parmesan is okay if it is a good imported, quality aged cheese. Otherwise, stay with the lactose-free Parmesan alternative.

Makes 8 servings
Preparation time: 35 minutes

5 tablespoons safflower oil margarine, Hollywood
2 garlic cloves, finely chopped
3 medium shallots, finely chopped
1/4 cup finely chopped fresh parsley
3/4 cup dry white wine
1 pound fresh sea scallops

1/2 cup bread crumbs, Pioneer
2 tablespoons grated Parmesan cheese alternative, Soyco,
    or imported aged Parmesan
1/2 teaspoon salt
Dash seasoned pepper
2 tablespoons safflower oil margarine, Hollywood, melted

Preheat the broiler. In a large sauté pan, over medium heat, melt the safflower margarine, add the garlic, shallots, 2 tablespoons of the parsley, and sauté for about 10 minutes. Be careful not to brown or burn. Add the white wine and simmer for an additional 8 to 10 minutes. Add the sea scallops to the pan and cook for an additional 6 minutes. While the scallops are cooking, stir the bread crumbs, Parmesan cheese alternative, salt, pepper, and the melted margarine until crumby. Set aside.

Remove the scallops from the pan and layer them into a large sauté dish. Sprinkle the bread-crumb mixture over the top of the scallops and place under the broiler for 2 to 4 minutes until golden brown and crisp.

*This makes an easy dinner accompanied by salad
and baked potatoes.*

Per Serving: Calories: 188 Cholesterol: 19mg Dietary Fiber: .3g Protein: 12g
Sodium: 403mg Carbohydrate: 8g Total Fat: 11g Saturated Fat: 2g
Calories from Fat: 57%, Calories from Carbohydrates: 17%, Calories from Protein: 26%

Scallop Bundles

These little bundles are very fancy, whether served as an appetizer or a main course. With the substitution of lactose-free ingredients, the consistency stays the same and the taste is wonderful. No one will guess you changed anything.

Makes 8 bundles
Preparation time: 30 minutes

1/2 cup safflower oil margarine, Hollywood
4 sheets phyllo dough
8 large whole sea scallops
1 tablespoon brandy
1 teaspoon minced fresh marjoram
Salt and freshly ground pepper, to taste
1 tablespoon safflower oil margarine, Hollywood
2 tablespoons minced shallots
1/2 cup dry white wine
2 tablespoons whipping cream alternative, Pastry Pride
1 large egg yolk
5 tablespoons safflower oil margarine, Hollywood
11/2 tablespoons fresh lemon juice

Melt the 1/2 cup safflower margarine in a saucepan or in the microwave. Do not allow to burn. Working with one sheet of phyllo dough at a time (keep the rest covered with a damp cloth), brush the sheet with the melted margarine. Place another sheet on top and brush again; repeat the process until all four sheets are used. Carefully cut the layers of phyllo dough into 4 equal squares.

In the center of each square place 1 large sea scallop, brush with the brandy, and sprinkle with fresh marjoram and salt and pepper. Draw up the sides of the phyllo dough around the scallop; pinch and twist to seal the little bundle. Place the bundles on a baking sheet. Return to the remaining phyllo dough and repeat the whole process, using up all the whole sea scallops and the sheets of phyllo dough.

Preheat the oven to 425° F. Brush the little bundles with more melted margarine, while they are lined up on the baking sheet. Bake in the oven for about 8 to 10 minutes. They should be a light golden brown.

While the bundles are baking, place 1 tablespoon margarine in a small saucepan and melt. Add the minced shallots and sauté until soft and tender, about 3 minutes. Add the white wine and bring to a boil, allowing the mixture to reduce to make about 1/4 cup. This should take about 5 minutes. Finally, mix in the whipping cream alternative, stir to blend, and remove from the heat.

Just before serving, return the sauce to medium-low heat. With a whisk, blend in the egg yolk; place the remaining 5 tablespoons margarine in the sauce and melt; add the lemon juice. Be careful not to boil the sauce, you just want to melt and blend the ingredients.

Ladle the finished sauce onto serving plates, and place the sea-scallop bundles on top. Serve hot.

Serve as a very fancy main dish or an appetizer.

Per Serving: Calories: 251 Cholesterol: 31mg Dietary Fiber: 0g Protein: 3g
Sodium: 275mg Carbohydrate: 7g Total Fat: 23g Saturated Fat: 5g
Calories from Fat: 84%, Calories from Carbohydrates: 10%, Calories from Protein: 6%

Shrimp Marinara

*T*his is a fresh and delicious Italian dish that the whole family can enjoy. Remember, imported Parmesan cheese is aged longer than American Parmesan, so the lactose content is lower. If you use an imported, aged Parmesan and grate it fresh, because of its minor lactose content it may not bother you. It is important to keep in mind that the level of tolerance for lactose is as individual as people are.

Makes 8 servings
Preparation time: 35 minutes

4 garlic cloves, sliced
3 tablespoons virgin olive oil, light
1 28-ounce can Italian tomatoes, peeled and chopped
1 teaspoon sugar
1/2 teaspoon dried oregano
2 tablespoons chopped fresh basil
1/4 teaspoon salt
1/8 teaspoon freshly ground pepper
1 pound angel hair pasta
1 pound shrimp, fresh or frozen
2 tablespoons parsley
1/2 cup Parmesan cheese alternative, Soyco

In a large skillet, sauté the garlic in the olive oil over medium heat until tender. Drain the canned tomatoes, reserving the juice. Add the tomatoes to the skillet and cook for about 3 minutes, stirring occasionally. Next put in the sugar, oregano, basil, salt, and pepper; stir and cook for 3 more minutes. Add the reserved tomato juice, bringing it to a boil. Reduce the heat and simmer for about 10 minutes. While the sauce is simmering, cook angel hair pasta according to the package directions. Drain and place on a serving platter. Add the shrimp to the sauté mixture and continue to cook for about 5 to 8 more minutes. Remove from the heat.

Ladle the sauce and shrimp over the pasta and serve. Garnish with fresh parsley and Parmesan cheese alternative.

*Warm lactose-free bread and a salad
complete this meal.*

Per Serving: Calories: 341 Cholesterol: 86mg Dietary Fiber: 3g Protein: 20g
Sodium: 164mg Carbohydrate: 49g Total Fat: 7g Saturated Fat: 1g
Calories from Fat: 19%, Calories from Carbohydrates: 58%, Calories from Protein: 23%

Main-Dish Casseroles and Hearty Dishes

When you become Lactose Intolerant, casseroles tend to drop by the wayside. Most are creamy and rich and include lactose-laden ingredients. In this section you'll find great casseroles and salads that bring back old favorites for the whole family. Whether you are Lactose Intolerant or not, you'll love these dishes.

Baked Cheesy Egg Casseroles

This makes a brunch special. For variety, you can use chopped green onions, top with shredded cheddar cheese alternative, mozzarella alternative, or use your imagination.

Makes 4 servings
Preparation time: 20 minutes

2 tablespoons safflower oil margarine, Hollywood
4 tablespoons grated Parmesan cheese alternative, Soyco,
   or imported aged Parmesan cheese
4 large eggs
Freshly ground pepper
1 tablespoon real bacon bits, Hormel
1/2 teaspoon chopped fresh parsley, for garnish

Preheat the oven to 325° F. Grease 4 shallow individual baking dishes with 1 tablespoon of the safflower margarine. Sprinkle 1 tablespoon of the Parmesan cheese alternative (or you can use fresh, imported grated Parmesan as long as it is well aged and your system can tolerate it) into each of the four individual baking dishes, covering the bottoms.

Into each dish, break 1 egg, keeping the yolk intact. Season with pepper and bacon bits. Top with 1 tablespoon margarine, evenly divided between the 4 dishes.

Bake in the oven, uncovered, until done to your taste (anywhere from 12 to 15 minutes). Garnish with parsley and serve.

Per Serving: Calories: 153 Cholesterol: 215mg Dietary Fiber: 0g Protein: 10g
Sodium: 286mg Carbohydrate: 10g Total Fat: 12g Saturated Fat: 3g
Calories from Fat: 72%, Calories from Carbohydrates: 2%, Calories from Protein: 26%

Baked Macaroni and Cheese Casserole

Macaroni and cheese was always part of our weekly dinner menu as our kids were growing up. My husband loved it! With the substitutions, you can achieve the same great taste and no one has to know it isn't the real thing. Again, if you watch the processing of the cheese, it is possible to use a "real" cheddar cheese. Remember, the longer the cheese ages, the lower the lactose content—it all comes down to your individual tolerance level.

Makes 8 servings
Preparation time: 45 minutes

8 ounces macaroni (elbow, rotini, or your choice)
    uncooked
6 tablespoons safflower oil margarine, Hollywood
3/4 cup bread crumbs, Pioneer
1 large shallot, minced
1 tablespoon all-purpose flour
Dash freshly ground pepper
1 1/2 cups 100% lactose-free 2% lowfat milk
2 cups shredded cheddar cheese alternative, TofuRella
Parsley, for garnish

In a large saucepan, cook the macaroni according to the manufacturer's instructions until tender but still firm. Drain and set aside.

Preheat the oven to 350° F. Generously grease a 2-quart casserole dish with 2 tablespoons of the safflower margarine. In the microwave, melt 2 tablespoons margarine. Remove from the microwave and add the bread crumbs, mixing only until coated; set aside. In a medium saucepan, heat the remaining 2 tablespoons margarine over medium-low heat. Add the minced shallot and cook until tender, about 3 to 5 minutes. With a wooden spoon, blend in the flour and pepper. Slowly stir in the lactose-free milk, and continue blending and stirring until the mixture becomes thickened. Remove from the heat and add the cheddar cheese alternative. Blend completely, stirring constantly.

Put the drained macaroni into the greased casserole dish. Slowly pour the cheese mixture over the cooked macaroni. Finish by sprinkling the bread-crumb mixture over the top.

Bake in the oven for about 20 minutes. Garnish with a sprig of parsley.

Main dish or side, this one's always a hit.

Per Serving: Calories: 386 Cholesterol: 4mg Dietary Fiber: 1g Protein: 17g
Sodium: 760mg Carbohydrates: 35g Total Fat: 21g Saturated Fat: 3g
Calories from Fat: 48%, Calories from Carbohydrates: 35%, Calories from Protein: 17%

Egg Salad

It's simple, it's easy, and it's quick. I use Best Foods Mayonnaise, because I think it's the best (on the East Coast, it's Hellmann's).

Makes 2 servings
Preparation time: 15 minutes

3 large eggs, whole
3 tablespoons mayonnaise, Best Foods or Hellmann's
Salt and pepper to taste

In a medium saucepan, place the eggs. Fill the pan with water, covering the eggs. Salt the water. Bring to a rapid boil, and time for 10 minutes (lower the heat slightly to prevent spilling over). Remove the eggs from the heat and submerge into cold water. To peel, gently tap on a hard surface to crack the shell. Carefully peel under cold running water.

Place the cooked eggs into a medium mixing bowl. Chop. Dust with salt and pepper to taste, and blend together with the mayonnaise. For variety add parsley, minced scallions, red onions, or mustard.

Great for sandwich fixin' or scooped into a salad.

Per Serving: Calories: 262 Cholesterol: 326mg Dietary Fiber: 0g Protein: 9g
Sodium: 229mg Carbohydrate: .9g Total Fat: 24g Saturated Fat: 5g
Calories from Fat: 84%, Calories from Carbohydrates: 1%, Calories from Protein: 15%

Lactose-Free Mushroom Quiche

Quiches freeze great. They can be made ahead, then reheated. Simply cover the quiche with foil and bake in a 325° F. oven for 40 minutes, or until thoroughly heated. For additional meals, pack quiches in individual freezer containers for fast lunches or dinners.

Makes 8 servings
Preparation time: 1½ hours

1/2 recipe Homemade Pie Crust (page 224)
1 tablespoon safflower oil margarine, Hollywood, softened
4 large eggs, slightly beaten
2 cups whipping cream alternative, Pastry Pride
3/4 teaspoon salt
1/4 pound fresh mozzarella, Del Pastore, shredded
1/4 cup safflower oil margarine, Hollywood
1/2 pound fresh mushrooms, thinly sliced
2 tablespoons minced shallots
1/4 teaspoon salt
1/8 teaspoon freshly ground pepper
1/4 cup real bacon pieces, Hormel

Prepare the pie shell in a quiche dish or pie plate, and coat with softened safflower margarine. Place in the refrigerator until ready to use.

In a large mixing bowl, with a wire whisk, blend the eggs, whipping cream alternative, salt, and cheese. Set aside. Preheat the oven to 425° F.

In a large skillet, over medium-high heat, melt the margarine. Add the mushrooms, shallots, salt, and pepper. Sauté until tender, approximately 5 minutes. Stir often, so as not to burn. After the mushroom mixture is cooked, stir into the creamed mixture. Add the bacon pieces and stir.

Remove the pie shell from the refrigerator, and pour the creamed mixture into it. Cook the quiche in the oven for 15 minutes, then turn down the temperature to 325° F., and cook for another 35 minutes. The quiche is done when a knife inserted in the center comes out clean. Allow the quiche to stand 10 minutes before serving.

Fresh bread and salad make this
a complete dinner.

Per Serving: Calories: 481 Cholesterol: 116mg Dietary Fiber: .4g Protein: 10g
Sodium: 655mg Carbohydrate: 26g Total Fat: 38g Saturated Fat: 21g
Calories from Fat: 71%, Calories from Carbohydrates: 21%, Calories from Protein: 8%

Stuffed Potatoes

This is a great quick lunch meal. You can let everyone stuff their own!

Makes 4 servings
Preparation time: 10 minutes

**4 large russet potatoes, scrubbed
4 tablespoons safflower oil margarine, Hollywood
Salt and pepper, optional
1 cup shredded cheddar cheese alternative, TofuRella
1 cup shredded mozzarella alternative, TofuRella
4 tablespoons real bacon pieces, Hormel**

Wash and scrub the potatoes. Pat dry. With a large fork, pierce each potato three times. In the microwave, place a paper towel and arrange the potatoes in a circular pattern. Cook on high for 12¹/₂ minutes. Test for doneness by inserting a fork into the potatoes. If they feel soft, they're done; if an area is hard, turn the potato around and give it another few minutes.

Take the cooked potatoes, place them in a soufflé dish or individual serving dishes. Cut open each potato, mashing and fluffing with a fork. Add the safflower margarine (1 tablespoon for each potato), blending into the potato. Sprinkle with salt and freshly ground pepper if desired. Sprinkle 1/4 cup each cheddar cheese and mozzarella alternative over the top of each potato. Sprinkle 1 tablespoon bacon pieces on top of each potato.

Return to the microwave on high for 1 to 2 minutes . . . just to melt the cheeses.

*Sour cream alternative or steamed vegetables
can add variety to this quick dish!*

Per Serving: Calories: 385 Cholesterol: 0mg Dietary Fiber: 2g Protein: 17g
Sodium: 1060mg Carbohydrate: 27g Total Fat: 25g Saturated Fat: 3g
Calories from Fat: 56%, Calories from Carbohydrates: 27%, Calories from Protein: 17%

The Grilled BLT Comeback

This cheesy bacon, lettuce, and tomato sandwich is one of my husband's favorites. Choose your preferred cheese substitute and invent your own concoctions. For variety, you can use a mozzarella alternative, mushrooms, and tomatoes.

Makes 1 serving
Preparation time: 15 minutes

4 slices bacon
1 large tomato
1 tablespoon safflower oil margarine,
    Hollywood
2 slices bread, lactose free
2 slices cheddar cheese alternative,
    TofuRella

Cook the bacon until crisp and drain on a paper towel. Slice the tomato. Spread the safflower margarine on one side of a slice of bread (sourdough, French, or Italian). Lay the slice of bread, margarine side down, in a small fry pan. Place 2 slices of the cheddar cheese alternative on top, followed by strips of bacon, a slice of tomato, and the other slice of bread. Spread the margarine on the top of the slice of bread that's facing up. Over low to medium heat, toast the sandwich. Flip the sandwich over and repeat on the other side. Remove from the fry pan when the cheese alternative is melted. Slice and serve.

Makes a great lunch or a light supper!

Per Serving: Calories: 343 Cholesterol: 6mg Dietary Fiber: 1g Protein: 11g
Sodium: 766mg Carbohydrate: 28g Total Fat: 22g Saturated Fat: 4g
Calories from Fat: 56%, Calories from Carbohydrates: 31%, Calories from Protein: 13%

The Ultimate Cheesesteak Sandwich

*W*hen you come from Philly, cheesesteaks are very important. To my husband, giving up such a ritual by moving to California, and because of his Lactose Intolerance, was unbearable! Now, he indulges whenever he wants. Remember, instead of the mozzarella alternative, you can use the fresh mozzarella because it is lactose free, and you can enjoy your old favorite!

Makes 4 servings
Preparation time: 30 minutes

2 tablespoons olive oil
8 ounces wafer-thin beef fillet steaks, frozen
2 medium shallots, chopped
1 large green pepper, minced
1 cup Italian spaghetti sauce, Prego Tomato and Basil, or
    Homemade (page 181)
2 ounces mozzarella alternative, TofuRella, or fresh
    mozzarella, lactose free, sliced or shredded
4 large French rolls, lactose free (see page 25)
4 teaspoons grated Parmesan cheese alternative, Soyco

In a large fry pan coated with 1 tablespoon olive oil, place the frozen steak layers in the pan and brown both sides. As the meat browns, separate the layers into paper-thin steaks.

In a separate medium fry pan, place another tablespoon of olive oil, coating the pan. Add the shallots and green pepper, and sauté until tender.

In a saucepan, warm the prepared tomato and basil sauce (or your homemade sauce). Return to the steaks, and top with sliced or shredded mozzarella alternative on as many pieces of steak as desired.

To assemble, split the rolls down the middle and lay them open. Layer the paper-thin cheesesteaks evenly in each roll, top with the shallots and peppers, and ladle the sauce on top. Sprinkle with the Parmesan cheese alternative and serve.

Per Serving: Calories: 334 Cholesterol: 40mg Dietary Fiber: 1g Protein: 16g

Sodium: 671mg Carbohydrate: 27g Total Fat: 18g Saturated Fat: 6g

Calories from Fat: 49%, Calories from Carbohydrates: 32%, Calories from Protein: 19%

Pastas and Italian Dishes

This is my favorite section! I think I should have been born Italian, as I can eat Italian food every day. When eating out, ask the waiter for a dish that contains no cheese or milk. Remember, linguine with olive oil and garlic is a "safe" dish. You can always leave the cheese off veal or chicken parmigiana. Watch your breads. If in doubt . . . leave it out!

A Real Pizza

(Bread Machine Recipe)

For time saving or if you don't have a bread machine, you can use Pillsbury pizza crust in the can. Just roll it out in the pan. The same is true of the sauce; store-bought is good as long as you read the label.

Makes 16 slices
Preparation time: 1½ hours

For the crust
2 tablespoons virgin olive oil, light
1 cup water, plus 2 tablespoons
3 cups bread flour
1 teaspoon salt
1 teaspoon sugar
2½ teaspoons bread machine yeast

For the sauce and topping
4 tablespoons virgin olive oil, light
4 garlic cloves, whole
3/4 cup finely chopped shallots
2 28-ounce cans peeled Italian tomatoes
10 whole fresh basil leaves
1/2 cup tomato paste
1/4 cup grated Parmesan cheese alternative, Soyco
1/4 teaspoon garlic salt
1/2 teaspoon dried basil
1/2 teaspoon dried oregano
1½ teaspoons sugar
PAM cooking spray
3 cups shredded fresh mozzarella, Del Pastore

Into a bread machine, place the first five ingredients in the order listed. With a spoon, make a small indentation in the ingredients and place the yeast into it (you don't want the yeast to come into contact with the liquids until it is mixing). Then follow the manufacturer's instructions for dough processing. (Skip this step if you are using the Pillsbury pizza crust in a can.)

While the bread machine is working, you can prepare the sauce for the pizza. Place 4 tablespoons olive oil into a large pot with the garlic cloves and shallots. Over medium heat, cook until both are tender, about 10 minutes. Stir occasionally, as you don't want to burn them, just lightly brown. Place the tomatoes and their juices into a blender and puree until smooth. When the garlic and shallots are cooked, pour in the tomato puree, place the heat on high, and bring to boiling for about 8 minutes. Turning the heat down, add the fresh basil and simmer the sauce for 25 to 30 minutes. Stir often. (Skip this step if you are using prepared sauce.)

When the sauce is finished, add the tomato paste, Parmesan cheese alternative, garlic salt, dried basil, dried oregano, and 1 1/2 teaspoons sugar. Pour the sauce back into the blender and process until smooth, about 15 seconds. It will take several small batches to completely blend all sauce in the blender.

When the dough is ready, preheat the oven to 400° F., place the oven rack at the lowest level, and spray two pizza pans (or two cookie sheets) with PAM. With floured hands, sprinkle some flour on the dough to reduce stickiness, divide the pizza dough in half, and work it a little until it's easier to handle. Pat into the shape of the pizza pans (or if using cookie sheets, make 12-inch circles). With a ladle, spread the prepared tomato sauce over the dough. Sprinkle the shredded fresh mozzarella over the entire pizza.

Place the pans in the oven and bake for 18 to 20 minutes until the crust is golden. Slice and serve.

Keep one or two in the freezer for quick dinners.

Per Serving (1 slice): Calories: 262 Cholesterol: 16mg Dietary Fiber: 2g Protein: 15g
Sodium: 428mg Carbohydrate: 24g Total Fat: 12g Saturated Fat: 5g
Calories from Fat: 41%, Calories from Carbohydrates: 36%, Calories from Protein: 23%

Baked Ziti

This mixture of firm tofu and cream cheese alternative creates the same consistency as ricotta. By adding the mushrooms, the tofu takes on their flavor. For another version, you can use cottage cheese alternative instead of tofu and cream cheese. All other ingredients should be the same.

Makes 12 servings
Preparation time: 1½ hours

6 cups Homemade Italian Sauce (page 181), or jarred
16 ounces ziti
8 ounces firm tofu
8 ounces cream cheese alternative, Tofutti
1 pound ground turkey
1 cup sliced mushrooms
1/2 cup grated Parmesan cheese alternative, Soyco
1/4 cup finely chopped parsley
1 large egg, slightly beaten
3/4 teaspoon salt
3/4 teaspoon freshly ground pepper
8 ounces mozzarella alternative, TofuRella

Prepare the homemade sauce or warm the jarred sauce. Prepare the ziti according to the manufacturer's directions. Drain and set aside.

Preheat the oven to 350° F. In a large bowl, beat the tofu and cream cheese alternative with an electric mixer until blended. Add a dash of salt and freshly ground pepper. Set aside.

In a Dutch oven or large stockpot, brown the ground turkey. During the last few minutes of browning, add the mushrooms and cook for a few minutes until tender. Remove the Dutch oven from the heat and add the tofu mixture, Parmesan cheese alternative, parsley, beaten egg, salt, and pepper. Stir to mix, adding half the prepared Italian sauce. When well mixed, toss in the drained ziti and coat well.

Turn the mixture out into a 9 × 13-inch glass baking pan. Spread the remaining Italian sauce over the top and layer the shredded mozzarella alternative over the sauce.

Place in the oven and bake for 20 minutes. Ziti will be bubbly and hot. Remove from the oven and allow to cool a few minutes before serving.

This dish allows you all your favorites!

Per Serving: Calories: 397 Cholesterol: 48mg Dietary Fiber: 6g Protein: 20g
Sodium: 910mg Carbohydrate: 50g Total Fat: 13g Saturated Fat: 2g
Calories from Fat: 30%, Calories from Carbohydrates: 50%, Calories from Protein: 20%

Cheddar Pasta Bake

*T*his dish makes a great warm pasta main dish for lunch or dinner. The cheddar flavor is wonderful. The lactose-free milk adds a creamy texture, and the bread-crumb topping finishes it off. Try adding canned chicken, turkey, tuna, or even crabmeat for variety. You can change the vegetables to your favorites, or use frozen. I prefer using fresh vegetables whenever possible.

Makes 12 servings
Preparation time: 45 minutes

11/2 pounds pasta, your choice of shape
3/4 cup safflower oil margarine, Hollywood
1 garlic clove, minced
1/2 cup all-purpose flour
6 cups 100% lactose-free 2% lowfat milk
1 tablespoon salt
1 teaspoon finely chopped fresh parsley
1 teaspoon dried oregano
8 ounces cheddar cheese alternative, TofuRella, shredded
1 pound zucchini, sliced 1/4 inch thick
2 cups diced tomatoes
11/2 cups frozen peas, thawed
11/2 cups bread crumbs, Pioneer (or your choice of
    lactose-free crumbs)

Preheat the oven to 350° F. Generously grease a large casserole dish with safflower margarine and set aside.

Cook the pasta according to the manufacturer's instructions, undercooking slightly. When pasta is done, drain and return to the warm pot.

In a large saucepan, over medium-high heat, melt half the safflower margarine (1/4 cup plus 2 tablespoons). Add the garlic and sauté until tender. Stir in the flour, blending for about 1 minute. Add the lactose-free milk and blend with the flour mixture until smooth. Add the seasonings and cook, stirring often until the mixture thickens and comes to a boil. Now, reduce the heat and simmer for about 10 minutes. Then add the cheddar cheese alternative and vegetables. Continue cooking, allowing the cheese to melt and blend. Remove from the heat and pour over the pasta. After mixing the sauce through the pasta, turn out into the greased casserole dish.

In a small saucepan, melt the remaining safflower margarine and add the bread crumbs. As the mixture starts to stick together, remove from the heat and sprinkle over the casserole. Sprinkle on additional parsley, if desired.

Bake in the oven for about 20 to 30 minutes. The casserole will be bubbly and the bread crumbs will have browned.

Serve as a main dish or side dish; the cheesy taste is great.

Per Serving: Calories: 508 Cholesterol: 10mg Dietary Fiber: 4g Protein: 18g
Sodium: 91mg Carbohydrate: 67g Total Fat: 19g Saturated Fat: 4g
Calories from Fat: 34%, Calories from Carbohydrates: 52%, Calories from Protein: 14%

Creamy Asparagus Pasta

This is a wonderful, creamy pasta dish. If you choose an aged, imported Parmesan cheese and freshly grate it, it is possible to use real cheese as long as you can tolerate it. Just don't overdo it!

Makes 6 servings
Preparation time: 15 minutes

8 ounces fettuccine
1 pound fresh asparagus
1 tablespoon safflower oil margarine, Hollywood
1/4 cup whipping cream alternative, Pastry Pride
1/2 cup grated Parmesan cheese alternative, Soyco,
   or aged Parmesan cheese
Dash freshly ground pepper

Prepare the pasta according to the package directions.

Wash the asparagus, break off the woody bases and using a potato peeler, peel several inches off the bottom of the stalks (this will make the asparagus tender, not tough and stringy). Slice the asparagus in diagonal 1-inch pieces and place in a small saucepan with enough boiling water to cover. Boil for 3 to 5 minutes until crispy-tender. Drain well and set aside.

When the fettuccine is done, drain it well and return it to the pot. Add the safflower margarine and toss continually until the margarine is melted and completely coats the fettuccine. Add the whipping cream alternative and repeat the tossing process.

Finally, spoon in the asparagus; sprinkle on the Parmesan cheese alternative and the ground pepper. In a serving dish, toss and serve immediately.

Serve this pasta dish with homemade bread and a light salad
for a quick, fresh-flavored dinner.

Per Serving: Calories: 239 Cholesterol: 0mg Dietary Fiber: 3g Protein: 11g
Sodium: 193mg Carbohydrate: 34g Total Fat: 7g Saturated Fat: 3g
Calories from Fat: 25%, Calories from Carbohydrates: 57%, Calories from Protein: 18%

Eggplant Parmesan

When selecting the ingredients for this dish, read the labels on the bread crumbs and the sauce (lactose, whey, and cheese are commonly used in these products). Prego, Barilla, and Classico brands are great. I double the recipe, making two pans and freezing one. Leftovers can be frozen in individual Tupperware containers for quick lunches or dinners.

Makes 6 servings
Preparation time: 1 hour

3 tablespoons virgin olive oil, light
1 medium egg, slightly beaten
1 cup bread crumbs, Pioneer, for coating
1 tablespoon dried parsley
1 teaspoon dried oregano
1 large eggplant, sliced 1/8 inch thick
8 ounces mozzarella substitute, Del Pastore
1 26-ounce jar Italian sauce, Prego Tomato & Basil
  (see page 26)

Preheat the oven to 400° F. Place the olive oil in a large fry pan over medium heat. In a large, wide-rimmed bowl, whisk the egg. In another large, wide-rimmed bowl, place the bread crumbs, parsley, and oregano, mixing well. Peel and slice the eggplant into pieces 1/8 inch thick. Dip the eggplant slices into the egg (allow excess to drip off), then coat with the bread-crumb mixture, gently shaking off the excess. Place in the fry pan, browning on both sides. Drain on paper towels, and set aside.

With a small grater, shred the mozzarella substitute finely (it melts much better). Warm the jarred (or homemade) sauce in a saucepan. Keep on low heat, stirring often.

In a casserole or lasagna pan, spread the warmed tomato sauce covering the bottom. Add a layer of fried eggplant, then cover with sauce, then sprinkle heavily with mozzarella substitute. Repeat the order, placing another layer of eggplant slices, sauce, and cheese on top of the first layer. Repeat the layers as desired, ending with a heavy layer of cheese on top.

Bake in the oven for 30 minutes. The cheese will be melted and the sauce should be bubbling. (You can sprinkle Parmesan cheese alternative, if you wish.)

Per Serving (without Parmesan): Calories: 278 Cholesterol: 35mg Dietary Fiber: 4g
Protein: 10g Sodium: 1131mg Carbohydrate: 34g Total Fat: 13g Saturated Fat: 3g
Calories from Fat: 39%, Calories from Carbohydrates: 47%, Calories from Protein: 14%

Lactose-Free
Fettuccine Alfredo

Quick, easy, and absolutely delicious. And who says you can't have a creamy sauce ... without lactose?

Makes 8 servings
Preparation time: 30 minutes

8 ounces fettuccine
1/4 cup safflower oil margarine, Hollywood
1/4 cup grated Parmesan cheese alternative, Soyco
2 tablespoons whipping cream alternative,
   Pastry Pride

1/4 teaspoon salt
1/8 teaspoon freshly ground pepper

Prepare the fettuccine as the package directs, drain, and keep warm.

In a warm serving dish, blend the safflower margarine, Parmesan cheese alternative, whipping cream alternative, salt, and pepper. Toss the warm fettuccine in a serving dish, coating it with the creamy mixture. Serve immediately. Sprinkle on additional cheese, if desired.

This easy dinner is always ready to fill the bill
for a fast feast.

Per Serving: Calories: 180 Cholesterol: 0mg Dietary Fiber: .7g Protein: 5g
Sodium: 190mg Carbohydrate: 22g Total Fat: 8g Saturated Fat: 2g
Calories from Fat: 40%, Calories from Carbohydrates: 49%, Calories from Protein: 11%

Homemade
Italian Sauce

*W*hile certain ready-made sauces are "safe," many aren't. This sauce
is easy to make and tastes terrific. It freezes great; you can reheat it
in a saucepan or crockpot.

Makes 24 servings
Preparation time: 30 minutes

3 29-ounce cans tomato sauce, Hunt's
1 12-ounce can tomato paste, Hunt's
1 medium onion, quartered
1/3 cup chopped fresh parsley
1/4 cup grated Parmesan cheese alternative, Soyco
1/4 cup dried oregano
1 1/2 teaspoons dried basil
2 whole bay leaves, Turkish
2 tablespoons safflower oil margarine, Hollywood
2 teaspoons celery flakes
3/4 cup port wine
3/4 teaspoon finely chopped garlic
Dash salt and freshly ground pepper

Place all the ingredients into a crockpot. Stir with a wooden spoon until blended well. No need to break up the safflower margarine; it will melt and blend.

Cook in the crockpot, uncovered, for 5 to 6 hours on high or for 10 to 12 hours on the low setting. The sauce can be ready in 2 to 3 hours, but the longer it simmers, the more the flavor of the spices is brought out.

(For a meat sauce, use 1/2 to 3/4 pound of the leanest ground beef or ground turkey, broken up with a fork. Add last to the sauce in the crockpot.)

Great over spaghetti, in lasagna, baked ziti,
or any Italian dish.

Per Serving (without meat): Calories: 73 Cholesterol: 0mg Dietary Fiber: 2g
Protein: 3g Sodium: 688mg Carbohydrate: 12g Total Fat: 2g Saturated Fat: .2g
Calories from Fat: 19%, Calories from Carbohydrates: 66%, Calories from Protein: 15%

Italian Meatballs

*T*hese meatballs freeze great. Just place them in Tupperware containers and freeze. Take them out in the morning, place them in the
crockpot on low for 8 to 10 hours, and dinner is ready. These are a
great crowd pleaser!

Makes 24 servings
Preparation time: 30 minutes

4 slices bread, cubed (remember to check the ingredients,
   see page 25)
2 medium eggs, slightly beaten
1 pound extra-lean ground beef
1/4 cup grated Parmesan cheese alternative, Soyco
2 tablespoons snipped parsley
1 teaspoon salt
1/4 teaspoon dried oregano, crushed
Dash freshly ground pepper
1/2 cup port wine
Homemade Italian Sauce (page 181)

Mix all the ingredients together in a large bowl. Blend very
well.

With damp hands, roll small balls from the mixture. Drop
the meatballs into a crockpot of prepared Italian sauce (or
jarred, see the "Safe" List, page 26), enough to cover the meatballs. If you don't have a crockpot, the meatballs can be
browned in a fry pan before being placed in a large pot of sauce
on the stove to cook.

Allow the meatballs to cook on high for at least 1 hour
before trying to stir. Use a wooden spoon and test before stirring to make sure the meatballs are holding together.

Cook in the crockpot on high for 5 to 6 hours. If you want to let the meatballs continue to cook while you are away, put the pot on low for 10 to 12 hours, without worrying about stirring.

Check the meatballs occasionally by stirring and scraping the edge of the pot. Cooking meatballs in a crockpot makes them soft and tender.

*Great as party appetizers, or with pasta
for dinner.*

Per Serving (with sauce): Calories: 175 Cholesterol: 31mg Dietary Fiber: 2g Protein: 9g
Sodium: 975mg Carbohydrate: 20g Total Fat: 6g Saturated Fat: 2.2g
Calories from Fat: 59%, Calories from Carbohydrates: 102%, Calories from Protein: 39%

Linguine with Garlic and Olive Oil

This is an easy, fast dinner, which you can also order in an Italian restaurant without worrying about lactose. Just ask the restaurant to eliminate the Parmesan, unless it's imported from Italy, is properly aged, and your tolerance level can handle it (or bring your own cheese). Any good Italian restaurant will amend their menu to accommodate you with this easy dish.

Makes 6 servings
Preparation time: 20 minutes

8 ounces linguine
1/4 cup olive oil
3 garlic cloves, minced
1/4 cup grated Parmesan cheese alternative, Soyco
1 tablespoon chopped fresh parsley

Cook the linguine as desired, according to the package instructions. Drain thoroughly, rinse with warm water, and drain again. Place in a large mixing bowl and keep warm.

In a sauté pan, place the olive oil and garlic. Sauté on low heat until the garlic is tender, about 3 minutes. Gently toss the linguine into the sauté pan and mix with the garlic and oil. Once mixed and warm, remove the pasta from the pan to a serving platter. Sprinkle with the Parmesan cheese alternative and parsley. Serve immediately.

For a little variety, steam shrimp or sauté scallops
and toss with the linguine.

Per Serving: Calories: 238 Cholesterol: 0mg Dietary Fiber: 1g Protein: 7g
Sodium: 84mg Carbohydrate: 29g Total Fat: 10g Saturated Fat: 1g
Calories from Fat: 39%, Calories from Carbohydrates: 49%, Calories from Protein: 12%

Mostaccioli with Basil Sauce

Creamy, cheesy, and sweet . . . all in one dish. For variety, instead of mostaccioli (a tubular pasta), you can use any favorite pasta shape, or toss in some steamed veggies. Make this dish your personal signature by creating touches of your own.

Makes 4 servings
Preparation time: 30 minutes

1 pound mostaccioli
2 tablespoons virgin olive oil, light
2 garlic cloves, minced
4 teaspoons dried basil, crushed
1/3 cup grated Parmesan cheese alternative, Soyco
4 ounces cream cheese alternative, Tofutti
1/2 cup cottage cheese alternative/acidophilus
1/3 cup water
1/3 cup dry white wine
1/4 cup chopped fresh parsley
Dash freshly ground pepper

Follow the manufacturer's directions for cooking the pasta. Drain and keep warm while you finish cooking the sauce.

In a medium skillet, place the olive oil; as it warms add the garlic and basil. Cook for about 1 minute. Reducing the heat to low, add all the cheese alternatives, while you stir constantly. Blend well until just about smooth. Then stir in the water, wine, parsley, and pepper. Allow the mixture to cook until it is thickened slightly, about 3 to 4 minutes.

Ladle the hot sauce over the finished pasta and serve immediately. Garnish with fresh parsley sprigs or fresh basil, if desired.

This is a quick and easy dinner dish.

Per Serving: Calories: 549 Cholesterol: 0mg Dietary Fiber: 3g Protein: 20g
Sodium: 223mg Carbohydrate: 87g Total Fat: 11g Saturated Fat: 2g
Calories from Fat: 18%, Calories from Carbohydrates: 66%, Calories from Protein: 16%

Stuffed Shells

Missing those stuffed creamy, cheesy Italian dishes? Not anymore! This recipe also freezes well in individual containers for quick meals in a hurry.

Makes 10 servings
Preparation time: 2¹/2 hours

2 cups spaghetti sauce, your choice (see page 26)
16 ounces large pasta shells
32 ounces cottage cheese alternative/acidophilus
12 ounces fresh mozzarella, Del Pastore, shredded
2 large eggs, slightly beaten
¹/3 cup bread crumbs, Pioneer
¹/4 cup chopped fresh parsley
1 teaspoon salt
¹/4 teaspoon freshly ground pepper
¹/2 cup grated Parmesan cheese alternative, Soyco

Prepare the spaghetti sauce, either Homemade (page 181) or your favorite jarred sauce (remember to read the labels carefully). Prepare the pasta shells according to the directions on the package. Drain well in a colander. Preheat the oven to 350° F.

In a large bowl, combine the cottage cheese alternative, 8 ounces of the mozzarella, eggs, bread crumbs, parsley, salt, and pepper. Stuff the pasta shells with rounded tablespoons of the cheese mixture.

In a 13 × 9-inch baking dish, spoon ¹/2 cup of the prepared sauce, covering the bottom. Carefully place the stuffed shells, seam side down, over the sauce, making one layer. Spoon the remaining sauce over the tops of the shells, sprinkle evenly the remaining 4 ounces of shredded mozzarella, and top with the Parmesan cheese alternative.

Bake in the oven for about 30 minutes. Let stand 5 minutes before serving.

Per Serving: Calories: 358 Cholesterol: 56mg Dietary Fiber: 3g Protein: 21g
Sodium: 729mg Carbohydrate: 46g Total Fat: 10g Saturated Fat: 4g
Calories from Fat: 25%, Calories from Carbohydrates: 51%, Calories from Protein: 24%

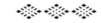

Pig in a Haystack

This little piggy accents a creamy fettuccine for a different twist on a simple dish.

Makes 8 servings

Preparation time: 30 minutes

1 pound fettuccine
8 ounces thin sliced bacon
1 cup shredded carrots
1 cup chopped fresh parsley
1 cup frozen peas, thawed
2 cups whipping cream alternative,
   Pastry Pride
2 cups grated Parmesan Cheese alternative,
   Soyco
Salt and pepper

Cook the fettuccine according to the manufacturer's directions. While the pasta is cooking, cook the bacon in a large fry pan until crispy. Place the bacon on a paper towel to drain.

Using about 1 tablespoon bacon fat, sauté the carrots, parsley, and peas in the large fry pan. This should take about 1 minute. With a whisk, blend the whipping cream alternative into the fry-pan mixture. Reduce the heat to a simmer and cook about 2 minutes. Sprinkle in the Parmesan cheese alternative, stirring to blend, only another minute (do not overcook or it will clump). The sauce should thicken slightly.

In a large serving bowl, place the cooked fettuccine and toss with the cream sauce from the fry pan. Crumble the bacon and toss into the fettuccine. Serve immediately, seasoning to taste with salt and pepper.

Per Serving: Calories: 714 Cholesterol: 24mg Dietary Fiber: 3g Protein: 31g
Sodium: 1055mg Carbohydrate: 62g Total Fat: 36g Saturated Fat: 20g
Calories from Fat: 47%, Calories from Carbohydrates: 36%, Calories from Protein: 17%

Cakes

Delicious, rich and creamy, gooey . . . those words can be banished forever . . . unless you read this section. You can have lactose-free rich and creamy and even gooey cakes. No one will realize there is anything different about these treats!

Black Forest Tower

This cake stands very tall and makes quite an entrance! Easy to assemble, it can be a quick fix for an impromptu dinner. The whipped topping border holds the cherries where you want them. The devil's food is very rich and moist because of the addition of lactose-free 2% lowfat milk instead of water.

Makes 12 servings
Preparation time: 30 minutes

1 package moist devil's food cake mix, Duncan Hines
3 large eggs, slightly beaten
1 1/3 cups 100% lactose-free 2% lowfat milk
1/2 cup vegetable oil
1 tube nondairy whipped topping, Squeeze Pro
4 2/3 cups (2 cans) cherry pie filling
Chocolate leaves or confectioners' sugar

Preheat the oven to 350° F. Generously grease and flour three 8-inch round cake pans.

Into a large mixing bowl, add the cake mix, eggs, lactose-free milk, and oil. Blend at low speed to combine ingredients; beat at medium speed for about 2 minutes. Pour immediately into the prepared pans and bake about 25 to 30 minutes. When a toothpick comes out clean, the cakes are done. Remove from the oven and cool on a wire rack.

When the cakes are completely cooled, remove from the pans, brushing off any crumbs, and place one layer on a serving plate. Around the edge of the layer, place a ribbon of whipped topping. Fill the center with cherry pie filling (enough to even out the layer).

Place the next cake layer on top and repeat the process. With the final layer, make a double row of whipped topping border and fill the center with the remaining pie filling. You can decorate with chocolate leaves, or just dust with confectioners' sugar.

Place the cake in the refrigerator to set until ready to serve.

This cake makes a grand finale to any meal.

Per Serving: Calories: 524 Cholesterol: 55mg Dietary Fiber: 2g Protein: 5g
Sodium: 399mg Carbohydrate: 71g Total Fat: 25g Saturated Fat: 14g
Calories from Fat: 43%, Calories from Carbohydrates: 54%, Calories from Protein: 3%

White Layers Under Clouds of Icing

Delicate, light, and wonderful, this cake can bloom—with edible flowers decorating the plate. You can make the cake layers 1 day ahead, wrapping with plastic wrap and storing at room temperature.

Makes 14 servings
Preparation time: 1 hour

For the cake
3/8 teaspoon salt
1 tablespoon, plus 1 teaspoon baking powder
23/4 cups cake flour
1/2 pound safflower margarine, Hollywood
2 cups sugar
2 teaspoons pure vanilla extract
1 cup, plus 2 tablespoons 100% lactose-free 2% lowfat
    milk
7 large egg whites, at room temperature

Seven-minute icing
2¼ teaspoons light corn syrup
3/8 teaspoon cream of tartar
2½ tablespoons water
3 large egg whites, at room temperature
2¼ cups sugar
1 teaspoon pure vanilla extract
Edible flowers, additional ornamental icing, or candy
  sprinkles, as decoration

Using three 9-inch round cake pans, lightly grease and flour all sides and the bottoms, then set aside. Place the oven rack in the center position and preheat the oven to 350° F.

In a mixing bowl, combine the salt, baking powder, and cake flour. Set aside.

Using a standing mixer with the paddle attachment, beat the safflower margarine for about 30 seconds. Once margarine is whipped, slowly add the sugar and beat until light, about 3 minutes. Add the vanilla, blending well.

Turn the speed down to the lowest and begin adding the cake flour mixture, alternating with the lactose-free milk. This should take about 3 additions each. Make sure to scrape down the sides of the mixing bowl often to ensure blending. Once completely blended, pour the batter into a large mixing bowl and set aside.

Clean the stationary bowl and make sure to dry it completely. Replace it in the stand and add the whisk attachment. Place the 7 egg whites into the bowl, and on the lowest speed beat them until they are frothy. Turn the speed up to the highest and continue to beat the whites just until stiff peaks form. Be careful not to dry them out.

In a gentle folding manner, using a rubber spatula, add the beaten egg whites into the cake batter. Fold carefully until just combined; do not beat. This is important to incorporate air and give height to the cake.

Gently scrape the cake batter into the prepared pans as evenly as possible. Smooth the batter out with the rubber spatula. Place in the oven and bake for about 25 to 30 minutes. Test for doneness by inserting a toothpick into the center of each pan. Cake is done when the toothpick comes out clean.

Remove the pans from the oven; allow to cool about 10 minutes before removing the layers from the pans. Finish cooling the layers completely on a wire rack.

For the seven-minute icing, begin by bringing a saucepan of water to a simmer. Meanwhile, find a large mixing bowl that is deep, heatproof, and will be able to sit over the saucepan. Place the corn syrup, cream of tartar, water, the 3 egg whites, and sugar into the bowl. With a handheld mixer on low, combine these ingredients.

Set the mixing bowl over the simmering water in the saucepan, but do not let it touch the water. Continue to beat the ingredients at medium speed for about 3 minutes, scraping the sides often. Kick the speed up to high for the next 4 minutes, beating until soft peaks form. Remove from the heat.

Add the vanilla and beat on high until the icing returns to soft peaks. Assemble your cake, spreading the layers with the icing, and add decorations, if desired. Remember to refrigerate this cake after frosting it.

Per Serving: Calories: 456 Cholesterol: 2mg Dietary Fiber: 0g Protein: 5g
Sodium: 346g Carbohydrate: 80g Total Fat: 15g Saturated Fat: 3g
Calories from Fat: 28%, Calories from Carbohydrates: 68%, Calories from Protein: 4%

Blueberry Coffee Cake

Luscious, plump blueberries fill this coffee cake, making it a perfect brunch treat.

Makes 10 servings
Preparation time: 20 minutes

1/4 cup sliced almonds
1/4 cup light brown sugar, firmly packed
11/2 cups all-purpose flour, sifted
3/4 cup granulated sugar
1 tablespoon baking powder
1/4 teaspoon ground nutmeg
1/2 teaspoon salt
1/3 cup safflower oil margarine, Hollywood
1 cup fresh blueberries, rinsed and drained
1 large egg, slightly beaten
1/2 cup 100% lactose-free 2% lowfat milk
1 teaspoon vanilla extract
Confectioners' sugar, for dusting

Preheat the oven to 350° F. Grease a 9-inch tube pan. In a small bowl, toss together the almonds and brown sugar. Liberally sprinkle in the bottom of the tube pan.

In a food processor, place the flour, sugar, baking powder, nutmeg, and salt. Pulse for a few times until incorporated. Break the safflower margarine into pieces and place into the food processor. Pulse until the mixture resembles coarse crumbs.

Remove from the food processor and place in a large bowl. Stir in the fresh blueberries, gently.

In a small bowl, blend together the beaten egg, lactose-free milk, and vanilla. Once blended well, add to the blueberry mixture just until combined.

Carefully pour the batter into the prepared pan. Place in the oven and bake until the cake is browned and a toothpick inserted in the cake comes out clean, about 45 minutes to 1 hour.

Remove from the oven and cool the pan on a wire rack for about 5 to 7 minutes. Run a knife around the rim edge of the pan to loosen the cake; invert onto a plate. Dust with confectioners' sugar and serve warm.

For a special touch, serve with blueberry sauce.

Per Serving: Calories: 238 Cholesterol: 22mg Dietary Fiber: 1g Protein: 4g
Sodium: 293mg Carbohydrate: 37g Total Fat: 9g Saturated Fat: 2g
Calories from Fat: 34%, Calories from Carbohydrates: 60%, Calories from Protein: 6%

Caramel Apple Pound Cake

This pound cake won't last . . . the aroma will fill your kitchen with unexpected visitors! I have baked this recipe in small 3 × 6-inch loaves for gifts, in a tube pan for a coffee cake effect, and in a regular large loaf pan. For a quick dessert, microwave a slice, just until warm, and top with homemade Rich Vanilla Lactose-Free Ice Cream (page 306). It will remind you of an apple cobbler with a faint hint of caramel.

Makes 10 servings
Preparation time: 25 minutes

3 large Red Delicious apples
1¹/4 cups light brown sugar, packed
³/4 cup coarsely chopped walnuts
4 tablespoons light corn syrup
3 tablespoons safflower oil margarine, Hollywood, melted
1¹/4 teaspoons ground cinnamon
1 package Betty Crocker Golden Pound Cake mix
²/3 cup water
2 large eggs, slightly beaten
Confectioners' sugar, for dusting

Preheat the oven to 375° F. Generously grease and flour the desired pan(s). Set aside.

Peel, core, and coarsely chop apples. Place in a large mixing bowl, stirring in the brown sugar, walnuts, corn syrup, melted safflower margarine, and cinnamon. Set aside and allow to get juicy.

Prepare the pound cake mix as directed on the box, using ²/3 cup water and 2 eggs. Pour half the batter into the prepared pan. Carefully spoon half the apple mixture on top, pour in the remaining batter, and finish with the apple mixture. (The apple mixture will eventually move down into the batter.)

Bake in the oven for about 1 hour 20 minutes, checking after 1 hour for doneness. When a toothpick inserted in the center comes out clean and the pound cake is golden brown, the cake is done. Cool on a wire rack and finish by dusting with confectioners' sugar.

Serve as breakfast bread, dessert, or as a treat anytime.

Per Serving: Calories: 434 Cholesterol: 43mg Dietary Fiber: 2g Protein: 5g
Sodium: 249mg Carbohydrate: 64g Total Fat: 19g Saturated Fat: 4g
Calories from Fat: 38%, Calories from Carbohydrates: 57%, Calories from Protein: 5%

Cherry Surprise

Always a crowd pleaser, this dish is quick and easy. For variety, you can use pecans instead of walnuts . . . or change the pie filling to blueberry, or apple, or any other favorite.

Makes 20 servings
Preparation time: 15 minutes

4²/3 cups (2 cans) cherry pie filling
1 package Duncan Hines Butter Golden cake mix
3/4 cup safflower oil margarine, Hollywood, melted
1¹/2 cups finely chopped walnuts

Preheat the oven to 400° F.

In an 11 × 15-inch glass baking dish, spread the cherry pie filling and sauce to cover the entire bottom of the dish. Sprinkle the cake mix (do not prepare the mix; use it dry) on top of the cherries. Spread the melted safflower margarine on top of the cake mix, smoothing it gently with a spoon. Sprinkle the nuts on top of the margarine, covering the entire top of the cake evenly.

Bake for about 40 minutes. Nuts will toast and become brown. Cool the cake for about 45 minutes before serving.

A perfect, rich dessert to finish any meal.

Per Serving: Calories: 296 Cholesterol: 0mg Dietary Fiber: 2g Protein: 3g
Sodium: 182mg Carbohydrate: 38g Total Fat: 15g Saturated Fat: 3g
Calories from Fat: 45%, Calories from Carbohydrates: 51%, Calories from Protein: 4%

Cinnamon Applesauce Coffee Cake

This breakfast coffee cake can moonlight as dessert. No leftovers here! (Remember to read the labels when using brand names, as companies tend to change ingredients when you least expect it.)

Makes 12 servings
Preparation time: 15 minutes

1 package Cinnamon Crumbcake mix, Duncan Hines
1 large egg, slightly beaten
2/3 cup 100% lactose-free 2% lowfat milk
1 cup cinnamon applesauce, Mott's
1/2 cup confectioners' sugar
1/4 teaspoon vanilla extract
2 teaspoons 100% lactose-free 2% lowfat milk

Preheat the oven to 350° F. and generously grease a 9 × 13-inch baking pan. In a large mixing bowl, empty the crumbcake mix and break up any lumps with a wooden spoon. Stir in the egg and the 2/3 cup lactose-free milk until a moist batter forms.

Knead the swirl packet from the mix package 10 seconds; open and squeeze over the batter. With a swirling motion, gently glide through the batter with a knife. Be careful not to blend fully.

Spoon about two thirds of the batter into the prepared pan. Spread the applesauce over the batter. Finish covering the top by dropping tablespoons of the remaining batter.

Open the topping packet and sprinkle evenly over the top. Bake the cake in the center of the oven for 25 to 30 minutes. The cake is done when a toothpick inserted in the center comes out clean. Cool.

In a small mixing bowl, place the confectioners' sugar, vanilla, and the 2 teaspoons lactose-free milk. Stir with a spoon until smooth and blended. Drizzle over the warm coffee cake and let the cake set 10 minutes.

Top a warm slice with a scoop of lactose-free ice cream.

Per Serving: Calories: 240 Cholesterol: 19mg Dietary Fiber: .3g Protein: 3g
Sodium: 263mg Carbohydrate: 43g Total Fat: 7g Saturated Fat: 1g
Calories from Fat: 25%, Calories from Carbohydrates: 70%, Calories from Protein: 5%

Creme-Filled Cupcakes

*M*issing *those Hostess cupcakes? Here's the lactose-free answer! All that's missing is the squiggle on top, and you can add that with vanilla decorating icing. If you are in a hurry, ready-to-spread chocolate fudge icing works well. Just remember to read the labels . . . certain brands are fine, such as Duncan Hines Homestyle dark chocolate frosting. For extra-special desserts, split a cupcake in half, place in a dessert bowl, scoop lactose-free ice cream on top, then drizzle on some Hershey's chocolate syrup, and top with nondairy whipping cream and a cherry.*

Makes 12 servings
Preparation time: 20 minutes

2 cups cake flour
Dash salt
1/2 cup unsweetened cocoa powder
1 teaspoon baking soda
11/2 cups sugar
10 tablespoons safflower oil margarine, Hollywood
3 large eggs, slightly beaten
1 teaspoon vanilla extract
1 cup 100% lactose-free 2% lowfat milk

For the filling
1/2 tube nondairy whipped topping, Squeeze Pro

For the glaze
1/2 cup safflower oil margarine, Hollywood
6 ounces semisweet chocolate, chopped

Preheat the oven to 350° F. and line a 12-cup muffin tin with paper cups.

In a mixing bowl, stir together the cake flour, salt, cocoa, and baking soda. Set aside. In a food processor, place the sugar and process until superfine.

Using an electric stationary mixer, beat the safflower margarine and the sugar until light and fluffy, about 5 minutes. Add the eggs, one at a time, and the vanilla, making sure to blend completely after each addition. Reducing the speed to the lowest, add 1/3 the flour mixture, then 1/3 cup of the lactose-free milk, repeat with the flour mixture, then lactose-free milk, and continue until both ingredients are just combined.

Spoon the batter into the paper muffin cups. Bake in the oven for about 12 to 15 minutes. The cupcakes are done when a toothpick inserted in the center comes out clean. Be very careful not to burn. Remove the cupcakes from the pan and place on a wire rack to cool.

When the cupcakes are completely cooled, open the icing tube or nondairy whipped cream topping. If you choose to use Cool Whip, simply fill a pastry tube with Cool Whip and attach a rosette or other large tip. Remove the paper cups from the cupcakes and insert the tip of the whipped cream tube into the bottom of the cupcake. Squeeze about 1 tablespoon whipping cream into the middle of each cupcake. Make sure that the tube is well into the center of the cupcake, and squeeze. Watch the cupcake spread slightly as it fills. Be careful not to overfill it. Return the cupcakes to the rack.

Prepare the chocolate glaze by placing a small saucepan with the 1/2 cup safflower margarine and the chopped chocolate over low heat. Stir with a wooden spoon until the chocolate is melted and very smooth. Remove from the heat and cool. Spread the glaze on top of each cupcake.

These make wonderful snacks or dessert treats!

Per Serving: Calories: 481 Cholesterol: 55mg Dietary Fiber: 2g Protein: 5g
Sodium: 306mg Carbohydrate: 56g Total Fat: 30g Saturated Fat: 12g
Calories from Fat: 52%, Calories from Carbohydrates: 44%, Calories from Protein: 4%

Lemon Cream Cake

This dense, lemony cake is a great dessert all by itself, or you can top it with scoops of sorbet, lactose-free ice cream, or Homemade Fresh Lemon Curd (page 338) for a wonderful treat.

Makes 12 servings
Preparation time: 30 minutes

PAM cooking spray, for coating pan
3 cups all-purpose flour
2 teaspoons baking powder
1/2 teaspoon salt
1 cup safflower oil margarine, Hollywood
2 cups sugar
4 large eggs
1 cup 100% lactose-free 2% lowfat milk
2 teaspoons grated lemon zest

For the glaze
1/3 cup fresh lemon juice
2 tablespoons safflower oil margarine, Hollywood
3/4 cup sugar

Preheat the oven to 350° F. Spray a 9-inch tube pan with PAM. Combine the flour, baking powder, and salt together in a large mixing bowl. Set aside.

Using a standing mixer, cream together the safflower margarine and sugar until light and fluffy, about 3 minutes. Add the eggs, one at a time, while continuing to beat. Once the eggs are well blended, lower the speed and incorporate the flour, baking powder, and salt, alternating with the lactose-free milk. Stir in the lemon zest.

Pour the batter into the PAM-sprayed tube pan evenly. Bake in the oven for about 50 to 55 minutes. The batter will be lightly browned. When a toothpick inserted in the center of the cake comes out clean, the cake is done. Cool the cake on a wire rack about 10 minutes, then remove from the tube pan, placing the cake back on the rack to finish cooling.

In a small saucepan over low heat, place the lemon juice, safflower margarine, and sugar. Dissolve the sugar and margarine into the lemon juice by stirring constantly. Once completely blended, remove from the heat and brush on the warm cake. Serve.

Serve with fresh fruit slices, lemon curd,
or sorbet.

Per Serving: Calories: 479 Cholesterol: 73mg Dietary Fiber: .01g Protein: 6g
Sodium: 354mg Carbohydrate: 72g Total Fat: 20g Saturated Fat: 4g
Calories from Fat: 37%, Calories from Carbohydrates: 58%, Calories from Protein: 5%

Cinnamon Cake

*T*his versatile cake can be served as a casual breakfast bread; or you can dress it up for an elegant dinner dessert: Scoop lactose-free ice cream on a wedge of cake, ladle warm pie filling or preserves on top, and finish with a mound of nondairy whipped cream!

Makes 16 servings
Preparation time: 30 minutes

1 tablespoon vinegar
1 cup 100% lactose-free 2% lowfat milk
4 large eggs, separated
2 cups granulated sugar
1 tablespoon ground cinnamon
1/2 teaspoon salt
1 teaspoon baking soda
2 teaspoons baking powder
21/2 cups all-purpose flour
1 cup safflower oil margarine, Hollywood
2 teaspoons vanilla extract
Confectioners' sugar, for dusting

Preheat the oven to 350° F. and generously grease a 12-cup bundt pan with Crisco solid shortening. Set aside. Place the vinegar into a 1-cup measure. Add enough lactose-free milk to make 1 cup. Stir and let stand until ready to use. (After standing this mixture will appear curdly; it is the substitute for buttermilk.) Separate the eggs, placing the yolks in one bowl and the whites in another. Do not whip or blend.

Place 1/2 cup of the sugar in a food processor along with the cinnamon. Pulse several times to blend and process to superfine. In a separate mixing bowl, blend all the dry ingredients, except the cinnamon sugar. Set aside.

Using a stationary heavy-duty mixer with the whisk attachment, beat the safflower margarine and vanilla until well blended and fluffy. Slowly beat into the fluffy mixture 1 cup of the granulated sugar. Continue to beat until the mixture is smooth, then add the egg yolks, one at a time, until completely blended. Next, alternate between adding the dry ingredients (already in the mixing bowl) and the lactose-free milk, blending very well after each addition.

In a separate bowl, using a hand mixer with clean beaters, beat the egg whites until they form soft peaks. Very slowly add the remaining 1/2 cup granulated sugar, while continuing to beat into stiff peaks. Fold the egg whites into the batter.

Into the prepared pan, spoon half the batter. Sprinkle half the cinnamon sugar on top of the batter. Cover with the remaining batter and top off with remaining cinnamon sugar.

Place the pan in the oven and bake for about 50 minutes. A toothpick inserted in the center should come out clean. Remove the cake pan to cool on a wire rack for 10 minutes. Then invert the cake onto a serving plate and dust with powdered sugar. Or, if you like, drizzle with Confection Sugar Glaze (page 334). Serve warm or completely cooled.

This is a perfect cake for any occasion!

Per Serving: Calories: 397 Cholesterol: 54mg Dietary Fiber: .2g Protein: 4g
Sodium: 330mg Carbohydrate: 41g Total Fat: 14g Saturated Fat: 3g
Calories from Fat: 41%, Calories from Carbohydrates: 54%, Calories from Protein: 5%

Pound Cake

*T*his basic pound cake can be used for so many things. It's great for breakfast (toasted with safflower margarine), as a snack (plain or dressed up with a sauce), or as a dinner dessert (topped with ice cream and/or sauce). The life span of fresh-baked pound cake is short, but if you have any leftover, toast some slices and serve with lactose-free ice cream. Or try cubes of cake tossed into lactose-free ice cream sundaes.

Makes 10 servings
Preparation time: 20 minutes

1 1/2 **cups cake flour**
1/4 **teaspoon salt**
3/4 **teaspoon baking powder**
3 **large eggs, slightly beaten**
1 1/2 **teaspoons vanilla extract**
3/4 **cup safflower oil margarine, Hollywood**
3/4 **cup sugar**

Preheat the oven to 350° F., and generously grease and flour a large loaf pan.

Sift the flour, salt, and baking powder together. Set aside. In a separate bowl, whisk the eggs and vanilla, and set aside. In a large stationary mixing bowl, beat the safflower margarine until light and airy. Slowly add the sugar, while beating. Once combined, add the egg mixture and continue to blend. Lower the speed and begin to add the flour mixture, while scraping the sides of the bowl often. Do not overmix; you just want to combine the ingredients.

Pour the batter into the prepared loaf pan. Place in the center of the oven on the middle rack and bake for approximately 1 hour and 10 minutes. The top should be golden brown, and a toothpick should come out clean when inserted in the middle of the loaf.

Cool on a wire rack for 8 to 10 minutes, remove from the pan, and cool completely.

Perfect for breakfast, snack, or dessert.

Per Serving: Calories: 261 Cholesterol: 64mg Dietary Fiber: .3g Protein: 3g
Sodium: 238mg Carbohydrate: 28g Total Fat: 16g Saturated Fat: 3g
Calories from Fat: 53%, Calories from Carbohydrates: 42%, Calories from Protein: 5%

Updike's Famous Fruitcake

*T*his cake is a family recipe that has become a tradition at Christmas. It is more of a moist raisin cake than a traditional fruitcake. Even people who hate fruitcake love this one!

Makes 36 servings
Preparation time: 1 hour

1 pound seedless raisins
2 cups pineapple juice
1 cup safflower oil margarine, Hollywood
2 cups sugar
4 cups all-purpose flour
4 teaspoons baking powder
1 tablespoon ground cinnamon
1 teaspoon salt
Dash each cloves and nutmeg
1 cup walnuts, coarsely crushed
1 cup crushed pineapple, drained, reserve the juice
4 ounces maraschino cherries, halved

Preheat the oven to 250° F. Select 5 to 6 small foil loaf pans. Set aside.

Place the raisins, pineapple juice, safflower margarine, and sugar in a large saucepan. Over medium heat, bring to a boil, stirring frequently. When well blended, remove from the heat and let cool. In a large bowl, sift the dry ingredients. Slowly add the cooled raisin mixture, including the liquid, stirring constantly. Stir in the walnuts, crushed pineapple, and cherries. The mixture will be a moist, doughlike blend.

Spoon the batter into the loaf pans, filling two thirds to three quarters full. Place the pans in the oven and bake for about 45 minutes. You need to watch the baking; the time may vary according to your oven temperature. The loaves are done when a toothpick inserted in them comes out clean.

Place pans on a rack to cool. When cool, wrap the loaves with plain or colored clear plastic wrap. Loaves can be frozen; just wrap them in foil over the clear wrap.

These make great gifts. Not to mention quick snacks from your freezer!

Per Serving: Calories: 213 Cholesterol: 0mg Dietary Fiber: .9g Protein: 3g
Sodium: 154mg Carbohydrate: 36g Total Fat: 8g Saturated Fat: 1g
Calories from Fat: 30%, Calories from Carbohydrates: 65%, Calories from Protein: 5%

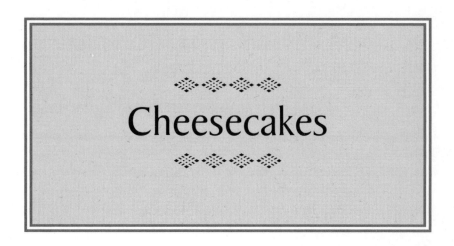

Cheesecakes

When was the last time you enjoyed a cheesecake without the painful consequences? Well, flip these pages and enjoy the new consequence-free cheesecakes!

Hydrox Cookie Cheesecake

Reading labels educates you on the packaged cookies you can and cannot eat. You cannot have Oreo cookies . . . but you can have Hydrox cookies! So, if you are a chocolate sandwich cookie lover, you'll still have the ability to enjoy them. And you'll love this cheesecake!

Makes 12 servings
Preparation time: 45 minutes

12 whole chocolate sandwich cookies, Hydrox
3 tablespoons safflower oil margarine, Hollywood, melted
24 ounces cream cheese alternative, Tofutti
5 teaspoons cornstarch
1/3 cup sugar
3 large eggs, slightly beaten
1 medium egg yolk
2/3 cup whipping cream alternative, Pastry Pride
2 teaspoons vanilla extract
1/3 cup crème de cacao
1 cup semisweet chocolate chips, lactose free
   (see page 28), melted
5 whole chocolate sandwich cookies, Hydrox, coarsely
   chopped

Preheat the oven to 350° F. Grease the bottom of a 9-inch springform pan.

In a food processor with the metal blade, crush the 12 whole cookies, then add the melted safflower margarine through the tube. Pulse to combine. Remove the crumb mixture and press into the springform pan, covering the bottom only.

Using a stationary heavy-duty mixer, combine the cream cheese, cornstarch, and sugar. Beat until smooth. One at a time, add the eggs and egg yolk, beating well after each addition. Stir in the whipping cream alternative, vanilla, and crème de cacao. Then add the melted chocolate chips. Remove the mixing bowl from the stand and fold in the 5 coarsely crumbled cookies. Pour the filling into the prepared crust.

Place the cheesecake into the oven for 15 minutes. Then lower the temperature to 200° F. and continue to bake for about 1 hour and 10 minutes. The cheesecake is done when the center no longer looks "wet" or shiny. Turn the oven off and remove the cake from the oven; run a knife around the rim of the springform pan to loosen. Return the cake to the oven for another hour. (Although the oven is off, additional cooking is done with the heat remaining in the closed oven.)

Remove the pan from the oven and cool on a wire rack. Place in the refrigerator and chill overnight, uncovered. Leave the cake in the springform pan until ready to serve. You can garnish with additional whole Hydrox cookies and nondairy whipping cream.

It's always cheesecake time!

Per Serving: Calories: 377 Cholesterol: 71mg Dietary Fiber: 9g Protein: 5g
Sodium: 334mg Carbohydrate: 24g Total Fat: 29g Saturated Fat: 11g
Calories from Fat: 69%, Calories from Carbohydrates: 26%, Calories from Protein: 5%

Lemon Swirl Cheesecake

*Y*es, this beauty was put to the test against "real" cheesecakes at the *Malibu Annual Pie Contest. I took home a third-place ribbon, and no one knew the cake was lactose free—your guests won't either!*

Makes 12 servings
Preparation time: 1 hour

1 cup walnuts
6 whole graham crackers, Nabisco Honey Maid
3 tablespoons safflower oil margarine, Hollywood, melted
2 teaspoons grated lemon zest
16 ounces cream cheese alternative, Tofutti
1/2 cup sugar
1/2 cup lemonade, frozen concentrate, thawed
2 teaspoons grated lemon zest
3/4 cup sour cream alternative, Tofutti
2 large eggs, slightly beaten
1 cup sour cream alternative, Tofutti
1 11¼-ounce jar lemon curd or Homemade Fresh
   Lemon Curd (page 338)
1 tube nondairy whipped topping, Squeeze Pro
Lemon slices, mint leaves, lemon zest, for garnish

Preheat the oven to 350° F. Place the walnuts in a single layer on a cookie sheet, and when oven is ready, toast for a few minutes. Remove from the oven and set aside. In a food processor, finely grind the graham crackers. Add the nuts, then the safflower margarine, and lemon zest through the top opening, and chop with the pulse action (on/off repetition). The dough should resemble moist crumbs. In a 9-inch springform pan, cover the entire bottom only with the moist crumbs, pressing them firmly in place with your fingertips. Place the pan in the oven on the center rack and bake for about 10 minutes until the crust is set. Set aside and cool.

Using a heavy-duty stationary mixer with the whisk attachment, beat the cream cheese alternative, sugar, thawed lemonade, lemon zest, and the 3/4 cup sour cream alternative until smooth. Add the eggs last, just blending into the filling. Pour the filling into the cooled crust and return it to the middle rack of the oven, baking for approximately 50 minutes. (It is difficult to determine when cheesecakes are done. The rule of thumb is to gently shake the pan; the center should move only slightly. Watch the cake carefully if you choose to leave it in a few extra minutes. You don't want to dry it out or burn it.) When the cake is done, remove it from the oven and place it on a wire rack to cool.

While the cake cools, place the sour cream alternative into a small mixing bowl and whisk until smooth. Into another small mixing bowl, empty the jar of lemon curd (or homemade lemon curd) and whisk until smooth. Set aside.

Release the cooled cake from the pan by running a small knife between the sides of the cake and the pan. Place alternating teaspoonfuls of lemon curd, then sour cream mixture, side by side around the top of the slightly warm cake. Make sure the top of the cake is completely covered; tap the pan to smooth out the teaspoonfuls of lemon curd when done. Give the cake a marble look by dragging a knife tip in a swirling motion through the pattern. Place the cake (still in the springform pan) in the refrigerator overnight, uncovered.

When ready to serve, remove the cake from the refrigerator. Loosen it from the pan with a small knife, as done previously. Release it from the pan, and place on a serving plate. With ready-to-use whipped topping (I like the kind in a pastry-type bag, for easier decorating), pipe the topping in a decorative border around the top edge of the cake. Border the bottom edge with topping also. Garnish with lemon slices, mint leaves, or curls of lemon zest, and serve immediately.

A classic lemon cheesecake.

Per Serving: Calories: 368 Cholesterol: 127mg Dietary Fiber: .8g Protein: 5g
Sodium: 101mg Carbohydrate: 34g Total Fat: 25g Saturated Fat: 13g
Calories from Fat: 58%, Calories from Carbohydrates: 36%, Calories from Protein: 6%

Pumpkin Cheesecake

This cheesecake is very rich and pumpkin-y. It is also a first-place winner at the annual Malibu Pie Festival! It can be sliced and frozen before you garnish it, so you can always be ready for the unexpected guest.

Makes 16 servings
Preparation time: 30 minutes

For the crust
11/2 cups cinnamon graham crackers, Nabisco
1/2 cup finely chopped walnuts
1/4 cup granulated sugar
1/2 teaspoon ground nutmeg
5 tablespoons safflower oil margarine, Hollywood,
   melted

For the filling
3 8-ounce tubs cream cheese alternative, Tofutti
3/4 cup light brown sugar, packed
3/4 cup granulated sugar
4 medium eggs, slightly beaten
1 16-ounce can pumpkin
1 1/4 teaspoons ground cinnamon
1 teaspoon vanilla extract
1/2 teaspoon ground nutmeg
1/4 teaspoon ground cloves

Preheat the oven to 350° F. Place the graham crackers, walnuts, 1/4 cup sugar, and nutmeg in a food processor and process until finely ground. Pulse in the melted safflower margarine only until the mixture starts to form together softly. Remove the mixture from the processor and firmly press it on the bottom and halfway up the sides of a 10-inch springform pan. Set aside.

In a large mixing bowl with an electric mixer (using the lowest speed), blend the cream cheese alternative until smooth. Add the sugars, alternating with the slightly beaten eggs until light, fluffy, and well blended. Add the remaining ingredients, in order, blending well after each addition and scraping the bowl often. Carefully pour the filling into the prepared crust. Bake for 1 hour and 20 minutes. Cheesecake is done when the center looks firm. If it has a shiny or "wet" look in the center, leave it in a little longer.

Cool completely at room temperature. Store in the refrigerator overnight, uncovered. When ready to serve, gently remove the springform, garnish with nondairy whipped topping, and dust with cinnamon.

Perfect for holiday feasts or fall dinners.

Per Serving: Calories: 171 Cholesterol: 53mg Dietary Fiber: 1g Protein: 4g
Sodium: 129mg Carbohydrate: 19g Total Fat: 10g Saturated Fat: 2g
Calories from Fat: 49%, Calories from Carbohydrates: 43%, Calories from Protein: 8%

The Ultimate Lemon Cheesecake

This classic lemon cheesecake tastes wonderful because it's made with fresh lemon juice and zest. It is both simple and elegant. Decorate with a dot of nondairy whipping cream or fresh fruit.

Makes 12 servings
Preparation time: 40 minutes

For the crust
13/4 cups graham cracker crumbs, Nabisco
1/4 cup light brown sugar, packed
1/2 cup safflower oil margarine, Hollywood, melted
1 teaspoon grated lemon zest

For the filling
32 ounces cream cheese alternative, Tofutti, cold
1 cup granulated sugar
1 cup whipping cream alternative, Pastry Pride, cold
2 teaspoons grated lemon zest
3 tablespoons fresh lemon juice
1 tablespoon water
1 teaspoon unflavored gelatin
Lemon slices, for garnish

Preheat the oven to 350° F. Begin by making the crust. Combine the graham crackers, brown sugar, melted safflower margarine, and the 1 teaspoon lemon zest into a food processor. With the metal blade in place, pulse the mixture until it forms a soft dough.

Press the soft graham-cracker crust into a 9-inch springform pan, covering the entire bottom and about 2 inches up the sides. Place in the oven and bake for about 10 minutes until the crust is set. Remove and cool completely.

Using a stationary mixer, combine the cream cheese alternative and granulated sugar at medium speed. Beat in about 1/2 cup of the whipping cream alternative along with the lemon zest and juice.

In a small saucepan, place the water. Sprinkle the gelatin over the water and allow it to soften for a few minutes. Then place it over low heat, stirring to dissolve completely. Slowly add the remaining 1/2 cup cream, whisking to blend. Once the gelatin mixture is completely blended, add it to the cream cheese mixture, beating until completely blended, about 1 to 2 minutes. Mixture will be fluffy.

Spoon the mixture into the cooled crust. Cover with aluminum foil and chill in the refrigerator overnight.

When you are ready to serve, run a knife around the rim of the springform pan to loosen the cake. Release the sides of the pan and place the cake on a serving platter. Decorate the top with lemon slices.

Serve with fresh fruit, fruit sauce, or just as is!

Per Serving: Calories: 292 Cholesterol: 0mg Dietary Fiber: .4g Protein: 1g
Sodium: 217mg Carbohydrate: 34g Total Fat: 18g Saturated Fat: 7g
Calories from Fat: 54%, Calories from Carbohydrates: 45%, Calories from Protein: 1%

Berry Vanilla Cheesecake

*T*his is a "Berry Special" cheesecake that can be completed up to 8 hours prior to serving, making it perfect for a dramatic finale to a no-fuss evening meal.

Makes 12 servings
Preparation time: 1 hour
Chill time: overnight

For the crust
1 1/2 cups crushed honey graham crackers, Nabisco, Honey Maid, or Keebler
1 cup chopped walnuts
1/4 cup sugar
1/4 cup safflower oil margarine, Hollywood, melted
1 teaspoon vanilla extract

For the filling
1/3 cup whipping cream alternative, Pastry Pride
2 whole vanilla beans, split lengthwise
24 ounces cream cheese alternative, Tofutti
1 cup sugar
1/2 cup sour cream alternative, Tofutti
2 teaspoons vanilla extract
4 large eggs, slightly beaten
6 ounces fresh blueberries
6 ounces fresh raspberries
1 tablespoon cornstarch

For the topping
1 cup sour cream alternative, Tofutti
1 1/2 teaspoons vanilla extract
3 tablespoons sugar
1/3 cup seedless raspberry jam
6 ounces fresh raspberries
6 ounces fresh blueberries

Preheat the oven to 350° F. In a food processor, process the graham crackers, nuts, and the 1/4 cup sugar. Pulse in the melted safflower margarine and vanilla until moist crumbs form. In a 9-inch springform pan, gently pat the crumb mixture over the bottom and up the sides of the pan. Place aluminum foil around the outside of the springform pan, and bake in the oven until the crust is lightly browned. This should take about 12 to 15 minutes. Remove from the oven and cool. (Do not turn the oven off, allow to continue temperature.)

In a saucepan, place the whipping cream alternative, the seeds from the vanilla beans, and the beans themselves. Stir and bring to a boil. Remove from the heat, cooling completely. Remove the beans and discard.

In a large bowl, beat all the cream cheese alternative with the sugar. After the mixture is smooth, add the cooled vanilla cream, sour cream alternative, vanilla, and the eggs (one at a time).

In a medium bowl, toss half the blueberries and half the raspberries with the cornstarch. Set aside.

Pour about two thirds of the filling mixture into the cooled crust. Place the berry mixture over the top and finish by pouring the remaining filling mixture over the berries, covering completely.

Place the cake in the oven and bake until golden brown, about 1 hour and 10 minutes. Cake will move slightly in center and begin to crack around the edges when done. (Do not turn the oven off.) Remove the cake from the oven and allow it to cool for about 10 minutes. You will notice that it will fall. That's to be expected.

As the cake is cooling, begin to prepare the final topping. In a small mixing bowl, combine the sour cream alternative, vanilla, and sugar. Blend until smooth. Evenly spoon the mixture all over the top of the cake. Return the cake to the oven and bake an additional 10 minutes.

Remove the cake from the oven (you can turn the oven off

now) and cool it on a wire rack. When the cake is completely cooled, place it in the refrigerator, uncovered, overnight.

Prior to serving, place the jam in a saucepan and melt over low heat. Stir constantly to avoid burning. Using about half to two thirds of the jam, spread it over the top of the cake. Decorate with the remaining berries, brushing them with the balance of the melted jam. Place the cake in the refrigerator until ready to serve. (Leave the sides on the pan until ready to serve. Then simply run a knife around the edge to loosen and pop the ring off.)

Per Serving: Calories: 431 Cholesterol: 61mg Dietary Fiber: 3g Protein: 7g
Sodium: 357mg Carbohydrate: 43g Total Fat: 27g Saturated Fat: 7g
Calories from Fat: 55%, Calories from Carbohydrates: 39%, Calories from Protein: 6%

Pies

Pies are a wonderful dessert. Unfortunately, crusts and fillings can hide lactose. The use of butter, creams, and other ingredients sometimes makes it difficult to be sure the pie is "safe." Have no fear—all the pies in this section have no hidden lactose. And they taste great—several of these recipes won prizes at the Malibu Pie Festival. So enjoy!

Homemade Pie Crust

If it's homemade, you know what's in it! (Check commercial refrigerated pie crusts for their ingredients; they often contain lactose). This is an easy recipe to make, and after a while you'll know by the feel of it if it will be light and flaky. The pastry blender is a must for easier mixing.

Makes two 10-inch pie crusts*
Preparation time: 30 minutes

2 cups all-purpose flour
1 teaspoon salt
2/3 cup solid all-vegetable shortening, Crisco, packed
Cold water, enough to moisten flour to make a soft dough

Sift the flour and salt. With a pastry blender cut in the shortening until it resembles crumbs. Slowly add the water, just enough until it begins to hold together. The mixture will be light and a little sticky.

With floured hands, form the dough into a round, flat circle. Divide the dough in half, working with one piece at a time. (The key here is not to handle the dough too much, since this makes it tough. The thinner the dough, the lighter and flakier your crust.) Dust with flour the area being used to roll dough out on, as well as the rolling pin. Dust the top and sides of the dough with a little flour, kneading slightly until a soft dough begins to form. Roll out on the floured area until you have a smooth, thin dough large enough to cover the bottom and sides

*This recipe makes a top crust and bottom crust for one 10-inch pie. Throughout this cookbook, you will see "1/2 recipe," that means just one crust; wrap the other one in plastic wrap and refrigerate for another use.

of a pie plate. Lift carefully and place in the pie plate. Allow it to hang over the edges.

After you have filled your pie, complete with a top crust, following the same routine that you did for the bottom crust. After placing the dough on top of the pie filling, pinch the edges of the bottom and top crusts together with your fingers, a fork, or whatever decorating tool you decide to use. Don't forget to brush the top crust with lactose-free milk, sprinkle with sugar, and make *vents*! If you don't provide vents to allow the steam to escape, you'll be scraping the pie off the inside of your oven!

This is the best pie crust … so light and flaky.

Per Serving: Calories: 260 Cholesterol: 0mg Dietary Fiber: 0g Protein: 3g
Sodium: 267mg Carbohydrate: 24g Total Fat: 16g Saturated Fat: 4g
Calories from Fat: 58%, Calories from Carbohydrates: 37%, Calories from Protein: 5%

(**Note:** These nutritional values are based on one recipe, which includes the top and bottom crusts.)

Apple Crumb Pie

Served warm or cool, this juicy pie is a terrific treat. It has won first prize at the annual pie contest in Malibu, California.

Makes 8 servings
Preparation time: 45 minutes

8 large apples, peeled, cored, and thinly sliced
2 tablespoons all-purpose flour
1 cup granulated sugar
1 teaspoon ground cinnamon
Dash ground nutmeg
1/2 recipe Homemade Pie Crust (page 224)
1/3 cup granulated sugar
3/4 cup all-purpose flour
6 tablespoons safflower oil margarine, Hollywood,
   chilled and chopped
1/2 cup confectioners' sugar
1/4 teaspoon vanilla extract
2 teaspoons 100% lactose-free 2% lowfat milk

In a large bowl, place the apples, flour, the 1 cup sugar, cinnamon, and nutmeg. Toss the apple slices until all are coated with the dry ingredients. The mixture will become juicy. Allow the apples to stand until ready to place in the crust. (The longer they stand, the juicier they become.)

Preheat the oven to 400° F. Prepare the pie crust pastry and line a pie plate. Stir the apples that have been sitting and fill the crust.

In a mixing bowl with a pastry cutter, blend 1/3 cup sugar, 3/4 cup flour, and the safflower margarine until crumby. Sprinkle generously over the top of the apples.

Bake in the oven for 35 to 40 minutes. The top will be light brown as will the edges of the crust. The pie is done when you insert a butter knife into it and the apples are soft. Try several spots to make sure.

Remove from the oven and cool on a wire rack. About 30 minutes after the pie is out of the oven, in a small mixing bowl, place the confectioners' sugar, vanilla, and lactose-free milk. Blend together until smooth. Drizzle over the crumb topping, in design or freely. Allow to set for a few minutes before cutting.

Serve warm with lactose-free ice cream.

Per Serving: Calories: 498 Cholesterol: 0mg Dietary Fiber: 4g Protein: 3g
Sodium: 221mg Carbohydrate: 85g Total Fat: 18g Saturated Fat: 4g
Calories from Fat: 32%, Calories from Carbohydrates: 65%, Calories from Protein: 3%

Award-Winning French Apple Pie

This pie won first place at the October 1993 Malibu Pie Festival and has always been a hit! Since it can be very juicy, you need to put aluminum foil below the rack in your oven to avoid a mess.

Makes 8 servings
Preparation time: 1 hour

8 large Red Delicious apples
1 cup sugar
2 tablespoons all-purpose flour
1 teaspoon ground cinnamon
Dash ground nutmeg
1/2 cup raisins
1 recipe Homemade Pie Crust (page 224)
1 tablespoon safflower oil margarine, Hollywood
2 tablespoons 100% lactose-free 2% lowfat milk
1 recipe Confection Sugar Glaze (page 334)

Peel, core, and thinly slice apples. Place in a large bowl with the sugar, flour, cinnamon, and nutmeg. Stir until the apples are coated. Sprinkle the raisins into the mixture. Allow to sit for several hours, even overnight. (Unless you have an apple peeling/coring/slicing machine—this device slices the apples thin enough that you don't have to wait. By the time you finish making the pastry dough, the apples will be juicy enough.)

Allowing the apples to make their own juice is the key to a juicy pie.

Preheat the oven to 400° F. Prepare the pie crust, lining the bottom of the pie plate with one thin smooth round of dough that curls over the edge of the plate. Fill with the apple-raisin mixture and juice, dot the top with safflower margarine and cover with the top pie crust. Arrange the top crust and crimp the top and bottom edges together, sealing in the apples and juice. Brush the finished top crust with the lactose-free milk, sprinkle with a little sugar, and finally slit air vents randomly to allow steam to escape.

Bake for 50 minutes, or until an inserted knife reveals soft apples. The top should be light brown in color and "crusty" when pierced. Cool the pie on a rack. After about 1 hour, glaze with Confection Sugar Glaze for the finishing touch.

Per Serving: Calories: 346 Cholesterol: 0mg Dietary Fiber: 4g Protein: 2g
Sodium: 140mg Carbohydrate: 66g Total Fat: 10g Saturated Fat: 2g
Calories from Fat: 24%, Calories from Carbohydrates: 73%, Calories from Protein: 3%

Blueberry Streusel Pie

The streusel topping is a great twist to the blueberry pie. The combination of cinnamon flavor, crunchy topping, and wonderfully gooey blueberry filling will guarantee this pie disappears fast! Using 100% lactose-free 2% lowfat milk makes the glaze creamier and very white in color.

Makes 10 servings
Preparation time: 20 minutes

4 cups fresh or frozen blueberries, rinsed and dried
3 tablespoons all-purpose flour
1 cup granulated sugar
1/2 teaspoon grated lemon zest
1/2 teaspoon ground cinnamon
Dash salt
1/2 recipe Homemade Pie Crust (page 224)
1 cup coarsely chopped walnuts
1 cup brown sugar, packed
1/2 teaspoon ground cinnamon
6 tablespoons safflower oil margarine, Hollywood,
   softened

For the glaze
1/2 cup confectioners' sugar
1/4 teaspoon vanilla extract
2 teaspoons 100% lactose-free 2% lowfat milk

Preheat the oven to 400° F. In a large bowl, place the blueberries, flour, sugar, lemon zest, cinnamon, and salt. Gently mix together until the blueberries are coated with the dry ingredients. Set aside.

Prepare the pie crust and line a 10-inch pie plate with the dough. Pinch the edges, working the dough as little as possible. Empty the blueberry mixture into the pie crust.

In a food processor, pulse the walnuts, brown sugar, cinnamon, and safflower margarine until crumby. Sprinkle over the top of the blueberry mixture in the pie crust, covering completely.

Bake in the oven for 35 to 40 minutes. The top will appear lightly golden. Allow to cool on a wire rack.

After about 10 minutes of cooling, prepare the glaze topping. In a small mixing bowl, blend the confectioners' sugar, vanilla, and lactose-free milk until smooth and creamy. Drizzle

over the top of the warm blueberry pie, in any desired pattern.
Let stand another 10 to 15 minutes before cutting.

A great quick dessert.

Per Serving: Calories: 439 Cholesterol: 0mg Dietary Fiber: 2g Protein: 5g
Sodium: 186mg Carbohydrate: 61g Total Fat: 22g Saturated Fat: 3g
Calories from Fat: 42%, Calories from Carbohydrates: 54%, Calories from Protein: 4%

Pumpkin Pie

*This recipe is a "family-hand-me-down" tradition for Thanksgiving
and Christmas get-togethers. While some ingredients are substituted, the pie's rich texture and wonderful flavor are not lost. This
recipe also won a first place at one of the annual Malibu Pie Festivals
in California.*

Makes 8 servings
Preparation time: 30 minutes

2 medium eggs, slightly beaten
13/4 cups canned solid pumpkin, Libby
3/4 cup sugar
1/2 teaspoon salt
3 teaspoons ground cinnamon
12/3 cups 100% lactose-free 2% lowfat milk
1/2 recipe Homemade Pie Crust (page 224)

Preheat the oven to 425° F. Mix the ingredients in the order given, blending well after each addition with an electric mixer. Pour into the unbaked pie shell. Bake in the 425° oven for 15 minutes. Then reduce the oven to 350° F. and bake for 45 minutes, or until done. To test for doneness, insert a butter knife in the center of the pie; if it comes out clean, the pie is done.

Top with nondairy whipped topping or homemade lactose-free ice cream.

Per Serving: Calories: 271 Cholesterol: 57mg Dietary Fiber: 2g Protein: 6g
Sodium: 312mg Carbohydrate: 38g Total Fat: 11g Saturated Fat: 3g
Calories from Fat: 36%, Calories from Carbohydrates: 56%, Calories from Protein: 8%

Pastries and Special Treats

Who can resist pastries? Well, depending on your tolerance level, you may *have* had to avoid them ... until now. Lactose doesn't exist in the pastries in this section; you'll find only delicious goodies without the consequences.

A Sweet Omelet Surprise

*W*ho *says lactose-free cooking can't be gourmet? This special dessert is definitely going to light up your evening. For a special touch, try adding your favorite preserves on top before pouring on the last of the liqueur and lighting it.*

Makes 4 servings
Preparation time: 35 minutes

4 large eggs, separated
1/4 cup 100% lactose-free 2% lowfat milk
4 tablespoons orange liqueur
1 tablespoon granulated sugar
1 tablespoon safflower oil margarine, Hollywood
2 tablespoons fresh, pure orange juice
Confectioners' sugar, for dusting

Preheat the oven to 350° F. In a mixing bowl, whisk the egg yolks, lactose-free milk, 1 tablespoon of the orange liqueur, and sugar. Set aside.

Place the egg whites in a separate bowl and beat with an electric mixer until just stiff. Be careful not to overbeat.

Gently fold stiff egg whites into the yolk mixture, a little at a time.

Using an ovenproof skillet, melt the safflower margarine over medium heat. Add the batter to the skillet and cover with a lid. Cook for about 2 1/2 minutes, uncover, and pierce the batter with a knife in order to have the heat circulate. Replace the lid and continue cooking for another 2 1/2 minutes.

Remove the lid, and place the skillet in the oven until the top appears set, about another 2 minutes.

Remove the omelet from the skillet, sprinkle with the orange juice, and dust with confectioners' sugar. Pour the warmed remaining 3 tablespoons of orange liqueur over and around the omelet. Carefully ignite, then serve with style!

A flaming success to top off a wonderful evening!

Per Serving: Calories: 176 Cholesterol: 214mg Dietary Fiber: 0g Protein: 7g
Sodium: 100mg Carbohydrate: 10g Total Fat: 8g Saturated Fat: 2g
Calories from Fat: 53%, Calories from Carbohydrates: 28%, Calories from Protein: 19%

Blueberry Scones

Liberally dusted with confectioners' sugar, these delicious scones are flaky and light. Using the substitution for buttermilk allows for the same original texture and taste as regular scones.

Makes 12 servings
Preparation time: 1 hour

11/2 teaspoons vinegar
1/2 cup 100% lactose-free 2% lowfat milk
11/2 cups blueberries, fresh or frozen
4 cups all-purpose flour
1/2 cup granulated sugar
11/2 teaspoons baking powder
1/2 teaspoon baking soda
Dash salt
1/2 cup safflower oil margarine, Hollywood
1 large egg white
1/2 teaspoon water
Confectioners' sugar, for dusting

Place the vinegar in a glass measuring cup and fill with the lactose-free milk to the 1/2-cup mark. Allow to stand for a few minutes. This makes a buttermilk substitute. Rinse and drain the blueberries.

Preheat the oven to 350° F. In a food processor, place the flour, sugar, baking powder, baking soda, and salt. Pulse a few times to incorporate. Break the safflower margarine up into pieces and add to the dry mixture. Pulse several times until the mixture resembles coarse crumbs. Add the buttermilk substitute, a little at a time, through the opening in the top of the processor. Pulse after each addition until a dough begins to form. Remove from the processor and roll out onto a floured surface, forming a circle about 1/4 inch thick.

Quickly add the berries to the dough and fold over to form a half-moon shape. Cut triangle shapes from the dough (or get creative and use biscuit cutters, large cookie cutters, etc.). Place the scones on cookie sheets.

In a small bowl, combine the egg white and water. Whisk together with a fork. Brush the mixture on top of the scones. Bake in the oven for about 18 to 20 minutes.

Remove from the oven and cool on a wire rack. Once cooled, liberally dust the scones with confectioners' sugar on all sides.

These make wonderful breakfast or brunch treats.

Per Serving: Calories: 268 Cholesterol: 1mg Dietary Fiber: 1g Protein: 5g
Sodium: 186mg Carbohydrate: 43g Total Fat: 9g Saturated Fat: 2g
Calories from Fat: 29%, Calories from Carbohydrates: 64%, Calories from Protein: 7%

Chocolate Dessert Crepes

*B*e very gentle when cooking crepes; they're fragile! The crepes and vanilla sauce can be made the day before to save time. Remember to stack the crepes with paper towels between the layers. Both the sauce and crepes need to be covered when refrigerated.

Makes 8 servings
Preparation time: 3 hours
Chill time: 1 hour

For the crepes
1/2 cup 100% lactose-free 2% lowfat milk
1 large egg, slightly beaten
1 tablespoon safflower oil margarine,
    Hollywood
1/2 teaspoon vanilla extract
2 1/2 tablespoons sugar
2 tablespoons unsweetened cocoa powder
2 tablespoons all-purpose flour
Dash salt
PAM cooking spray, for coating pan

For the Vanilla Sauce
2 cups whipping cream alternative,
    Pastry Pride
1/2 stick vanilla bean, split lengthwise
2 large eggs, slightly beaten
1/2 cup sugar

For the filling
4¹/2 ounces semisweet chocolate, chopped
   (see substitutes, page 28)
1 tablespoon dark rum
2 tablespoons whipping cream alternative,
   Pastry Pride
2 large egg yolks, slightly beaten
¹/4 cup sugar
3 large egg whites
Dash salt

Fresh berries, for garnish

THE CREPES: In a blender, place the lactose-free milk, egg, melted safflower margarine, and vanilla. Blend well. Next add the sugar, cocoa powder, flour, and salt. Continue to blend until smooth; remove and chill at least 1 hour.

Using a skillet with a 6"-diameter bottom, spray with PAM. Warm the pan over low heat, while removing batter from refrigerator. Whisk the batter to blend thoroughly. Using a swirling motion, coat the bottom of the heated skillet with 2 tablespoons of batter. After about 2 minutes, the edges of the crepe will be very dry. Carefully loosen those edges and turn over with a spatula. Allow the crepe to cook another minute, then remove to a paper towel. Continue the same process with the remaining batter, stacking finished crepes between sheets of paper towels. You may need to brush the skillet with additional margarine or spray with PAM between the crepes. Cool.

THE VANILLA SAUCE: In a medium saucepan, place the whipping cream alternative, the seeds from the vanilla bean, and the vanilla bean itself. When the mixture simmers, remove it from the heat. With a whisk, blend in the eggs and the sugar in a large bowl. Slowly blend in the hot mixture. Return all to the saucepan and, over low heat, cook until it thickens, about 4 minutes. Stir constantly, so as not to burn. Do not boil the mixture. Remove from the heat, strain, and chill.

THE FILLING: Bring a saucepan of water to a boil and remove from the heat. Turn the heat down and as the water simmers, place a heatproof bowl on top and place the chopped semisweet chocolate in the bowl. Stir until the chocolate is melted and smooth. Remove the bowl from over the saucepan, and allow the chocolate to cool for about 5 minutes. Whisk the rum and whipping cream alternative into the chocolate. Set aside.

In a mixing bowl with an electric mixer, beat the yolks and sugar until thick and pale yellow, about 3 minutes. Empty the bowl into the chocolate, whisking to blend.

Using a chilled bowl, with clean dry beaters on the electric mixer, beat the whites and the salt until stiff peaks form. Fold the whites into the chocolate a third at a time.

TO ASSEMBLE: Preheat the oven to 400° F. Lay the crepes out on baking sheets lined with parchment paper. On half of each crepe place 1/3 cup chocolate filling, flip the other half over the filling, lightly. When all the crepes are filled and flipped, place them in the oven. Bake for about 6 minutes, just until set. Remove from the oven, and place the crepes on a serving plate, and drizzle chilled vanilla sauce on top. Garnish with fresh berries.

Serve with fresh berries or offer different flavored sauces.

Per Serving: Calories: 471 Cholesterol: 134mg Dietary Fiber: 1g Protein: 6g
Sodium: 134mg Carbohydrate: 49g Total Fat: 29g Saturated Fat: 20g
Calories from Fat: 54%, Calories from Carbohydrates: 41%, Calories from Protein: 5%

Chocolate Raspberry Tart

*F*or the Lactose Intolerant, the milk chocolate void is the hardest to fill. This recipe combines whipping cream alternative and lactose-free semisweet chocolate to achieve that milk chocolate taste. In the chocolate division of the annual Malibu Pie Festival, this tart came in second, and no one knew it was lactose free! This is a dessert that can be assembled at your leisure over 2 days. Your guests will be very impressed.

Makes 12 servings
Preparation time: 45 minutes
Chill time: 1 hour

For the crust
2 cups whole almonds
6 tablespoons light brown sugar, packed
1/4 teaspoon ground cinnamon
5 tablespoons safflower oil margarine, Hollywood, melted

For the filling
3/4 cup whipping cream alternative, Pastry Pride
6 ounces semisweet chocolate, chopped (see substitutes, page 28)
1 pint fresh raspberries
1/4 cup seedless raspberry jam
Confectioners' sugar and chocolate curls, for garnish if desired

Preheat the oven to 325° F. Toast the almonds in a single layer on a cookie sheet in the oven for a few minutes. Cool. In a food processor, finely grind the almonds, brown sugar, and cinnamon. Through the top opening, pour in the melted safflower margarine while the processor is running. The dough is ready when moist clumps form. Remove the dough and press it with your fingertips into the bottom and up the sides of a 9-inch tart pan with a removable bottom. Place the pan in the oven and bake for about 30 minutes until lightly browned and firm. Place the pan on a wire rack and cool completely.

In a medium heavy-gauge saucepan, bring the whipping cream alternative to a simmer. Remove from the heat and add the chocolate, stirring constantly until melted, blended, and smooth. Pour into the cooled crust. Chill in the refrigerator for about 1 hour (you can do this overnight, but cover it).

Rinse and dry the raspberries. Remove the tart from the refrigerator and, beginning with the outside edge, arrange the raspberries closely in the tart. Place the jam in a small saucepan and melt it over low heat. Remove from the heat and carefully brush the jam over the raspberries on top of the tart. When ready to serve, remove the tart from the pan and place on a serving plate. You can dust the top with confectioners' sugar or decorate it with chocolate leaves.

Per Serving: Calories: 345 Cholesterol: 0mg Dietary Fiber: 5g Protein: 6g
Sodium: 72mg Carbohydrate: 28g Total Fat: 26g Saturated Fat: 8g
Calories from Fat: 64%, Calories from Carbohydrates: 30%, Calories from Protein: 6%

Éclairs

Using the right ingredients, you can even have these delicious treats! All the gooey, chocolate pastries, like éclairs, you loved before lactose became a problem can be part of your choices again. Remember to use quality substitutes and read all labels.

Makes about 10 éclairs
Preparation time: 3 hours

1 cup water
1/2 cup safflower oil margarine, Hollywood
1/4 teaspoon salt
1 cup all-purpose flour
4 large eggs
1 4.6-ounce package vanilla pudding, Jell-O,
    cook and serve
3 cups 100% lactose-free 2% lowfat milk
2 1-ounce squares semisweet chocolate (see substitutes,
    page 28)
2 tablespoons safflower oil margarine, Hollywood
1 cup confectioners' sugar
3 tablespoons 100% lactose-free 2% lowfat milk

Preheat the oven to 375° F. Generously grease 2 large baking sheets. Set aside.

In a large saucepan, bring the water, the 1/2 cup safflower margarine, and salt to boil over medium heat. Remove the saucepan from the heat, stir in the flour, mixing with a wooden spoon until a ball of dough forms. Add the eggs, one at a time, blending well after each addition. Allow the batter to cool slightly, a few minutes, for easier handling.

Place the batter into a pastry bag fitted with a plain, wide round tip. Pipe the batter onto the baking sheets in straight 3-inch lines about 2 inches apart, making about 10 éclairs.

Place in the oven and bake for about 40 minutes, or until light brown. Remove from the oven, cut a little slit in the side of each éclair, and bake an additional 10 more minutes. Turn the oven off, allowing the éclairs to remain in the oven for another 10 minutes to dry. Place them on a wire rack to cool.

Prepare Jell-O vanilla pudding, using the 3 cups lactose-free milk, following the instructions on the package.

In a saucepan, melt the semisweet chocolate and the 2 tablespoons safflower margarine, stirring continually until smooth. Add the confectioners' sugar and the 3 tablespoons lactose-free milk, stirring constantly until completely blended and smooth.

To assemble: Slice the cooled éclairs lengthwise about one third from the top. Fill the bottom of the shell with the prepared vanilla pudding. Replace the top of the shell. Spread the chocolate glaze on top. Refrigerate until ready to serve.

Your favorite éclairs—without the lactose.

Per Serving (1 éclair): Calories: 474 Cholesterol: 91mg Dietary Fiber: 2g Protein: 8g
Sodium: 319mg Carbohydrate: 59g Total Fat: 26g Saturated Fat: 10g
Calories from Fat: 47%, Calories from Carbohydrates: 47%, Calories from Protein: 6%

Lactose-Free Cannoli

Using cottage cheese alternative as a substitute for ricotta, you can have cannoli for dessert. I always make the shells and filling ahead of time, and then fill them right before serving. That way, it eliminates the chance of the shells getting soggy. This is a wonderful dessert.

Makes 20 cannoli
Preparation time: 1½ hours

1⅓ cups all-purpose flour
¼ teaspoon salt
2 tablespoons solid all-vegetable shortening, Crisco
5 tablespoons white wine
½ teaspoon sugar
Shortening for frying cannoli
24 ounces cottage cheese alternative, Soyco or
  L. acidophilus
1 teaspoon vanilla extract
¼ cup sugar
1 cup whipping cream alternative, Pastry Pride
Confectioners' sugar, for dusting

On a clean surface, mound the flour and make an indentation in the center. Place the salt, 2 tablespoons shortening, wine, and sugar into the indentation. Using a fork, slowly incorporate the flour into the center until almost all of it is blended. Using floured hands, complete kneading the dough until it is smooth. Divide the dough into two equal balls.

Roll one ball out to the thickness of an egg noodle. Cut into squares measuring about 3½ inches. Roll the dough squares around cannoli tubes (you can find these at gourmet or kitchen shops), and seal by moistening one edge with water and pressing it closed.

Melt the shortening in a large saucepan to 400° F. With the melted shortening filling the saucepan about 1 inch deep, deep-fry the cannoli tubes. They will fry quickly, so do not leave them unattended. Use tongs to turn them for equal browning. Total frying time should be approximately 30 to 45 seconds.

When the cannoli are completely browned, remove to a paper towel to allow them to drain. After they have cooled several minutes, hold one end of the tube with a potholder and carefully slip the fried cannoli off the tube, using a fork. Set the tubes aside to cool completely before using them again. Allow the cannoli shells to cool completely also before filling them.

For the filling, blend together the cottage cheese alternative, vanilla, sugar, and whipping cream alternative (the amount of sugar you add can be adjusted according to your individual taste). When the mixture is well blended, fill a pastry bag, using desired tip. Hold the cannoli shell and place the tip of the pastry bag in one end, squeeze, and fill the shell. Place the shells on a plate. If desired, garnish the ends of the shells with lactose-free chocolate chips or chopped pistachio nuts. Generously dust with confectioners' sugar. Serve chilled.

An elegant finale to any dinner, especially Italian!

Per Serving (I cannoli): Calories: 102 Cholesterol: 0mg Dietary Fiber: 0g Protein: 2g
Sodium: 74mg Carbohydrate: 12g Total Fat: 5g Saturated Fat: 3g
Calories from Fat: 45%, Calories from Carbohydrates: 47%, Calories from Protein: 8%

Peach Cobbler

The wonderful smell that fills your kitchen when you bake this will have everyone circling the oven! You can use frozen peaches if you desire, but fresh peaches are the best. Top a warm square of this cobbler with homemade Rich Vanilla Lactose-Free Ice Cream (page 306) for a very special dessert.

Makes 20 servings
Preparation time: 45 minutes

3/4 teaspoon vinegar
1/4 cup 100% lactose-free 2% lowfat milk
1 cup safflower oil margarine, Hollywood
2 1/2 cups light brown sugar, packed
1/2 cup granulated sugar
4 tablespoons vanilla extract
1 teaspoon ground nutmeg
2 teaspoons ground cinnamon
2 tablespoons cornstarch
1/4 cup water
3 cups all-purpose flour
1/2 cup solid all-vegetable shortening, Crisco, packed
1/2 teaspoon baking soda
1 1/2 tablespoons baking powder
Dash salt
5 pounds fresh peaches, peeled and sliced

In a glass measuring cup, place the vinegar and pour enough lactose-free milk to measure 1/4 cup. Let stand. This makes a buttermilk substitute.

In a saucepan, melt the safflower margarine, brown sugar, and granulated sugar. Stir constantly over medium-low heat until the sugars dissolve and form a liquid. Add the vanilla, nutmeg, and cinnamon; stir to mix. Lower the heat and allow to simmer for about 10 minutes. In a small bowl, mix together the cornstarch and water. Add to the simmering sugar mixture and continue to cook for another 10 minutes. Set aside.

Preheat the oven to 350° F. In a food processor, place the flour, Crisco, baking soda, baking powder, and salt. Pulse together to blend until coarse crumbs form. Through the tube at the top of the processor, pulse in the buttermilk substitute, a little at a time, until you have a soft dough. Be careful not to overwork the mixture.

Take half the dough and press it into a 9 × 13-inch glass baking dish, covering the bottom and sides. Prick with a fork in several spots. Bake the crust in the oven for 8 to 10 minutes until lightly browned.

Remove the crust from the oven and fill with the peaches. Cover with the brown sugar sauce. Flatten the remaining unbaked crust into a rectangle and lay it over the top of the peaches and sauce. Prick in several places with a fork, venting for steam. Cover with foil. Return the dish to the oven and bake for about 45 minutes. Remove the foil and bake for another 15 minutes. Serve warm.

Serve this for brunch or as a summer dinner dessert.

Per Serving: Calories: 338 Cholesterol: 0mg Dietary Fiber: 2g Protein: 3g
Sodium: 214mg Carbohydrate: 51g Total Fat: 15g Saturated Fat: 3g
Calories from Fat: 38%, Calories from Carbohydrates: 59%, Calories from Protein: 3%

Cream Puff Extravaganza

My daughter, Chrissy, made this dessert for a large group, and it was quite the scene stealer. She put it down on the dessert table and it was gone in literally one minute! Instead of ready-to-use nondairy whipped topping, you can use Cool Whip if you prefer. You can also omit the strawberries and serve the cream puff ring plain.

Makes 10 servings
Preparation time: 3 hours

1 cup water
1/2 cup safflower oil margarine, Hollywood
1 cup all-purpose flour
4 large eggs, slightly beaten
1 tube nondairy whipped topping, Squeeze Pro
3 pints fresh strawberries, sliced
1/2 cup semisweet chocolate chips, lactose free
   (see page 28)
1 tablespoon safflower oil margarine, Hollywood
11/2 teaspoons light corn syrup
11/2 teaspoons 100% lactose-free 2% lowfat milk

Preheat the oven to 400° F.; generously grease and flour a large cookie sheet. In a saucepan over medium heat, place the water and the 1/2 cup safflower margarine. Stir until the margarine melts and the mixture comes to a boil. Remove the saucepan from the heat and stir in the flour with a wooden spoon. Continue stirring until the mixture pulls from the sides of the saucepan, forming a soft dough. One at a time, add the 4 eggs, blending completely after each addition. The batter will be smooth and satiny.

As a guide, turn a 7-inch plate upside down on the prepared cookie sheet and draw the outline in the flour. Use this guide to drop cream puff dough by tablespoonfuls within the circle. The mixture should make about 10 mounds, just barely touching each other within the ring. (You may need to use a rubber spatula to push the batter off the tablespoon and onto the cookie sheet.)

Bake the ring in the oven until golden, approximately 40 minutes. Turn the oven off and allow the ring to remain in the oven for another 15 to 17 minutes. Remove the ring from the oven and place it on a wire rack to cool. When the ring is completely cool, use a long, serrated knife to slice it in half horizontally. Carefully lift the top off. Remove any moist dough inside. Using the whipped topping, fill the bottom of the ring completely with the "cream." Top with the sliced strawberries, allowing them to protrude outside the ring. Replace the top of the cream puff ring.

In a small saucepan, over low heat, stir the chocolate chips, the 1 tablespoon safflower margarine, corn syrup, and lactose-free milk until melted and blended. Remove from the heat when mixture is smooth and shiny. With a tablespoon, spoon the mixture over the top of the cream puff ring. Place in the refrigerator until ready to serve. For added decoration, fill the center of the ring with whole strawberries.

A wonderful dessert to serve a crowd.

Per Serving: Calories: 373 Cholesterol: 85mg Dietary Fiber: 2g Protein: 5g
Sodium: 133mg Carbohydrate: 29g Total Fat: 28g Saturated Fat: 17g
Calories from Fat: 65%, Calories from Carbohydrates: 30%, Calories from Protein: 5%

Lactose-Free Tiramisù

This is a special dessert, especially designed for the Lactose-Intolerant sweet tooth. It's rich, creamy, and wonderful. Traditional tiramisù contains mascarpone cheese, but this recipe uses alternative ingredients to achieve a comparable texture and taste. This dessert is great to make the day before. This allows proper chilling and set up time.

Makes 18 servings
Preparation time: 1 hour
Chill time: 6 hours

2 cups Marsala wine
12 large egg yolks
1 1/2 cups sugar
1/2 cup water
2 teaspoons instant espresso coffee, any brand
1 pound cream cheese alternative, Tofutti
6 tablespoons whipping cream alternative, Pastry Pride
1/4 cup sour cream alternative, Tofutti
9 ounces any lactose-free ladyfinger cookies,
    split in half
2 tablespoons unsweetened cocoa powder
Hershey's chocolate syrup and nondairy whipped topping,
    Squeeze Pro, to garnish

First, whisk together in a large metal bowl 1 1/2 cups of the Marsala, all the egg yolks, and 3/4 cup of the sugar. Place the metal bowl over a saucepan that has simmering water in it. With a handheld electric mixer, and using a candy thermometer, beat the mixture until it reaches 160° F. on the thermometer, approximately 12 to 15 minutes. Remove the bowl from the saucepan and set aside. You have now created zabaglione, a custardlike mixture.

Bring the water to a boil. In a large bowl, mix together the hot water and espresso until the coffee is completely dissolved. Then add the remaining 3/4 cup sugar, the cream cheese alternative, whipping cream alternative, and the sour cream alternative. Beat with an electric hand mixer until completely blended.

In the bottom of a 9 × 13 × 2-inch glass baking dish, layer a single row of ladyfinger halves, flat side up. Using about 1/4 cup Marsala, brush the wine over the ladyfinger halves. Next spread the "cream cheese" mixture over the wine-soaked ladyfingers. And finally top with half the zabaglione mixture. Cover with another layer of ladyfingers, flat side up, and repeat the process. After placing the last coating of zabaglione, dust with the cocoa powder liberally.

Cover the baking dish and chill in the refrigerator for at least 6 hours.

To serve, simply slice the tiramisù into squares and place on dessert plates. For added beauty, decorate with drizzles of chocolate syrup and dots of whipped topping. Or dust the dessert plate with the cocoa powder.

This dessert is a very special after-dinner spectacular!

Per Serving: Calories: 202 Cholesterol: 194mg Dietary Fiber: .2g Protein: 4g
Sodium: 49mg Carbohydrate: 27g Total Fat: 7g Saturated Fat: 3g
Calories from Fat: 35%, Calories from Carbohydrates: 57%, Calories from Protein: 8%

Turtle Truffle Tart

*T*his tart will help satisfy that candy-bar craving, for sure. Being Lactose Intolerant leaves you quite limited in the candy-bar department. Milk chocolate is out, and most candy bars use milk chocolate. This recipe combines all your favorites, so you aren't missing anything.

Makes 16 servings
Preparation time: 45 minutes

11/3 cups all-purpose flour
1/3 cup sugar
1/2 cup safflower oil margarine, Hollywood, chilled and sliced
1 large egg, slightly beaten
1 teaspoon vanilla extract
11/2 cups semisweet chocolate chips, lactose free (see page 28)
3/4 cup whipping cream alternative, Pastry Pride
14 ounces Caramels (page 296)
3 cups coarsely chopped pecans

Preheat the oven to 400° F. In a food processor with the knife blade, place the flour, sugar, and safflower margarine. Process until crumby, about 1 minute. With the processor running, pour the egg and vanilla through the top of the processor until a smooth, soft dough forms.

Remove the dough from the processor and press into an 11-inch tart pan with a removable bottom, covering the bottom and up the sides. Pierce the bottom of the crust with a fork several times. Bake in the oven for 10 minutes until a light golden brown. Remove and cool.

In a small saucepan, place the chocolate chips and 1/4 cup of the whipping cream alternative. Over low heat, melt and blend the whipping cream and chips until smooth.

Remove the chocolate from the heat and place 1 cup of the melted chocolate-and-cream mixture in the tart crust, evenly. Place in the refrigerator and chill for about 30 minutes.

While the tart is chilling, in a medium saucepan over low heat, melt the caramels and the remaining whipping cream. Stir, constantly blending, until creamy and smooth. Toss in the pecans, continue stirring and fold out into the chilled tart.

Using a resealable sandwich bag, spoon the leftover melted chocolate into the bag. Microwave on high for 30 seconds, only until soft and fluid. Snip a small corner of the bag and use it as a pastry bag. Twist the top of the bag to force the melted chocolate down through the open corner. Liberally drizzle melted chocolate over the top of the tart, in any desired pattern.

Allow to chill at least 1 hour before serving. You can make this dessert the day before and chill until ready to serve. Allow to stand 30 minutes for easier slicing.

A really special sweet-tooth satisfier!

Per Serving: Calories: 396 Cholesterol: 13mg Dietary Fiber: 3g Protein: 4g
Sodium: 80mg Carbohydrate: 38g Total Fat: 28g Saturated Fat: 8g
Calories from Fat: 61%, Calories from Carbohydrates: 36%, Calories from Protein: 3%

Updike Nut Roll

This nut roll is a holiday tradition in our family. It's great as a breakfast bread or dessert treat. However, it does not freeze well. Besides, it won't last that long—everyone enjoys it!

Makes 96 slices
Preparation time: 2 to 2¹/2 hours

1 envelope yeast
¹/2 cup sugar
2 cups water, warmed
2 teaspoons salt
³/4 cup safflower oil margarine, Hollywood,
   cut in pieces
2 large eggs, slightly beaten
6 cups all-purpose flour, approximately
2 cups coarsely chopped walnuts
2 cups sugar
¹/4 cup safflower oil margarine, Hollywood, melted

In a large bowl or roasting pan, mix the yeast and ¹/2 cup sugar in the warm water. Add the salt, safflower margarine, eggs, and enough flour to make a soft dough. Cover with a damp dish towel and place in a warm area to rise, about 30 minutes.

In a food processor or nut chopper, chop the walnuts finely. Place in a bowl and add 2 cups sugar. Mix thoroughly. Set aside.

Punch down the dough. Cover and repeat rise two more times. Then divide the dough into smaller portions. Roll each small portion out to a thickness of ¹/2 inch or ¹/4 inch, brush with melted margarine, and sprinkle the nut mixture in a thin layer over the entire area. Roll the dough up like a jelly roll. Seal the top edge with some margarine and brush the complete top of the loaf with melted margarine. Let rise one last time on an ungreased cookie sheet.

Preheat the oven to 450° F. Then bake the loaf for about 15 minutes, or until golden brown. The dough should be cooked inside. Use a toothpick to test doneness.

Cool on wire racks completely. Wrap in plastic wrap. To serve, cut the roll into 1/4-inch thick slices to reveal the pinwheel design.

Slice thin for serving; it will look like a pinwheel.

Per Serving (1 slice): Calories: 47 Cholesterol: 4mg Dietary Fiber: 0g Protein: 1g
Sodium: 60mg Carbohydrate: 7g Total Fat: 2g Saturated Fat: .3g
Calories from Fat: 32%, Calories from Carbohydrates: 60%, Calories from Protein: 8%

Cookies

Sweets and treats are important to everyone, but especially to someone with Lactose Intolerance. It is hard to find cookies without lactose. But just because you can't tolerate lactose well doesn't mean that craving sweets goes away! So, enjoy the following recipes—they're guaranteed to satisfy the biggest sweet tooth.

Almond Spritzer Cookies

Using Crisco shortening instead of butter or margarine makes these cookies very light ... and definitely lactose free! This is a wonderful recipe because it can be changed so easily! Place a few drops of food coloring in the batter to make a "rainbow of cookies." Change the decorator cookie disc for different shapes, or use another flavor extract for a totally different taste.

Makes 72 cookies
Preparation time: 15 minutes

11/2 cups solid all-vegetable shortening, Crisco, packed
11/2 cups sugar
2 large eggs, slightly beaten
21/4 teaspoons almond extract
1/2 teaspoon baking powder
1/2 teaspoon salt
4 cups all-purpose flour, dip and sweep method

Preheat the oven to 375° F. Line up ungreased cookie sheets.

In a large stationary mixing bowl, place the shortening and sugar. Beat until light and fluffy. Gradually add the eggs, almond extract, baking powder, and salt until all is incorporated. Slowly add the flour, mixing well after each addition.

Using a cookie press (such as Super Shooter), fill the cylinder with dough. Choose a decorator disc and assemble, following the manufacturer's directions. Place the cookies on the cookie sheets. Decorate the cookies with colored sugars, jimmies, etc., if desired.

Bake in the oven for about 8 to 10 minutes until the edges

are golden brown. Allow the cookies to cool on the cookie sheets 2 to 3 minutes before removing them to a wire rack.

Anytime, anyplace, these almond cookies are wonderful!

Per Serving (1 cookie): Calories: 80 Cholesterol: 6mg Dietary Fiber: 0g Protein: 1g
Sodium: 19mg Carbohydrate: 10g Total Fat: 4g Saturated Fat: 1g
Calories from Fat: 48%, Calories from Carbohydrates: 48%, Calories from Protein: 4%

Caramel-Drizzled Brownies

*W*ho says the Lactose Intolerant have to be deprived? These brownies are great just by themselves, or you can warm them up (put them in the microwave for 45 seconds) and top them with homemade Rich Vanilla Lactose-Free Ice Cream (page 306).

Makes 16 brownies
Preparation time: 20 minutes

2 large eggs, slightly beaten
1 cup sugar
1 teaspoon vanilla extract
1/2 cup safflower oil margarine, Hollywood
1/4 teaspoon salt
1/2 teaspoon baking powder
2/3 cup all-purpose flour
1/2 cup cocoa powder
1/2 cup chopped walnuts
12 Caramels (page 296)
1 tablespoon 100% lactose-free 2% lowfat milk

Preheat the oven to 375° F. and grease a 9 × 9 × 2-inch baking pan.

With an electric mixer, beat the eggs, sugar, vanilla, and safflower margarine until light and fluffy. On low speed, blend in the salt, baking powder, flour, and cocoa. Do not overblend; it's okay to have a few small lumps. Drop in the walnut pieces, and mix on lowest speed for a few seconds.

Spread the batter into the prepared pan and bake in the oven for 20 to 25 minutes. If you insert a toothpick into the center, it should come out clean.

During the last few minutes of cooking, begin making the caramel drizzle. In a small saucepan over low heat, place the caramels and lactose-free milk. Stir constantly, blending the caramels and milk until smooth. When the brownies come out of the oven, drizzle the caramel sauce over the top. Remove from the oven; cool in the pan on a wire rack. Slice into squares, when ready to serve.

Make some additional caramel sauce to
top off a brownie sundae.

Per Serving (1 brownie): Calories: 189 Cholesterol: 27mg Dietary Fiber: 1g
Protein: 3g Sodium: 116mg Carbohydrate: 27g Total Fat: 9g Saturated Fat: 2g
Calories from Fat: 42%, Calories from Carbohydrates: 53%, Calories from Protein: 5%

Raspberry Brownies

Chocolate, safflower margarine, and lactose-free 2% lowfat milk all give richness to these luscious brownies.

Makes 20 brownies
Preparation time: 20 minutes

6 1-ounce squares semisweet chocolate, lactose free
   (see page 28)
1 cup safflower oil margarine, Hollywood
6 large eggs, slightly beaten
3 cups sugar
3 teaspoons vanilla extract
1/2 teaspoon salt
2 cups all-purpose flour
2 cups chopped walnuts
3/4 cup seedless raspberry jam

For the Velvet Chocolate Glaze
1 1-ounce square unsweetened baking chocolate,
   melted
2 tablespoons safflower oil margarine, Hollywood
2 tablespoons light corn syrup
1 cup confectioners' sugar
1 tablespoon 100% lactose-free 2% lowfat milk
1 teaspoon vanilla extract

For the decoration
Unsweetened cocoa powder
Hershey's chocolate syrup
Fresh raspberries

In a double boiler, bring water to a boil and remove from the heat. Place semisweet chocolate together with the safflower margarine in the top of the double boiler, over the hot water. Stir until melted, blending until smooth. Cool.

Blend the eggs, sugar, vanilla, and salt briefly in a food processor with the metal blade. Then add the melted chocolate, flour, and walnuts, pulsing until blended.

Preheat the oven to 325° F. Turn the batter into a well-greased 9 × 13-inch or 11 × 15-inch baking pan. Bake for about 40 minutes until done. Upon removing the pan from the oven, immediately spread the raspberry jam on top of the hot brownies. Let them cool in the pan. Top the brownies with the Velvet Chocolate Glaze or Betty Crocker lactose-free chocolate fudge frosting. Cut into bars.

To make the Velvet Chocolate Glaze: In a double boiler, bring water to a boil and remove from the heat. Melt the chocolate in the top of the boiler, set over the hot water. Blend the margarine and corn syrup with the melted chocolate. Stir in the confectioners' sugar, lactose-free milk, and vanilla, blending well. Spread on top of the raspberry jam.

Decorate the serving plate with a dusting of cocoa and/or a drizzle of chocolate syrup before placing a brownie slice on it. Garnish with fresh raspberries and enjoy!

Very rich—a great finale to dinner.

Per Serving (1 brownie): Calories: 550 Cholesterol: 53mg Dietary Fiber: 3g
Protein: 7g Sodium: 158mg Carbohydrate: 75g Total Fat: 30g Saturated Fat: 10g
Calories from Fat: 45%, Calories from Carbohydrates: 50%, Calories from Protein: 5%

Chocolate Chip Cookies

The dough for this recipe or the baked cookies themselves can be frozen in a tightly covered container. I usually double the recipe, so I always have "spares" tucked away in the freezer!

Makes 72 cookies
Preparation time: 20 minutes

1 cup solid all-vegetable shortening, Crisco, packed
1/4 cup brown sugar, packed
1 1/2 cups sugar
2 large eggs, slightly beaten
2 teaspoons vanilla extract
1/2 teaspoon salt
1 teaspoon baking soda
2 1/4 cups all-purpose flour, dip and sweep method
2 cups semisweet chocolate chips, lactose free (see page 28)
Chopped nuts (optional)

Preheat the oven to 375° F. Using a standing or hand mixer, combine the shortening, both sugars, the eggs, and vanilla in a large bowl. Cream together until well blended. Add the salt and baking soda, and gradually add the flour, mixing well. With a wooden spoon, stir in the chocolate chips (and nuts, if desired).

Drop by tablespoon (for large cookies) or teaspoon (for smaller cookies) onto ungreased cookie sheets. Bake for 9 to 11 minutes until golden brown.

These are delicious warm . . . just reheat in the microwave for 15 to 20 seconds.

Per Serving: (1 cookie, without nuts): Calories: 81 Cholesterol: 6mg Dietary Fiber: .3g Protein: .8g Sodium: 35mg Carbohydrate: 11g Total Fat: 4g Saturated Fat: 2g Calories from Fat: 45%, Calories from Carbohydrates: 51%, Calories from Protein: 4%

Chocolate-Dipped Fingers

These very fragile cookies have a "buttery" taste that is our secret! They keep a very long time, but I guarantee they'll be gone before you know it. They're great cookies for gift-giving because they look so special.

Makes 48 cookies
Preparation time: 1 hour
Chill time: 2 hours

3/4 cup, plus 1 tablespoon all-purpose flour
1 cup cornstarch
1/8 teaspoon salt
1¼ cups confectioners' sugar, dip and sweep method
1 cup safflower oil margarine, Hollywood
1 teaspoon vanilla extract
6 ounces semisweet chocolate chips, lactose free
   (see page 28)

Whisk together the flour, cornstarch, and salt in a bowl. Set aside.

Using a food processor with the metal blade, process 1/2 cup of the powdered sugar until very fine. With the motor running, add pieces of safflower margarine through the tube. Continue to process until smooth and creamy. Pulse in the vanilla, and scrape the bowl to make sure the blending is completed. Add the dry ingredients, pulsing only until blended.

Remove the dough from the food processor, wrap in plastic wrap, and put into the refrigerator for about 2 hours. This will chill the dough for easier handling.

Preheat the oven to 375° F. Move the racks in the oven to the top and bottom thirds. Lightly grease the cookie sheets.

Using a small portion of dough at a time (keeping the rest refrigerated), knead with floured hands until manageable. Form a large ball, flatten slightly, and roll out on a lightly floured surface. Using a back-and-forth motion, roll the flattened ball to form a "rope." Cut lengths of the "rope" measuring about 2 1/2 inches and place them on the cookie sheets about 1 1/2 inches apart. If you have any leftovers, blend them into the next batch of dough.

Place the cookie sheets into the oven and bake the cookies for about 10 to 15 minutes. Halfway through the baking, rotate the cookie sheets—top to bottom, front to back. This will give a more even baking to the cookies. The cookies are done when they are just turning brown on the edges.

Place 3/4 cup of the confectioners' sugar in a wide, shallow bowl. Place the bowl near the wire racks you will cool the cookies on.

Remove the cookie sheets from the oven. Allow the cookies to cool a few minutes on the sheets, then remove with a pancake turner and dip in the confectioners' sugar. Very gently roll the cookies in the sugar, covering all sides. Place them on the wire racks to cool. A second dipping should be done when they are completely cool.

Using a double boiler, bring the water in the bottom to a rapid boil. Remove from the heat and place the top of the double boiler over it, filled with the chocolate chips. Stir constantly, blending the melting chocolate until smooth and creamy. Remove the top portion (melted chocolate) from the double boiler, tilt, and dip the end of each cookie into the melted chocolate. Place on wax paper or aluminum foil on the counter to cool. Allow to set a few minutes. These cookies can be stored in an airtight container, layered between sheets of wax paper.

An extra-special cookie!

Per Serving (1 cookie): Calories: 80 Cholesterol: 0mg Dietary Fiber: .2g Protein: .4g
Sodium: 45mg Carbohydrate: 9g Total Fat: 5g Saturated Fat: 1g
Calories from Fat: 54%, Calories from Carbohydrates: 44%, Calories from Protein: 2%

Cinnamon Sugar Cookies

These cookies are easy and quick . . . great to fill the cookie jar! Using Crisco instead of butter or margarine makes them extra light, and lactose free. I like to bake them in my convection oven for a more even browning. If you have a convection oven, simply reduce the heat by 50° F. and stagger the cookie sheets.

Makes 36 cookies
Preparation time: 20 minutes

1 cup solid all-vegetable shortening, Crisco, packed
11/2 cups sugar
1 teaspoon vanilla extract
2 large eggs
22/3 cups all-purpose flour
2 teaspoons cream of tartar
1 teaspoon baking soda
1/4 teaspoon salt
2 tablespoons ground cinnamon
1/2 cup sugar

Preheat the oven to 400° F. Lightly grease cookie sheets. In a heavy-duty mixer with the dough paddle attachment, combine all ingredients except the cinnamon and sugar. Beat until incorporated. With a wooden spoon, take 2 teaspoons of the cinnamon and swirl it through the batter.

In a small bowl, combine the remaining cinnamon and the sugar (last 2 ingredients) and mix well. Mold teaspoonfuls of dough into rounded balls and roll them in the cinnamon sugar, covering completely. Drop the cinnamon-sugar balls on the greased cookie sheets and bake for 8 to 10 minutes. The edges should be light brown.

Allow to cool for 2 minutes on the cookie sheets before removing to wire racks for complete cooling.

These delightful cookies make great
gift-giving.

Per Serving (1 cookie): Calories: 131 Cholesterol: 12mg Dietary Fiber: .2g Protein: 1g
Sodium: 54mg Carbohydrate: 19g Total Fat: 6g Saturated Fat: 1g
Calories from Fat: 39%, Calories from Carbohydrates: 57%, Calories from Protein: 4%

Karen's Jam Crescents

These cookies are very fragile and delicate. You can't freeze them or keep them for days. But don't worry, they are so good they won't be around long!

Makes 36 cookies
Preparation time: 40 minutes
Chill time: 1 hour

2 1/2 cups all-purpose flour
1/4 cup granulated sugar
1/8 teaspoon salt
8 ounces cream cheese alternative, Tofutti
1 cup safflower oil margarine, Hollywood
2 tablespoons sour cream alternative, Tofutti
1/2 cup lactose-free pure fruit preserves, any kind
Confectioners' sugar, for dusting

In a large mixing bowl, mix the flour, sugar, and salt with a pastry blender. Cut in the cream cheese alternative and safflower margarine until it resembles cornmeal. With a fork stir in the sour cream alternative until it holds the dough together. Form a ball and wrap it in wax paper. Refrigerate for 1 hour.

Preheat the oven to 325° F; lightly grease two cookie sheets. Divide the dough into quarters. Working a quarter at a time, roll out the dough on a floured surface to about a 10-inch to 13-inch square. Using a 3-inch round cookie cutter, cut as many circles as possible from the square. Fill each circle with 1 teaspoon preserves, fold in half, moisten the edges, and seal with a floured fork. With the fork, poke holes in the top of each cookie for venting.

Bake for 18 to 20 minutes until lightly browned. Dust with powdered sugar before serving.

Per Serving (1 cookie): Calories: 110 Cholesterol: 0mg Dietary Fiber: .1g Protein: 2g
Sodium: 91mg Carbohydrate: 11g Total Fat: 7g Saturated Fat: 1g
Calories from Fat: 57%, Calories from Carbohydrates: 39%, Calories from Protein: 4%

Molasses Mountains

Even people who don't like molasses love these cookies. They are soft, chewy, and full of great flavor.

Makes 36 cookies
Preparation time: 3 hours
Chill time: 2 hours

2²/3 cups all-purpose flour
2 teaspoons baking soda
1 teaspoon ground cinnamon
1 teaspoon ground ginger
1/2 teaspoon ground cloves
1/2 teaspoon salt
1 cup light brown sugar, firmly packed
1/2 cup safflower oil margarine, Hollywood
1/4 cup molasses
2 large egg whites, slightly beaten
1/2 cup granulated sugar

Place the first six ingredients in a mixing bowl and stir together; set aside. Using a food processor with a metal blade attachment, blend the brown sugar, safflower margarine, molasses, and egg whites completely. Add the entire mixing bowl of dry ingredients, processing again until completely blended, scraping the bowl often. Remove from the processor and wrap in plastic wrap in the shape of a ball. Chill for about 2 hours.

Preheat the oven to 375° F. Shape the dough into 36 balls. Put the granulated sugar into a wide bowl. Dip each ball in cold water, shake and then roll in the sugar. Place the balls on ungreased cookie sheets, leaving room between. Bake for about 8 to 10 minutes. Cool on wire racks.

Great old-fashioned taste!

Per Serving (1 cookie): Calories: 89 Cholesterol: 0mg Dietary Fiber: .1g Protein: 1g
Sodium: 131mg Carbohydrate: 16g Total Fat: 3g Saturated Fat: .5g
Calories from Fat: 27%, Calories from Carbohydrates: 68%, Calories from Protein: 5%

Mom's Icebox Cookies

These cookies are light and wonderful, and they freeze great. They're a family favorite. The recipe is a Christmas tradition that my mother-in-law taught me. For a different taste and texture, you can add ground nuts as a last step in the mixing, or change the 2 cups sugar to 1 cup granulated sugar and 1 cup brown sugar.

Makes 48 cookies
Preparation time: 30 minutes
Chill time: 1 hour

4 cups all-purpose flour
1 teaspoon baking soda
4 teaspoons baking powder
1¹/2 cups solid all-vegetable shortening, Crisco
2 cups sugar
2 medium eggs, slightly beaten
2 teaspoons vanilla extract
Sprinkles, for decoration (optional)

Sift the flour first, then measure. Mix the flour with the baking soda and powder; sift again. In a large bowl, cream the shortening on high speed, add the sugar, eggs, vanilla, and beat well. Add the dry ingredients and blend. Shape into 4 long rolls and wrap in wax paper or plastic wrap. Chill for at least 1 hour in the refrigerator.

Preheat the oven to 425° F. Remove one roll from the refrigerator; slice into ¹/4-inch slices. Place on ungreased cookie sheets, decorate with colored sprinkles, if desired. Repeat with the other rolls. Bake the cookies for 3 minutes, or until the edges are very light brown. Cool on a wire rack; store in tightly closed container until ready to serve.

Per Serving (1 cookie): Calories: 129 Cholesterol: 9mg Dietary Fiber: 0g Protein: 1g
Sodium: 59mg Carbohydrate: 16g Total Fat: 6g Saturated Fat: 1g
Calories from Fat: 44%, Calories from Carbohydrates: 52%, Calories from Protein: 4%

No-Bake Orange Squares

*T*hese easy-to-make squares require no baking. The ingredients are simple to have on hand, so there's no reason to panic if you get last-minute company! (Before you begin your dinner preparation, you can make this dessert and slip it into the refrigerator; it'll be ready to serve after dinner.)

Makes 24 servings
Preparation time: 45 minutes
Chill time: 2 hours

11/4 cups chocolate wafer cookies, lactose free
1/3 cup safflower oil margarine, Hollywood, cut into
   pieces
1/2 teaspoon vanilla extract
1 tablespoon 100% lactose-free 2% lowfat milk
2 teaspoons grated orange zest
1/3 cup safflower oil margarine, Hollywood
11/2 cups confectioners' sugar
1 tablespoon safflower oil margarine, Hollywood,
   melted
1 tablespoon unsweetened cocoa powder

Using the metal blade in a food processor, pulse the chocolate wafers until finely ground. Pulse in the 1/3 cup safflower margarine only until combined. Remove and pat into place in an ungreased 9-inch square baking dish. Place in the refrigerator until the crust is firm.

In a large mixing bowl, combine the next 5 ingredients (vanilla through confectioners' sugar). Using the medium speed on a hand mixer, beat until the filling is light and fluffy. Scrape the sides of the bowl often to ensure complete blending. Remove the chilled crust from the refrigerator and spread this filling over the top. Place the baking dish back into the refrigerator until ready to complete the dessert.

Melt the 1 tablespoon safflower margarine in the microwave (about 45 seconds on high). Place the melted margarine in a small mixing bowl, add the unsweetened cocoa, and blend together with a wooden spoon. This will make your chocolate glaze. Remove the baking dish from the refrigerator and drizzle the chocolate glaze over the top of the filling.

Return the baking dish to the refrigerator and chill until the dessert is firm, approximately 2 hours. Slice into squares for serving. Always store in the refrigerator.

*Simple and quick . . . and always
ready for company.*

Per Serving: Calories: 132 Cholesterol: 0mg Dietary Fiber: .1g Protein: .9g
Sodium: 128mg Carbohydrate: 17g Total Fat: 8g Saturated Fat: 1g
Calories from Fat: 50%, Calories from Carbohydrates: 48%, Calories from Protein: 2%

Oatmeal Raisin Cookies

These cookies go fast! Make a double batch and freeze them in a tight container, so you're always ready for hungry people. For variety, omit the raisins and add chocolate chips, drizzle with melted chocolate, or just dip one side of the cookie in chocolate.

Makes 48 cookies
Preparation time: 20 minutes

2 cups quick-cooking oats
1 1/2 cups all-purpose flour, dip and sweep
   method
1 cup light brown sugar, packed
1/2 cup finely chopped walnuts
1 cup solid all-vegetable shortening, Crisco
1/2 cup granulated sugar
2 large eggs, slightly beaten
1 teaspoon salt
1 teaspoon baking soda
1 teaspoon vanilla extract
1 cup raisins

For the glaze
1/4 teaspoon vanilla extract
2 teaspoons 100% lactose-free 2% lowfat milk
1/2 cup confectioners' sugar

Preheat the oven to 375° F. Into the large mixing bowl of a heavy-duty mixer, place all the ingredients except those for the glaze. Mix slowly at first, then beat at medium speed until completely blended. Make sure to continually scrape the sides of the bowl for better blending.

Drop by teaspoonfuls on ungreased cookie sheets, leaving about 1 inch between. Bake for about 12 minutes until golden brown. If you prefer chewy cookies, remove them when the edges are browning but the center is still "wet-looking." With a wide spatula, carefully remove the cookies to a wire rack for cooling.

With a spoon, mix the glaze ingredients in a small mixing bowl. Blend until smooth and creamy. Fill a resealable sandwich bag with the glaze, forcing it to one corner. Snip the corner of the bag to allow the glaze to stream out in a tiny line. Once the cookies are cooled, decorate the tops. Allow to stand a few more minutes so glaze will set.

Layer lactose-free ice cream between 2 cookies
for a cool treat.

Per Serving (1 cookie): Calories: 121 Cholesterol: 9mg Dietary Fiber: .2g Protein: 2g
Sodium: 75mg Carbohydrate: 16g Total Fat: 6g Saturated Fat: 1g
Calories from Fat: 40%, Calories from Carbohydrates: 53%, Calories from Protein: 7%

Orange Cookies

These quick orange cookies are a wonderful change for the lunchbox or after-school-snack bunch!

Makes 72 cookies
Preparation time: 15 minutes

1 tablespoon vinegar
1 cup 100% lactose-free 2% lowfat milk
1 cup solid all-vegetable shortening, Crisco
1¹/2 cups light brown sugar, packed
2 large eggs, slightly beaten
2 tablespoons grated orange zest
¹/4 cup fresh orange juice
1 teaspoon vanilla extract
3¹/2 cups all-purpose flour, dip and sweep method
2 teaspoons baking powder
1 teaspoon baking soda
¹/4 teaspoon salt
1 cup toasted walnuts, chopped

Preheat the oven to 350° F. Lightly grease 2 cookie sheets (recoating as needed). In a measuring cup, place the vinegar and fill with lactose-free milk to make 1 cup—this makes a substitution for sour milk or buttermilk. Let stand until ready to use.

Using a stationary mixer with the whipping attachment, cream the shortening and brown sugar until well blended. Beat in the eggs, one at a time. Add the orange zest, orange juice, vanilla, and lactose-free milk mixture and beat until blended. Add the flour, baking powder, baking soda, and salt, slowly. Fold in the nuts.

Drop the dough from a teaspoon onto the cookie sheets and bake in the oven for 15 minutes. Cool on a wire rack.

Stuff that cookie jar!

Per Serving (1 cookie): Calories: 73 Cholesterol: 6mg Dietary Fiber: .1g Protein: 1g
Sodium: 40mg Carbohydrate: 8g Total Fat: 4g Saturated Fat: .8g
Calories from Fat: 48%, Calories from Carbohydrates: 45%, Calories from Protein: 7%

Peanut Butter Passion Cookies

My family goes crazy over these cookies. For a fancy touch, you can top them with semisweet chocolate curls or drizzle with melted chocolate pieces. For a favorite treat, place a scoop of homemade lactose-free ice cream between two cookies, wrap the "sandwich" in plastic freezer wrap, and place it in the freezer.

Makes 36 cookies
Preparation time: 2 hours 15 minutes

21/4 cups all-purpose flour
1 cup peanut butter, any style
2/3 cup honey
1/2 cup sugar
1/2 cup solid all-vegetable shortening, Crisco
2 large eggs, slightly beaten
1/2 teaspoon baking powder
1/4 cup sugar, for rolling

Preheat the oven to 350° F. Using a large Kitchen-Aid mixer (or heavy-duty mixer) with the dough paddle, combine all the ingredients at medium speed until well blended. Remove the dough from the mixer and with damp hands mold the dough into 1-inch balls. Drop balls one at a time into a small bowl with sugar and roll, coating the entire ball. Place the balls on a cookie sheet. With a floured fork, press down deeply, flattening the ball and forming a criss-cross "pattern."

Bake in the oven for about 15 minutes, just until cookies are slightly browned. Using a large spatula move the cookies immediately to a wire rack for cooling.

Per Serving (1 cookie): Calories: 134 Cholesterol: 12mg Dietary Fiber: .4g Protein: 3g
Sodium: 43mg Carbohydrate: 17g Total Fat: 7g Saturated Fat: 2g
Calories from Fat: 43%, Calories from Carbohydrates: 49%, Calories from Protein: 8%

Peanut Butter Pinwheels

*A*nyone *for dunkin'? These delicious treats feature a great combination of chocolate and peanut butter. They are special enough to give as gifts (freeze 'em ahead), or just to stock the cookie jar.*

Makes 48 cookies
Preparation time: 2 hours
Chill time: 2 hours or overnight

For the peanut butter cookie dough
3/4 cup peanut butter, creamy style
1/3 cup safflower oil margarine, Hollywood
3/4 cup granulated sugar
3/4 cup light brown sugar, packed
3/4 teaspoon baking soda
1 large egg, slightly beaten
3 tablespoons 100% lactose-free 2% lowfat milk
1 teaspoon vanilla extract
2 cups all-purpose flour

For the chocolate cookie dough
1/2 cup safflower oil margarine, Hollywood
1/2 cup solid all-vegetable shortening, Crisco
1 cup granulated sugar
1/3 cup sweet ground chocolate, Ghirardelli
1/4 teaspoon baking soda
1/8 teaspoon salt
1 large egg, slightly beaten
2 tablespoons 100% lactose-free 2% lowfat milk
1 teaspoon vanilla extract
21/2 cups all-purpose flour

In this recipe, you are really making two separate cookie doughs, and incorporating them in the final stage.

In a large stationary mixer with a dough paddle, beat the peanut butter and safflower margarine on high for 30 seconds. Add the sugars, baking soda, egg, lactose-free milk, vanilla, and flour. Beat slowly at first until flour becomes incorporated, then turn speed up to medium until thoroughly blended. Divide the dough in half and wrap in plastic wrap. Refrigerate about 1 hour.

Using the same mixer, place all remaining ingredients in a clean mixing bowl with clean dough-paddle attachment. Turn the mixer on slow speed until the flour becomes incorporated, then turn to medium speed until all ingredients are well combined. Divide the dough in half and wrap as the peanut butter dough. Chill in the refrigerator for 1 hour.

Place a piece of wax paper about 12 inches long on a clean, flat rolling area. Take one portion of the chocolate cookie dough (working one half at a time) from the refrigerator, unwrap it, and place it on the wax paper. Cover it with a similar-size piece of wax paper. Roll the dough to a rectangular shape, and set aside. Take a portion of the peanut butter cookie dough and repeat the process between another two sheets of wax paper. Remove the top sheets of wax paper from each of the cookie doughs and carefully invert one over the other. Peel off the top wax paper and, beginning on the long side, roll up the dough as a jelly roll. Lightly wet the seam and pinch to seal. Cut the roll in half across the middle (for easier handling) and wrap in plastic wrap overnight. Repeat the complete process with the remaining dough.

When ready to bake, preheat the oven to 375° F. Work with one roll at a time, for easier handling. Slice each roll into 1/4-inch thick slices and place on ungreased cookie sheets, at least 2 inches apart. Bake for about 8 minutes until bottoms are lightly browned. It will be hard to tell if they are done because of the chocolate outer edge, but the tops will begin to dry a little. Watch them carefully. Allow the cookies to set on the cookie sheets a few minutes before trying to remove them; this will allow set-up time. With a large pancake flipper or spatula transfer the cookies to wire racks and cool completely.

A cookie-jar hit for peanut butter lovers!

Per Serving (1 cookie): Calories: 153 Cholesterol: 9mg Dietary Fiber: .2g Protein: 3g
Sodium: 88mg Carbohydrate: 19g Total Fat: 8g Saturated Fat: 2g
Calories from Fat: 44%, Calories from Carbohydrates: 50%, Calories from Protein: 6%

Simply Butterscotch Cookies

The simple blending of safflower oil margarine and brown sugar makes these cookies rich and savory.

Makes 36 cookies
Preparation time: 1 hour
Chill time: 1 hour

1/2 cup safflower oil margarine, Hollywood
2/3 cup light brown sugar, packed
1 large egg, slightly beaten
1 1/3 cups all-purpose flour, dip and sweep method
3/4 teaspoon baking soda
3/4 teaspoon vanilla extract
1/3 cup coarsely chopped walnuts

Preheat the oven to 375° F. In a saucepan, melt the safflower margarine. Blend the brown sugar into the melted margarine until completely dissolved. Remove from the heat and place in a mixing bowl. Add the egg to the warm mixture and beat until light and fluffy. Stir in the flour and baking soda. Add the vanilla and nuts, blending. Chill in the refrigerator for about 1 hour. This will make it easier to handle.

Remove from the refrigerator, roll teaspoonfuls of dough into balls and place on ungreased cookie sheets. Bake in the oven for 8 to 10 minutes. Remove and immediately place on a wire rack to cool.

This rich butterscotch taste is wonderful anytime.

Per Serving (1 cookie): Calories: 56 Cholesterol: 0mg Dietary Fiber: .1g Protein: .8g
Sodium: 53mg Carbohydrate: 6g Total Fat: 3g Saturated Fat: .5g
Calories from Fat: 52%, Calories from Carbohydrates: 43%, Calories from Protein: 5%

Special Occasion Almond Cookies

Every so often I like to surprise everyone with "Just Because" cookies! For Valentine's Day there's hearts . . . for Christmas, angels, bells, and snowflakes . . . for St. Patrick's Day, shamrocks. These cookies make great holiday gifts. For added pizzazz, after dipping the cookies in the melted chocolate, sprinkle on some colored sugar crystals or jimmies, or drizzle with an icing.

Makes 36 cookies
Preparation time: 45 to 60 minutes
Chill time: 2 hours

1 cup safflower oil margarine, Hollywood
3 ounces cream cheese alternative, Tofutti
1 large egg, slightly beaten
1 1/2 teaspoons almond extract
3/4 cup sugar
3 cups all-purpose flour
1 cup semisweet chocolate chips, lactose free (see page 28)
1/4 cup safflower oil margarine, Hollywood

Combine the first 5 ingredients in a large mixing bowl and beat at medium speed until the batter is light and fluffy. Make sure to incorporate all the ingredients by scraping the sides of the bowl often. Slowly add the flour, blending well after each addition. When the flour is completely incorporated, remove the dough from the bowl and divide it into two balls. Wrap in plastic wrap and place in the refrigerator until firm and easy to handle. This will take about 2 hours.

Preheat the oven to 375° F. Do not grease the cookie sheets. On a clean, smooth surface, sprinkle extra flour as well as flour a rolling pin. Taking one ball of cookie dough at a time from the refrigerator, roll it out onto the prepared surface. You want a thickness of about 1/4 inch. Flour the desired cookie cutters and cut out shapes from the dough. For flakier cookies, handle the dough as little as possible.

Place the cut-out cookies on the ungreased cookie sheets, leaving about 1 inch between them. Bake in the oven for about 7 to 10 minutes. You don't want these cookies brown, so remove them when you see the edges start to brown lightly. Allow the cookies to cool a few minutes on the cookie sheets before removing them to a wire rack, where they need to cool completely.

Once you have completed baking all the cookies and they have cooled, place the chocolate chips and 1/4 cup margarine in a small saucepan. Over low heat, melt both, stirring constantly to blend well together. This should take about 4 to 6 minutes.

Remove from the heat, and prop up one side of the pan a little higher than the other. This will create a "well" in the chocolate. Take each cooled cookie and dip into the chocolate (dip only half or part of the cookie). Place the dipped cookie on wax paper and put in the refrigerator to set until firm. To store these special cookies, keep them in a covered container in the refrigerator.

Per Serving (1 cookie): Calories: 135 Cholesterol: 6mg Dietary Fiber: .3g Protein: 2g
Sodium: 68mg Carbohydrate: 15g Total Fat: 8g Saturated Fat: 2g
Calories from Fat: 53%, Calories from Carbohydrates: 43%, Calories from Protein: 4%

The Butter Cookie

Although these are plain cookies, you can be creative with them. One time my daughter "tie-dyed" her cookies! What a hit they made with her friends. Just stir in the food coloring instead of blending it with a mixer. You can also make these cookies ahead (without decorations) and freeze them in a covered container. Then defrost and finish decorating.

Makes 36 cookies
Preparation time: 1 hour
Chill time: 2 to 3 hours

1 tablespoon vanilla extract
2 tablespoons fresh orange juice
1 large egg, slightly beaten
1 cup safflower oil margarine, Hollywood
1 teaspoon baking powder
1 cup sugar
2 1/2 cups all-purpose flour

For the frosting
4 cups powdered sugar
1/2 cup safflower oil margarine, Hollywood
31/2 teaspoons 100% lactose-free 2% lowfat milk
2 teaspoons vanilla extract

In a stationary mixer using the dough paddle, place the first 7 ingredients. Beat on low speed, incorporating all ingredients by scraping the bowl often, about 2 minutes. (At this time, if you wish to color the dough, simply remove some of the batter and add drops of food coloring to the batter, or place equal portions of the dough in separate bowls and color differently.) Separate the dough into two or three balls, wrap in plastic wrap, and refrigerate until firm. This can take anywhere from 2 to 3 hours.

Preheat the oven to 400° F., and line up several ungreased cookie sheets. Flour a "rolling surface" and using one ball of dough at a time, roll out to about 1/4-inch thickness. Dip cookie cutters into the flour for easier handling. Cut shapes out of the dough and place on the cookie sheets about 1 inch apart. At this time, you can sprinkle colored sugar crystals on top of the cookies if desired. (You can frost and decorate later also.)

Place the cookie sheets into the preheated oven and bake for 6 to 9 minutes. The edges will be lightly browned when cookies are ready to be removed. Allow the cookies to stay on the cookie sheets for a few minutes to make it easier to remove them without breaking. Place them on wire racks to cool completely.

When the cookies are completely cooled, decorate them with a frosting. Using a small bowl, blend the powdered sugar, 1/2 cup margarine, lactose-free milk, and vanilla on the low speed of a hand mixer. Scrape the bowl often and blend about 2 minutes. The frosting will be light and fluffy. (If you like, you can add a few drops of food coloring to the frosting and blend in.)

Frost the cooled cookies, decorate with jimmies, sugar crystals, raisins, chocolate chips, or coconut flakes. Be creative!

Per Serving (1 cookie): Calories: 175 Cholesterol: 6mg Dietary Fiber: 0g Protein: 1g
Sodium: 89mg Carbohydrate: 26g Total Fat: 8g Saturated Fat: 1g
Calories from Fat: 41%, Calories from Carbohydrates: 57%, Calories from Protein: 2%

The Plain Coffee Cookie

*The cream cheese alternative adds a rich taste to this simple cookie.
The subtle coffee flavor makes these perfect to serve anytime.*

Makes 24 cookies
Preparation time: 45 minutes
Chill time: 15 minutes

1 tablespoon whipping cream alternative, Pastry Pride
2 teaspoons vanilla extract
2 tablespoons instant coffee granules
1 medium egg yolk
2 ounces cream cheese alternative, Tofutti
1/2 cup safflower oil margarine, Hollywood
11/4 cup confectioners' sugar
1 tablespoon brown sugar, firmly packed
13/4 cup all-purpose flour, sifted
1/2 teaspoon baking powder
1/2 teaspoon salt

Preheat the oven to 350° F. and prepare baking sheets by covering with aluminum foil.

In a large bowl, place the whipping cream alternative, vanilla, and coffee granules. Stir until the coffee is dissolved. Whisk in the egg yolk. Place the cream cheese alternative and safflower margarine in the mixture and beat with an electric mixer until smooth. On low speed, blend the powdered and brown sugars into the mixture. Finally, add the flour, baking powder, and salt gradually, blending well after each addition.

Gather up the dough and form a ball. Place the dough in the refrigerator for about 15 minutes, or just until firm enough to handle.

Divide the chilled dough into 24 even balls. In a small bowl, place additional confectioners' sugar to use as a coating. Roll each ball in the confectioners' sugar, coating it completely. Place the sugared balls on the baking sheets about 1 inch apart. With a glass bottom dipped in confectioners' sugar, flatten the balls into discs about 2¹/₂ inches wide.

Bake the cookies for about 12 to 15 minutes; the bottoms will start to turn golden brown. Place them on a wire rack to cool. Store in an airtight container.

*These give a special touch to a dish of
Rich Vanilla Lactose-Free Ice Cream.*

Per Serving (1 cookie): Calories: 105 Cholesterol: 9mg Dietary Fiber: 0g Protein: 1g
Sodium: 103mg Carbohydrate: 14g Total Fat: 5g Saturated Fat: 1g
Calories from Fat: 43%, Calories from Carbohydrates: 52%, Calories from Protein: 5%

The Chocolate Coffee Spritzer

Coffee liqueur and chocolate give these cookies great flavor; what a gift they'd make for your coffee-loving friends! The substitution of Crisco shortening for butter or margarine makes them light, and dipping the cookies in melted lactose-free chocolate chips makes them "safe" as well.

Makes 48 cookies
Preparation time: 15 minutes
Set-up time: 20 minutes

1¹/2 cups solid all-vegetable shortening, Crisco, packed
1¹/2 cups sugar
2 large eggs, slightly beaten
4 teaspoons coffee liqueur
1/2 teaspoon baking powder
1/2 teaspoon salt
4 cups all-purpose flour, dip and sweep method
2 ounces semisweet chocolate chips, lactose free
   (see page 28)
1 tablespoon solid-all vegetable shortening, Crisco

Preheat the oven to 375° F. Line up ungreased cookie sheets. In the bowl of a large stationary mixer, place the shortening, sugar, eggs, and coffee liqueur. Whip until light and fluffy. Add the baking powder and salt, and gradually add the flour, mixing well after each addition.

Fill a cookie press, choosing the desired disc (a star or heart shape is recommended), and press out onto an ungreased cookie sheet.

Bake in the oven for 8 to 10 minutes until the edges are light brown.

Allow to cool for 2 to 3 minutes on the cookie sheets before removing them to a wire rack.

When the cookies are completely cooled, line the counter or a flat surface with wax paper. Place the semisweet chocolate chips and shortening into the top of a double boiler. Over low heat, melt the chocolate, stirring constantly. As it combines with the shortening, the chocolate will become glossy. Remove from the heat. Tip the pan holding the melted chocolate, and dip one part of each cookie into the melted chocolate. Allow excess chocolate to drip off the cookies before placing them on the wax paper to allow the chocolate to set. Let stand for 20 to 30 minutes. (If you have trouble with the chocolate setting up, place the cookies in the refrigerator, chilling them until the chocolate sets.)

For very special cookies, you can sprinkle the chocolate parts of the cookies with decorator sugars or jimmies before the chocolate sets.

For a wonderful gift, fill a special coffee mug with cookies, tied with a bow.

Per Serving (1 cookie): Calories: 130 Cholesterol: 9mg Dietary Fiber: .1g Protein: 1g
Sodium: 29mg Carbohydrate: 15g Total Fat: 7g Saturated Fat: 2g
Calories from Fat: 48%, Calories from Carbohydrates: 47%, Calories from Protein: 5%

The Chocolate Cookie Express

These giant cookies make quite an impression. You can bake them in smaller sizes and stuff your cookie jar . . . but they won't last! When choosing chocolate chips, read the labels. I love to use Ghirardelli semisweet chocolate chips because of the flavor and taste, but I have found other chips that are less expensive and just as flavorful that are lactose free.

Makes 20 large cookies
Preparation time: 45 minutes
Chill time: 20 minutes

2²/3 cups semisweet chocolate chips, lactose free
    (see page 28), for melting
1³/4 cups sugar
4 large eggs, slightly beaten
1/4 cup safflower oil margarine, Hollywood,
    melted
1 teaspoon instant espresso coffee granules
1 tablespoon vanilla extract
1/2 cup cake flour
1/4 teaspoon salt
1 teaspoon baking powder
2¹/3 cups semisweet chocolate chips,
    lactose free
1 cup chopped toasted walnuts

In the top of a double boiler, melt the 2²/3 cups chocolate chips over simmering water. Stir the chips until they are smooth and glossy. Remove from the heat and set aside to cool.

In a large bowl, beat the sugar and eggs for about 4 to 5 minutes until mixture is thick. Add the melted chocolate chips, melted safflower margarine, espresso coffee, and vanilla. In a separate bowl, mix the cake flour, salt, and baking powder. Add to the chocolate mixture, blending completely. With a wooden spoon, stir in the 2 1/3 cups chocolate chips and the toasted walnuts. For easier handling, refrigerate the dough for about 20 to 30 minutes.

Preheat the oven to 350° F. Place parchment paper on cookie sheets and drop the batter onto the parchment by regular ice cream scoopfuls, spacing them evenly (or just divide the dough into 20 equal mounds). Then, using a moist glass bottom or simply pressing with your fingers, make large round cookies.

Bake for about 15 minutes in the oven. Watch carefully so as not to burn. The tops will be dry and cracked when done. Remove the cookies from the oven, slide the parchment off the cookie sheet onto the counter for cooling. When cool, remove the cookies from the parchment.

Special gift or "spoil yourself" cookies.

Per Serving (1 cookie): Calories: 354 Cholesterol: 43mg Dietary Fiber: 3g Protein: 5g
Sodium: 85mg Carbohydrate: 48g Total Fat: 20g Saturated Fat: 8g
Calories from Fat: 46%, Calories from Carbohydrates: 49%, Calories from Protein: 5%

Chocolate Mountains

A great chocolate cookie: moist and chewy . . . reminiscent of a brownie. For variety, you can change the type of nuts. The cookies will be soft coming out of the oven, but they firm up as they cool.

Makes 60 cookies
Preparation time: 20 minutes

1 cup semisweet chocolate chips, lactose free (see page 28)
2 tablespoons safflower oil margarine, Hollywood
3 tablespoons all-purpose flour, dip and sweep method
1/4 teaspoon baking powder
2 large eggs, slightly beaten
1/2 cup sugar
1 teaspoon vanilla extract
11/3 semisweet chocolate chips, lactose free
11/2 cups coarsely chopped walnuts

Boil water in the bottom of a double boiler. Remove from the heat and place the cup chocolate chips and the safflower margarine in the top of the double boiler and put on top of the pan with boiling water. Stir the chips and margarine together until well blended. (If the water cools before the melting is complete, return the pan to the heat and bring to a boil again. Be careful not to allow the water to mix with the chocolate or burn the bottom of the top pan . . . this makes the chocolate unusable.) Once the chocolate is melted and blended, remove the pan from the heat and set aside.

In a small mixing bowl, mix the flour and baking powder together. In a large mixing bowl, with a hand mixer beat the eggs, sugar, and vanilla on high until light and fluffy. Turn the speed down to the lowest and add the melted chocolate. Carefully blend, adding the flour mixture next. Once completely blended, use a wooden spoon to add the 1¹/3 cups chocolate chips and the nuts.

Preheat the oven to 350° F. Line each cookie sheet you are going to use with aluminum foil. Drop by teaspoon (the cookies should be very small, but you can mound them as high as possible). You should be able to fit about 15 cookies on a large baking sheet. Bake about 6 minutes on the top rack of the oven; rotate the cookie sheet to the bottom rack, turning the sheet front to back. Bake for an additional 3 minutes until the tops are dry. Cool the cookies on the foil, "peeling" them off when cool.

Per Serving (1 cookie): Calories: 69 Cholesterol: 7mg Dietary Fiber: .6g Protein: lg
Sodium: 8mg Carbohydrate: 7g Total Fat: 5g Saturated Fat: 2g
Calories from Fat: 55%, Calories from Carbohydrates: 38%, Calories from Protein: 7%

The Raspberry Linzer Heart

These are my favorite cookies. They have a wonderful flavor and a rich taste. For lighter cookies, remember to sift that flour.

Makes 48 cookies
Preparation time: 25 minutes

11/2 cups all-purpose flour, sifted
1/2 teaspoon ground cinnamon
3/4 cup granulated sugar
Dash salt
1 teaspoon grated lemon zest
2/3 cup safflower oil margarine, Hollywood,
    chilled and chopped
21/4 cups finely ground hazelnuts
1 large egg yolk
1/2 jar raspberry seedless jam
1/4 cup confectioners' sugar, for coating

In a food processor with the metal blade, combine the flour, cinnamon, sugar, salt, and lemon zest. Pulse several times to combine. Add pieces of chilled safflower margarine, and pulse until the mixture resembles fine crumbs.

Place the crumb mixture into a large bowl and stir in the hazelnuts and egg yolk. Combine until well blended, then turn out onto a floured surface and very quickly knead until the mixture forms a soft dough and sticks together.

Preheat the oven to 375° F. Split the dough in half, wrap in plastic wrap, and place one half in refrigerator while you work with the other half. Roll the dough out on the floured surface to about 1/4 inch thick. Using cookie cutters, cut the dough into shapes and place on ungreased cookie sheets. Cut the centers out from half the cutouts you make. These will be the tops of the sandwich-style cookies. Repeat the process with the chilled dough in the refrigerator.

Bake in the oven until the cookies are light brown, or about 8 to 10 minutes. Cool on a wire rack. Once cooled, spread the jam on a solid cookie, top with one of the cutout-center cookies to make a "sandwich." Dust the tops with confectioners' sugar.

Store these cookies in an airtight container to keep them fresh longer.

For special company, as a gift, or just for you!

Per Serving (1 cookie): Calories: 87 Cholesterol: 4mg Dietary Fiber: .3g Protein: 1g
Sodium: 26mg Carbohydrate: 8g Total Fat: 6g Saturated Fat .7g
Calories from Fat: 61%, Calories from Carbohydrates: 34%, Calories from Protein: 5%

Candies

It is very difficult to find candy without lactose. Sweets are important to everyone, but especially so to someone with Lactose Intolerance. Grabbing a candy bar at the store becomes quite a chore. Check the labels—milk chocolate, along with lactose, is everywhere. The recipes in this section are lactose-free versions of some great favorites.

Caramels

You can use this recipe to make a variety of treats. Wrap your finished caramels in colored plastic wrap and tie with colorful bows to create a special gift for the Lactose Intolerant.

Makes about 80 pieces
Preparation time: 30 minutes

2 tablespoons safflower oil margarine, Hollywood
1 cup light corn syrup
3 cups sugar
2 cups whipping cream alternative, Pastry Pride
3/4 cup safflower oil margarine, Hollywood
1 tablespoon vanilla extract

With the 2 tablespoons safflower margarine, grease a 9-inch pan. In a heavy-gauge saucepan, combine the corn syrup, sugar, and whipping cream alternative. Over low heat, stir until blended and the sugar is completely dissolved. Increase the heat and, using a candy thermometer, bring the mixture to 238° F. The mixture will be light tan in color and at the soft-ball stage.

Remove the pan from the heat. Immediately stir in the 3/4 cup safflower margarine and vanilla. After stirring several times, pour the mixture into the prepared pan. Allow to cool at room temperature. Slice into bite-size pieces and wrap in clear plastic wrap. Stored in a cool, dry place, the candies will keep for weeks.

Melt several of these and coat an apple on a stick.
Caramel apples bring back great childhood memories!

Per Serving (1 piece): Calories: 79 Cholesterol: 0mg Dietary Fiber: 0g Protein: 0g
Sodium: 31mg Carbohydrate: 12g Total Fat: 4g Saturated Fat: 2g
Calories from Fat: 43%, Calories from Carbohydrates: 57%, Calories from Protein: 0%

Granna Hadley's Famous Fudge

This original recipe was handed down through generations of our family. This fudge has a distinctive peanut butter flavor, but it is light and delicious.

Makes 24 pieces
Preparation time: 45 minutes

1 tablespoon safflower oil margarine, Hollywood
2 squares unsweetened baking chocolate (see page 28),
** broken**
1 cup 100% lactose-free 2% lowfat milk
2 cups sugar
1 teaspoon vanilla extract
5 ounces peanut butter
6 ounces marshmallow cream, Kraft

Generously grease an 8 × 8-inch baking pan, loaf pan, or small baking dish of your choice with additional safflower margarine. Set aside.

In a 2-quart saucepan, slowly melt the margarine, then add the chocolate. Slowly alternate between adding a little lactose-free milk, then a little sugar at a time, until completely dissolved. Cook slowly, stirring occasionally, on a low boil until it forms a soft dough (about 30 minutes). Remove from the heat; stir in the vanilla, peanut butter, and marshmallow cream.

Pour the mixture into the prepared pan. Allow the fudge to set. No need to refrigerate it. After the fudge has set, slice it as desired.

Per Serving (1 piece): Calories: 143 Cholesterol: 1mg Dietary Fiber: .7g Protein: 2g
Sodium: 42mg Carbohydrate: 25g Total Fat: 5g Saturated Fat: 2g
Calories from Fat: 30%, Calories from Carbohydrates: 65%, Calories from Protein: 5%

The Lactose-Free Almond Bar

This is the equivalent of a Hershey's almond bar, but it's lactose free. Its dark chocolate flavor will definitely satisfy that sweet tooth.

Makes 24 pieces
Preparation time: 20 minutes
Chill time: 1 hour

12 ounces semisweet chocolate chips, lactose free (see page 28)
1 ounce unsweetened chocolate
1 cup almonds, whole

Line a shallow pan with wax paper. Melt the semisweet chocolate chips and unsweetened chocolate in a large saucepan over low heat. Stir often. Be careful not to burn. When the mixture is smooth, remove from the heat and add the almonds. Pour into the prepared pan and chill in the refrigerator for about 1 hour until set. When the chocolate is set, break it into pieces or wedges and store in an airtight container in the refrigerator.

Per Serving (1 piece): Calories: 109 Cholesterol: 0mg Dietary Fiber: 2g Protein: 2g
Sodium: 2mg Carbohydrate: 11g Total Fat: 8g Saturated Fat: 3g
Calories from Fat: 59%, Calories from Carbohydrates: 35%, Calories from Protein: 6%

The Lactose-Free Chunky

The Chunky bar is my husband's favorite candy, so I have tried to duplicate it here, lactose free—this is as close as I have been able to get. It is definitely wonderful to be able to enjoy this substitute, knowing there's no lactose in it to bother you.

Makes 36 pieces
Preparation time: 30 minutes
Chill time: 30 minutes

12 ounces semisweet chocolate chips, lactose free (see page 28)
1 ounce unsweetened chocolate
1 cup coarsely chopped cashews
1/2 cup coarsely chopped peanuts
1/2 cup raisins

Prepare cookie sheets by lining them with wax paper. Using a large saucepan, melt the semisweet chocolate chips and unsweetened chocolate over low heat. Stir often, so as not to burn. When the chocolate is melted and smooth, remove the pan from the heat and add the nuts and raisins. Drop by teaspoonfuls onto wax paper–lined cookie sheets. Place in the refrigerator to set. Once the candies are set, place them in an airtight container and store in the refrigerator.

Per Serving (1 piece): Calories: 88 Cholesterol: 0mg Dietary Fiber: 1g Protein: 2g
Sodium: 2mg Carbohydrate: 9g Total Fat: 6g Saturated Fat: 2g
Calories from Fat: 56%, Calories from Carbohydrates: 38%, Calories from Protein: 6%

The Peanut Butter Cup Frenzy

Lactose Intolerance deprives you of the simple pleasure of running into a store and buying a Reese's peanut butter cup when that chocolate craving hits you. You can't just pick up a candy bar, you have to *read* labels and settle for something else. Well, I won't settle! I've made lots of chocolates, and I've surprised my husband with candy bars he thought he would never be able to eat again. These peanut butter cups are wonderful.

Makes 36 pieces
Preparation time: 1 hour
Chill time: 1 hour and 50 minutes

3/4 cup chunky peanut butter
2 tablespoons whipping cream alternative, Pastry Pride, very cold
1/4 teaspoon vanilla extract
1/4 cup sour cream alternative, Tofutti
1/4 cup confectioners' sugar, plus 2 tablespoons
3 cups semisweet chocolate chips, lactose free (see page 28)

In a medium bowl, place the peanut butter, whipping cream alternative, vanilla, sour cream alternative, and confectioners' sugar. Stir well and refrigerate, covered, for about 1 hour. (You can place it in the refrigerator overnight—the colder it gets, the better.)

Using mini-muffin foil cups, line up 36 cups on cookie sheets and set aside. In a double boiler, melt the chocolate chips over simmering water. Stir constantly to make sure it doesn't burn. The chips will be smooth and glossy. When done, remove from the heat.

Using about 1 teaspoon of the melted chocolate per foil cup, drop it in the center of the cup and roll it around the cup to completely cover it. You can use a small paintbrush or a small spatula to spread the chocolate evenly if necessary. Set the chocolate by placing the cookie sheets lined with foil cups into the refrigerator for about 20 to 25 minutes. Reserve the unused melted chocolate for later.

After the chocolate shells are set, fill each one with the peanut butter mixture that has chilled in the refrigerator. Leave a little space between the filling and top of the rim of the chocolate shell.

Return the reserved melted chocolate to the double boiler and remelt it. Carefully spoon enough melted chocolate over the filling in each foil cup to cover completely. Smooth out the tops and return to the refrigerator to set, about 20 to 25 minutes. Keep the peanut butter cups in the refrigerator in airtight containers for freshness.

Per Serving (1 piece): Calories: 106 Cholesterol: 0mg Dietary Fiber: 1g Protein: 2g
Sodium: 29mg Carbohydrate: 11g Total Fat: 7g Saturated Fat: 3g
Calories from Fat: 55%, Calories from Carbohydrates: 38%, Calories from Protein: 7%

Chocolate Lollipops

*B*oth white chocolate and the chocolate found at candy-making supply stores are off limits for Lactose-Intolerant people. However, by using this adapted recipe, a fancy chocolate lollipop can surprise your special Lactose Intolerant chocolate lover without anyone knowing the difference.

Makes 12 lollipops
Preparation time: 45 minutes
Chill time: Overnight

Safflower oil, Hollywood
8 ounces semisweet chocolate, chopped
8 ounces bittersweet chocolate, chopped (or omit and use
   8 more ounces semisweet chocolate)

Supplies*
2 plastic lollipop molds containing 6 shapes each
12 lollipop sticks
12 lollipop bags (check size with mold shapes)
12 lengths of ribbon

Carefully oil the lollipop molds with the safflower oil. A light coating is all that is needed. Place a saucepan of water over medium heat and bring to a simmer. I find it easier to work with half the chocolate at a time. With this in mind, place the 8 ounces semisweet chocolate (or mix 4 ounces semisweet and 4 ounces bittersweet) in a bowl large enough to set over the simmering saucepan. Stir until the chopped chocolate melts and

*All supplies are available at candy-supply stores. Fancy ribbons can be found at craft or fabric stores. Using a glue gun, tack on a couple of gold bells to the center of a bow on a Christmas lollipop. Be creative.

becomes smooth. Remove the bowl from over the saucepan and drizzle the melted chocolate by spoonfuls into the lollipop molds. Drop the lollipop sticks into position, turning the sticks in order to cover with chocolate. Repeat the complete procedure with the 8 ounces bittersweet chocolate.

Tap the molds gently to remove any air bubbles. You should see them rise to the top of the molds (this will be the back of the lollipop shape when they are done).

Place the molds carefully into the refrigerator. Keep them refrigerated until they are firm. Best results are achieved overnight, but at least 3 hours of refrigeration is advised.

Once the lollipops are firm, invert the molds and pop out carefully. Wrap in individual lollipop bags, tie with ribbon and/or decorate. Keep the lollipops refrigerated until ready to eat.

You can make these special treats up to 3 days ahead. Just store them in the refrigerator.

Per Serving (I lollipop): Calories: 180 Cholesterol: 0mg Dietary Fiber: 2g Protein: 2g
Sodium: 4mg Carbohydrate: 24g Total Fat: IIg Saturated Fat: 7g
Calories from Fat: 50%, Calories from Carbohydrates: 47%, Calories from Protein: 3%

"Ice Cream" and Creamy Desserts

There's lactose in ice cream. If you have Lactose Intolerance, that's not a news flash. It was probably one of the first things you found you couldn't tolerate well. Here are recipes to tantalize your taste buds, and remind you that you can have "ice cream," puddings, and even special treats wrapped around that "ice cream." Just make sure you follow these recipes carefully and you won't feel deprived anymore!

Rich Vanilla Lactose-Free Ice Cream

*T*his *"ice cream" is so good, my entire family favors it over the storebought. Now there's no reason you can't say yes to pie à la mode! To create variety, while the ice cream machine is running, during the last few minutes you can add chocolate syrup, nuts, broken-up candies, or fresh fruit.*

Makes 8 servings (about 1 quart)
Preparation time: 15 minutes
Freeze time: 2 hours

2 large eggs, slightly beaten
1/2 cup sugar
2 cups whipping cream alternative, Pastry Pride, cold or frozen
1 cup 100% lactose-free 2% lowfat milk, cold
2 teaspoons vanilla extract

In a chilled, medium mixing bowl, whisk the eggs until light and fluffy, about 2 minutes. Add the sugar a little at a time, making sure it is completely blended before adding more. Pour in the whipping cream alternative, lactose-free milk, and vanilla all at once, whisking until completely blended.

Start your ice cream maker, following the manufacturer's instructions. Add the mixture immediately and freeze according to directions.

I have a Krups electric ice cream and yogurt maker. The "tub" is kept in the freezer until you are ready to pour in the mixture. The tub is the last thing I set in place. Then I use a large funnel in the opening at the top of the ice cream maker, and pour in the mixture carefully while the tub is running. I allow it to run for at least 30 minutes. I then transfer it to a freezer container and freeze for at least 2 hours.

Hint: If you use the whipped topping frozen, it will simulate the hardness of real ice cream better. Using Cool Whip in this recipe makes the "ice cream" very, very sweet. So, if you choose to use Cool Whip, reduce the amount of sugar in the recipe considerably.

Milk shakes, "ice cream" sodas, and sundaes are now all possible!

Per Serving: Calories: 294 Cholesterol: 56mg Dietary Fiber: 0g Protein: 3g
Sodium: 92mg Carbohydrate: 26g Total Fat: 20g Saturated Fat: 16g
Calories from Fat: 61%, Calories from Carbohydrates: 36%, Calories from Protein: 3%

Lactose-Free Pumpkin Pie Ice Cream

This "ice cream" is a very special favorite in our family. It tastes so much like pumpkin pie, it's remarkable. Even people who don't like pumpkin pie love it.

Makes 8 servings (about 1 quart)
Preparation time: 45 minutes
Chill time: 2 hours

2 large eggs, slightly beaten
1/2 cup sugar
2 cups whipping cream alternative, Pastry Pride, frozen
1 cup 100% lactose-free 2% lowfat milk, cold
1 cup canned pumpkin
1 teaspoon ground nutmeg
1 teaspoon ground cinnamon

In a chilled mixing bowl, whisk the eggs until light and fluffy, about 2 minutes. Add the sugar, a little at a time, whisking until completely blended after each addition. Pour in the whipping cream alternative and lactose-free milk all at once and blend with the whisk. In a side mixing bowl, pour 1 cup of the cream mixture, blend with the pumpkin and spices, and finally return to the chilled mixing bowl to complete the blending of all ingredients.

Transfer to the ice cream maker and follow manufacturer's instructions.

I have a Krups electric ice cream maker and upon completing the mixture, I assemble the parts of the ice cream maker, leaving the frozen "tub" until last. I put a wide funnel in the top opening of the assembled machine and pour the mixture carefully into it while it's running. I allow it to run for at least 30 minutes. Then I turn it into a freezer container and freeze for at least 2 hours before serving.

Great to serve at holiday time.

Per Serving: Calories: 306 Cholesterol: 56mg Dietary Fiber: 1g Protein: 3g
Sodium: 93mg Carbohydrate: 29g Total Fat: 20g Saturated Fat: 16g
Calories from Fat: 59%, Calories from Carbohydrates: 37%, Calories from Protein: 4%

Frozen Lemon à la Raspberry Parfait

This combination is wonderful: The tang of fresh lemons contrasts with the fresh cold berries, the smooth whipped "cream," and the ultimate favorite—chocolate . . . all topped with more raspberry. How can this one go wrong?

Makes 12 servings
Preparation time: 5 hours
Chill time: 7 hours to overnight

1/2 cup fresh lemon juice
31/2 teaspoons grated lemon zest
1/2 cup safflower oil margarine, Hollywood, melted
6 large egg yolks, slightly beaten
2 cups sugar
3 cups whipping cream alternative, Pastry Pride, chilled
3 1-ounce squares semisweet chocolate (see page 28),
   chopped
2 pints fresh raspberries, rinsed

Bring a saucepan of water to a simmer and remove from the heat. Using a metal mixing bowl that will fit over the saucepan later, whisk the lemon juice, lemon zest, melted safflower margarine, egg yolks, and 13/4 cups of the sugar until they are well blended. Place the metal bowl over the simmering water in the saucepan and whisk the mixture for about 8 minutes until a candy thermometer reaches 180° F. Pour the lemon mixture into a larger bowl and place in the refrigerator (whisking several times intermittently) for about 20 minutes.

In another large bowl, whip the whipping cream alternative until soft peaks form. Add the remaining 1/4 cup sugar slowly, while continuing to beat to stiff peaks. Remove about 13/4 cups of the whipped "cream" mixture, placing it in a covered small bowl in the refrigerator. Fold the remaining "cream" into the chilling lemon mixture and freeze, covered, overnight. (If you want to make it early in the day for a dinner dessert, then allow at least 6 hours.)

In a medium saucepan, place the remaining 1/2 cup whipping cream alternative. Over low heat bring it to a simmer and remove from the heat. Add the chopped chocolate and stir constantly until all the chocolate is melted and smooth.

Using 12 fancy parfait or dessert dishes, divide the chocolate mixture among them. Cool completely in refrigerator. Place a few tablespoons of raspberries on top of the cooled chocolate. Spoon reserved, chilled whipped "cream" over the berries, and top with more berries. Return to the refrigerator, covered, and chill for at least 1 to 4 hours. When ready to serve, cover with the frozen lemon mixture and a few berries to garnish. For added flair, add a garnish of shaved chocolate that hints of the surprise at the bottom of the dish!

An elegant summer dessert in berry season.

Per Serving: Calories: 661 Cholesterol: 106mg Dietary Fiber: 5g Protein: 4g
Sodium: 145mg Carbohydrate: 78g Total Fat: 41g Saturated Fat: 25g
Calories from Fat: 53%, Calories from Carbohydrates: 45%, Calories from Protein: 2%

Orange Sorbet

This sorbet is so rich and creamy you won't believe it's not made with milk. Sherbets are made with milk, but true sorbets are lactose free because they are made from fruit juices and purees.

Makes 8 servings
Preparation time: 20 minutes
Chill time: 1 hour

3/4 cup water
3/4 cup sugar
3 tablespoons Grand Marnier
3 tablespoons freshly grated orange zest
2 cups fresh orange juice

Over high heat in a saucepan, combine the water and sugar. Stir constantly until the sugar dissolves and a syrup forms, about 5 minutes. Remove from the heat. In a large mixing bowl, combine the warm syrup, Grand Marnier, orange zest, and orange juice until well blended. Place in the refrigerator to chill for about 1 hour. Remove from the refrigerator and place in ice cream maker. Process according to the manufacturer's directions.

*Float balls of sorbet in fruit punch; serve between courses
or as dessert!*

Per Serving: Calories: 121 Cholesterol: 0mg Dietary Fiber: .2g Protein: .5g
Sodium: 2mg Carbohydrate: 28g Total Fat: .1g Saturated Fat: 0g
Calories from Fat: 1%, Calories from Carbohydrates: 97%, Calories from Protein: 2%

Raspberry Sorbet

Raspberry is my favorite flavor, but any fruit can be used for this recipe, and vodka or another liqueur can be substituted. You can also use a 12-ounce package of frozen raspberries instead of fresh.

Makes 6 servings
Preparation time: 20 minutes
Chill time: 1 hour

3 cups fresh raspberries (12 ounces frozen)
1/3 cup water
1/3 cup sugar
2 tablespoons fresh lemon juice
1/4 cup Chambord or other raspberry liqueur

Rinse and dry the raspberries. Place them in a food processor and puree; strain and measure 2 cups puree for the sorbet. Set aside.

In a medium saucepan, over high heat, stir together the water and sugar until blended. The sugar should completely dissolve, making a syrup. This should take about 5 minutes or so. Remove from the heat and measure the syrup. You should have about 1/2 cup.

Combine the warm syrup, raspberry puree, fresh lemon juice, and the Chambord or other raspberry liqueur in a bowl. Stir to combine completely. Place in the refrigerator to chill, about 1 hour.

Transfer the chilled mixture to your ice cream maker and follow the manufacturer's instructions.

A perfect fresh summer dessert.

Per Serving: Calories: 106 Cholesterol: 0mg Dietary Fiber: 4g Protein: .6g
Sodium: 1mg Carbohydrate: 22g Total Fat: .3g Saturated Fat: 0g
Calories from Fat: 3%, Calories from Carbohydrates: 94%, Calories from Protein: 3%

Spiked Orange Sherbet

Here, the subtle flavor of orange is perked up with orange liqueur for a wonderful, refreshing sherbet.

Makes 6 servings
Preparation time: 30 minutes
Chill time: 1 to 2 hours

2/3 cup orange juice, frozen concentrate
2 tablespoons fresh lemon juice
1/2 teaspoon grated orange zest
1 cup sugar
21/2 cups 100% lactose-free 2% lowfat milk, cold
1/4 cup orange liqueur

In a mixing bowl, blend together the orange juice, lemon juice, orange zest, and sugar. Add the lactose-free milk slowly, stirring as you do. Pour into your ice cream maker and follow the manufacturer's directions.

Just before the sherbet is finished, add the orange liqueur of your choice. Remove from the ice cream freezer, place in a covered container, and freeze until ready to serve. Allow 1 to 2 hours of freezing for a firmer sherbet.

Top a fresh summer fruit salad with
homemade sherbet.

Per Serving: Calories: 270 Cholesterol: 8mg Dietary Fiber: .3g Protein: 4g
Sodium: 53mg Carbohydrate: 54g Total Fat: 2g Saturated Fat: 1g
Calories from Fat: 8%, Calories from Carbohydrates: 86%, Calories from Protein: 6%

The "Wine-ing" Raspberry Sherbet

The addition of Framboise, a wonderful raspberry wine, adds an elegant touch to a simple dessert. Remember that presentation is sometimes just as important as the dish itself. By using chilled stemware glasses, you'll give the illusion of elegance!

Makes 6 servings
Preparation time: 25 minutes
Chill time: 1 to 2 hours

2 packages frozen raspberries
2/3 cup sugar
2 cups 100% lactose-free 2% lowfat milk
2 tablespoons light corn syrup
2 tablespoons fresh lemon juice
1/4 cup Framboise raspberry liqueur
Additional Framboise and fresh raspberries,
    for garnish

Thaw the frozen raspberries. Place them in a food processor or blender and puree. Strain the seeds; set the pureed raspberries aside.

In a medium saucepan, over medium-low heat, stir the sugar, lactose-free milk, and corn syrup until the sugar completely dissolves. Allow the mixture to cool.

Once cooled, add the pureed raspberries and fresh lemon juice to the sugar mixture. Place it in an ice cream maker and freeze according to the manufacturer's directions. Just before the sherbet is done, pour in the Framboise, and continue processing in the ice cream maker a little longer. Remove the sherbet and place it in a covered container in the freezer until ready to serve, at least 1 to 2 hours.

While the sherbet is chilling, toss the fresh raspberries in additional Framboise (enough to completely coat the berries and soak in), allowing them to marinate for about 30 minutes. When ready to serve, scoop the raspberry sherbet into chilled Manhattan or champagne glasses and spoon the marinated raspberries and juices over the sherbet. Serve immediately.

An easy recipe for a very special dessert!

Per Serving: Calories: 202 Cholesterol: 7mg Dietary Fiber: 3g Protein: 3g
Sodium: 50mg Carbohydrate: 40g Total Fat: 2g Saturated Fat: 1g
Calories from Fat: 9%, Calories from Carbohydrates: 84%, Calories from Protein: 7%

Homemade Rice Pudding

*D*esserts made with milk are the ones most Lactose-Intolerant people tend to give up right away. But using a quality substitute, you can serve puddings to everybody. The lactose-free milk gives this homey rice pudding the creamy, rich texture and flavor everyone loves. It's important to remember that 100% lactose-free 2% lowfat milk gives you a richer, thicker pudding than nonfat milk does.

Makes 6 servings
Preparation time: 1 hour

3 cups 100% lactose-free 2% lowfat milk
1/3 cup raisins
1/3 cup long-grain rice
1/4 cup sugar
1 teaspoon ground cinnamon
1 teaspoon vanilla extract
Safflower oil margarine, for coating the dish
1/4 teaspoon ground nutmeg

Place the lactose-free milk into a medium saucepan, and bring to a boil. Be careful not to burn. Stirring constantly, add the raisins and rice, lower the heat to low, and cover the saucepan. Cook for approximately 35 to 40 minutes, stirring several times. The mixture will look curdled and most of the milk will evaporate. Stir in the sugar, 3/4 teaspoon of the cinnamon, and the vanilla. Blend completely.

Preheat the oven to 300° F. Generously grease a 2-quart ovenproof casserole dish with the safflower margarine. Stir the pudding mixture and turn it into the prepared dish. Take the remaining 1/4 teaspoon cinnamon along with the ground nutmeg and sprinkle over the top of the pudding.

Place the dish in the oven and bake for 20 to 25 minutes, stirring several times to ensure complete baking. The pudding will be creamy with a golden brown top.

Serve the pudding in dessert dishes while it's warm . . . sprinkle additional cinnamon, if desired. Top with nondairy whipped topping and a plump raisin for a special touch!

Refrigerate for a terrific cold treat.

Per Serving: Calories: 161 Cholesterol: 10mg Dietary Fiber: .7g Protein: 5g
Sodium: 64mg Carbohydrate: 29g Total Fat: 3g Saturated Fat: 2g
Calories from Fat: 15%, Calories from Carbohydrates: 73%, Calories from Protein: 12%

Quick Pudding Surprise

This is a very easy dessert to make that doesn't look that way—and it's delicious!

Make 8 servings
Preparation time: 10 minutes

3 cups 100% lactose-free 2% lowfat milk, cold
1 4.6-ounce package chocolate pudding mix, Jell-O
1 cup canned cherry pie filling
Nondairy whipped topping, for garnish
Chocolate sprinkles, for garnish

Into a large mixing bowl, pour the cold lactose-free milk. With the mixer on the lowest speed, blend in the pudding mix. Continue to blend for about 2 minutes until it thickens.

Arrange 8 fancy dessert dishes in front of you. Add a spoonful of cherry pie filling to the bottom of each dish, next add a large spoonful of pudding, then a squirt of whipped topping. Then begin again with layers of cherry pie filling, pudding, and whipped topping. End up with the whipped topping and garnish with chocolate sprinkles and a reserved cherry from the filling.

Quick, easy, and always ready for the unexpected guest!

Per Serving: Calories: 158 Cholesterol: 8mg Dietary Fiber: 1g Protein: 3g
Sodium: 364mg Carbohydrate: 32g Total Fat: 2g Saturated Fat: 1g
Calories from Fat: 11%, Calories from Carbohydrates: 81%, Calories from Protein: 8%

Lactose-Free Tapioca Pudding

A pudding that warms your heart in an old-fashioned way. Patience is important when making this dessert. It has a long and slow cooking time.

Makes 8 servings
Preparation time: 20 minutes

2 cups 100% lactose-free 2% lowfat milk
2 cups whipping cream alternative, Pastry Pride
1/3 cup sugar
1 teaspoon vanilla extract
1/2 cup pearl tapioca

Preheat the oven to 300° F. Grease a 1 1/2-quart ovenproof baking dish. Set aside. In a medium mixing bowl, blend all ingredients, finishing with the tapioca. Pour the mixture into the prepared baking dish.

Bake in the oven until creamy, approximately 2 to 2 1/2 hours. This recipe cooks long and slow. At the end of cooking, a golden skin will appear on the surface of the pudding. Remove from the oven and dish out into dessert bowls. Serve warm.

Top the tapioca pudding with nondairy
whipped topping.

Per Serving: Calories: 308 Cholesterol: 5mg Dietary Fiber: .1g Protein: 2g
Sodium: 91mg Carbohydrate: 32g Total Fat: 19g Saturated Fat: 16g
Calories from Fat: 56%, Calories from Carbohydrates: 41%, Calories from Protein: 3%

Frozen Chocolate Peanut Butter Cups

These little treats never seem to last long enough to sit at room temperature. My family enjoys them as a frozen dessert.

Makes 8 servings
Preparation time: 45 minutes
Chill time: 3½ hours

Paper or foil baking cups (cupcake size)
6 ounces semisweet chocolate chips, lactose free (see page 28)
1 tablespoon solid all-vegetable shortening, Crisco
1 cup whipping cream alternative, Pastry Pride, cold
1 jar marshmallow cream
3 ounces cream cheese alternative, Soya Kaas, cold
1/2 cup chunky peanut butter
Peanuts or chocolate curls, for garnish

Arrange paper or foil cups in a muffin pan. Over low heat, in a heavy 1-quart saucepan, carefully stir the chocolate chips and shortening until melted and smooth.

Remove from the heat and, starting at the top edge of the paper/foil cups, begin drizzling 1 heaping teaspoon at a time down the inside of the cup. Cover the entire inside of the cup as evenly as possible; it may take about 3 teaspoons per cup. Smooth out the bottom of the cup if necessary. Place the cups in the refrigerator until firm, approximately 30 minutes.

While the cups are chilling, start assembling the filling. In a small, chilled mixing bowl, beat the whipping cream alternative until stiff peaks form. In a separate, large mixing bowl (you can use same beaters), on low speed blend the marshmallow cream, cream cheese alternative, and peanut butter until smooth. Scrape the bowl often to ensure complete blending. Carefully fold the stiff whipping cream into the peanut butter mixture.

Remove one chocolate cup at a time from the refrigerator. With cool hands, carefully unwrap the paper/foil wrapper from the chocolate cup. Fill the finished chocolate cup with the peanut butter mixture. Cover with plastic wrap gently and freeze until firm, at least 3 hours. Repeat the process until all the cups are filled and place them in the freezer.

To serve, garnish with peanuts and/or chocolate curls. If you let the cups stand at room temperature a few minutes, they'll be easier to eat.

Per Serving: Calories: 397 Cholesterol: 0mg Dietary Fiber: 2g Protein: 5g
Sodium: 126mg Carbohydrate: 43g Total Fat: 25g Saturated Fat: 13g
Calories from Fat: 54%, Calories from Carbohydrates: 41%, Calories from Protein: 5%

Strawberry Angel Cloud

Lactose Intolerance won't be a problem with this takeoff on the traditional strawberry shortcake. The angel food cake mix contains no problem ingredients (do not purchase the "fat-free" version—it contains whey).

Makes 16 servings
Preparation time: 20 minutes

1 package angel food cake mix, Duncan Hines
3 baskets fresh strawberries
1 quart Rich Vanilla Lactose-Free Ice Cream (page 306)
Nondairy whipped topping, for garnish

Early in the day, prepare the angel food cake according to the instructions on the box. Cool as directed and place in a covered cake plate.

When ready to serve dessert, rinse the strawberries, pat dry, slice, and place in a bowl (you may want to reserve a few whole strawberries for garnishing). Slice the angel food cake, placing each slice in a serving bowl (fancy soup bowls make it very special). Scoop lactose-free ice cream on top of the cake, spoon some strawberries over the "ice cream" and cake, and cover the entire dessert with whipped topping. Decorate with 1 whole strawberry on top.

Per Serving: Calories: 261 Cholesterol: 28mg Dietary Fiber: .6g Protein: 4g
Sodium: 279mg Carbohydrate: 38g Total Fat: 10g Saturated Fat: 8g
Calories from Fat: 35%, Calories from Carbohydrates: 59%, Calories from Protein: 6%

The Brownie Express

In our home we have "Mommy Specials." These are desserts I have surprised my kids and their friends with since they were little. This dish has been voted number one . . . and the "kids," now in their twenties, are still clamoring for "Mommy Specials"!

Makes 24 servings
Preparation time: 15 minutes

1 package Duncan Hines chewy brownies
1 medium egg
1/3 cup water
1 tablespoon 100% pure coffee extract
1/3 cup vegetable oil, Crisco
2/3 cup semisweet chocolate chips, lactose free
    (see page 28)
1 quart Rich Vanilla Lactose-Free Ice Cream
    (page 306)
1/4 cup chocolate syrup, Hershey's
Nondairy whipped topping, for garnish
12 maraschino cherries, for garnish

Preheat the oven to 350° F. Grease the bottom only of a 9 × 13-inch pan with solid vegetable shortening (Crisco). In a large bowl, combine the brownie mix, egg, water, coffee extract, vegetable oil, and chocolate chips, and mix with a large wooden spoon. When well mixed, fold into the prepared pan. Allow to cook for 25 to 28 minutes, or until done. Cool on a rack.

Within 1 hour (while still warm), cut the brownies and place in a dessert dish. Scoop homemade lactose-free ice cream on top of the warm brownie, drizzle the chocolate syrup over the top, and garnish with nondairy whipped topping and a maraschino cherry. This is a Brownie Express!

Per Serving: Calories: 401 Cholesterol: 28mg Dietary Fiber: 2g Protein: 2g
Sodium: 176mg Carbohydrate: 69g Total Fat: 14g Saturated Fat: 7g
Calories from Fat: 30%, Calories from Carbohydrates: 68%, Calories from Protein: 2%

Special Drinks

Any milk drinks, or mixtures using milk, are always the most logical to drop from your list if you have Lactose Intolerance. It is so hard to pass an ice cream shop and not remember the thick, foamy milk shakes of days gone by. Well, now you can hurry by that shop and get home to toss your homemade lactose-free ice cream into the blender, drown it with 100% lactose-free 2% lowfat milk, press that button, and watch your dreams swirl into reality!

It's important to use fresh ingredients whenever possible. I can't stress that enough. Fresh, ripe fruits bring out a strong flavor that can't be imitated. Enjoy your choices ... these recipes are just the beginning!

A Cool Peach Drink

*F*resh peaches, full of flavor and taste, are wonderful in this drink. For a special touch, add a shot of peach schnapps when adding the lactose-free ice cream.

Makes 2 servings
Preparation time: 20 minutes

1 cup (about 1 to 2 peaches) fresh peaches, peeled and chopped
1/8 teaspoon almond extract
Dash salt
1 cup 100% lactose-free 2% lowfat milk
1 cup Rich Vanilla Lactose-Free Ice Cream (page 306)

After peeling and chopping the peaches (save a few pieces for garnish), measure them and place in a blender. Add the almond extract, salt, and lactose-free milk, press LIQUEFY, and blend until smooth. Scoop the lactose-free ice cream into the blender and process on GRATE for one cycle. Pour into chilled serving glasses and serve immediately.

Per serving: Calories: 396 Cholesterol: 66g Dietary Fiber: 2g Protein: 7g
Sodium: 155mg Carbohydrate: 42g Total Fat: 23g Saturated Fat: 17g
Calories from Fat: 51%, Calories from Carbohydrates: 42%, Calories from Protein: 7%

Eggnog

*A*s long as you use this recipe, you can enjoy that "ole holiday cheer" and no one will notice the lactose is missing.

Makes 10 servings
Preparation time: 20 minutes
Chill time: 8 hours

6 large eggs, slightly beaten
2 cups 100% lactose-free 2% lowfat milk
1/3 cup sugar
2 tablespoons light rum
2 tablespoons bourbon
1 teaspoon vanilla extract
1 cup whipping cream alternative, Pastry Pride
2 tablespoons sugar
Nondairy whipped topping, for garnish
Ground nutmeg, for garnish

Blend the eggs, lactose-free milk, and the 1/3 cup sugar in a large saucepan over medium heat. Continue stirring until the mixture is thick enough that it coats the back of a metal spoon. Immediately remove from the heat, and place the pan in a bowl of ice water to cool the mixture down, while continuing to stir another 2 minutes. Add the rum, bourbon, and vanilla, pour into a container, and refrigerate for 8 hours. (You can chill it overnight.)

When ready to serve, whip the whipping cream alternative and the 2 tablespoons sugar until soft peaks form. Place the chilled egg mixture into a chilled punchbowl and fold in the whipping cream mixture. As you serve each portion, top it with nondairy ready-to-use whipped topping and sprinkle with nutmeg. Serve at once.

Per Serving: Calories: 204 Cholesterol: 132mg Dietary Fiber: 0g Protein: 5g
Sodium: 87mg Carbohydrate: 17g Total Fat: 11g Saturated Fat: 8g
Calories from Fat: 53%, Calories from Carbohydrates: 35%, Calories from Protein: 12%

Frozen Strawberry Champagne

No lactose to worry about in this festive drink. What an elegant way to top off a meal. You can substitute raspberries or blackberries for the strawberries.

Makes 8 servings
Preparation time: 25 minutes
Chill time: 1 hour

11/2 pints fresh, ripe strawberries (reserve several
    strawberries for garnish)
1/2 cup sugar
3 tablespoons water
1/2 teaspoon unflavored gelatin
1 cup champagne, cold
Mint sprigs, optional

Rinse, pat dry, and slice strawberries. Place them in a bowl with the sugar. Set aside.

In a small saucepan, place the water and sprinkle the gelatin in it. Allow to stand for about 1 minute before placing the saucepan over low heat. Cook, stirring until the gelatin dissolves completely. Remove from heat and set aside.

In a food processor with the knife blade attachment, place the strawberries, sugar, and any accumulated juice. Process the mixture until smooth, about 2 minutes. In a bowl pour the strawberries, gelatin mixture, and cold champagne, mixing well.

Using an electric ice cream maker, pour the entire mixture into the cylinder. Follow the manufacturer's instructions, but allow the strawberry mixture to freeze about 1 hour in the cylinder.

Spoon the finished drink into stemware, garnish with a whole strawberry and mint sprigs, if desired. Serve immediately.

Elegant, refreshing, and very easy to make!

Per Serving: Calories: 90 Cholesterol: 0mg Dietary Fiber: 1g Protein: .4g
Sodium: 1mg Carbohydrate: 17g Total Fat: .2g Saturated Fat: 0g
Calories from Fat: 3%, Calories from Carbohydrates: 95%, Calories from Protein: 2%

Brandy Alexander

A *few minor adjustments and a frosty favorite can perk up your
night. The bar can be lactose free without a hint to your guests!*

Makes 8 servings
Preparation time: 10 minutes

2 ounces brandy
1/4 cup chocolate syrup, Hershey's
1/4 cup whipping cream alternative, Pastry Pride
1 quart Rich Vanilla Lactose-Free Ice Cream (page 306)

Prechill the glasses. Place all ingredients into a blender. On
the highest speed, blend until mixture is smooth.
Pour into chilled glasses and serve.

*For a special touch, top each glass with a dab of nondairy
whipped topping and shaved dark chocolate.*

Per Serving: Calories: 358 Cholesterol: 56mg Dietary Fiber: 0g Protein: 3g
Sodium: 109mg Carbohydrate: 33g Total Fat: 22g Saturated Fat: 18g
Calories from Fat: 58%, Calories from Carbohydrates: 39%, Calories from Protein: 3%

Strawberry Smoothie

Most versions of this very popular drink contain lactose. With this recipe you can make one to enjoy without suffering later. For variety, try substituting fresh blueberries, raspberries, or blackberries . . . or mix your berries.

Makes 2 servings
Preparation time: 10 minutes

1 cup crushed ice
1 tablespoon sugar
1 teaspoon lemon juice
3/4 cup fresh strawberries
1 cup 100% lactose-free 2% lowfat milk

Use a blender and place all the ingredients into it, in the order shown. Cover and press LIQUEFY. Process until smooth. Pour into chilled glasses and serve.

Per Serving: Calories: 107 Cholesterol: 10mg Dietary Fiber: 1g Protein: 4g
Sodium: 67mg Carbohydrate: 16g Total Fat: 3g Saturated Fat: 2g
Calories from Fat: 23%, Calories from Carbohydrates: 61%, Calories from Protein: 16%

The Float

Who can resist a "lactose-free float"? Choose your favorite soda, scoop that homemade lactose-free ice cream in it, and ENJOY!

Makes 1 serving
Preparation time: 5 minutes

6 ounces root beer (or soda of choice), chilled
2 scoops Rich Vanilla Lactose-Free Ice Cream (page 306)

Into a large chilled glass, pour the root beer. Top the soda with two generous scoops of the lactose-free ice cream. Serve immediately.

Per Serving: Calories: 364 Cholesterol: 56mg Dietary Fiber: 0g Protein: 3g
Sodium: 114mg Carbohydrate: 44g Total Fat: 20g Saturated Fat: 16g
Calories from Fat: 49%, Calories from Carbohydrates: 48%, Calories from Protein: 3%

The Ultimate Milk Shake

The best memory I have since I began experimenting with lactose-free recipes is of my husband's face as he was sipping away on a large, cold, chocolate milk shake after having avoided them for over seven years! There isn't any reason why you can't enjoy a milk shake. Always keep homemade lactose-free ice cream in your freezer, and this dessert is just waiting for you.

Makes 3 servings
Preparation time: 10 minutes

1 cup 100% lactose-free 2% lowfat milk, cold
1 pint Rich Vanilla Lactose-Free Ice Cream (page 306)

At high speed in a covered blender, place the lactose-free milk and homemade lactose-free ice cream. Blend until smooth. Pour into large chilled glasses and serve.

CHOCOLATE MILK SHAKE: Add 3 tablespoons chocolate syrup (Hershey's) to the above ingredients before blending.

BANANA MILK SHAKE: Add 1 large ripe banana to the above ingredients before blending.

STRAWBERRY MILK SHAKE: Add 1/2 to 1 pint fresh, ripe, sliced strawberries to the above ingredients before blending.

A wonderful treat, lactose free!

Per Serving: Calories: 436 Cholesterol: 81mg Dietary Fiber: 0g Protein: 6g
Sodium: 164mg Carbohydrate: 39g Total Fat: 28g Saturated Fat: 22g
Calories from Fat: 58%, Calories from Carbohydrates: 36%, Calories from Protein: 6%

Sauces and Frostings

Sauces and frostings are important additions to many dishes. Unfortunately, Lactose-Intolerant people usually have to eliminate them from their diet. Well, whether it's a creamy sauce for vegetables or a delicious dessert sauce or frosting . . . you aren't limited anymore. Try some of these recipes and expand them with your own creations.

Confection Sugar Glaze

Here's a simple sugar glaze to brighten any dessert or baked goodie. The use of 100% lactose-free 2% lowfat milk instead of water makes the glaze whiter and thicker.

Makes about 1/2 cup
Preparation time: 15 minutes

1/2 cup confectioners' sugar, packed
1/4 teaspoon vanilla extract
2 teaspoons 100% lactose-free 2% lowfat milk

Combine all the ingredients in a small mixing bowl. Stir rapidly with a large wooden spoon until smooth and free-flowing (you can add a little more lactose-free milk if needed).

Let the glaze stand for a few minutes to ensure set. (If it is too watery, allow it to stand a few minutes; it should firm up.) Drizzle over pies, cookies, cakes, etc., in desired pattern.

Decorates cakes, pies, cookies, breads—anything!

Per Tablespoon: Calories: 240 Cholesterol: 1mg Dietary Fiber: 0g Protein: .3g
Sodium: 6mg Carbohydrate: 60g Total Fat: .3g Saturated Fat: .1g
Calories from Fat: 1%, Calories from Carbohydrates: 99%, Calories from Protein: 0%

Fresh Strawberry Cream

This strawberry cream can be used to frost a chiffon or angel food cake, or as a delicious dip for fresh fruit.

Makes 32 servings
Preparation time: 15 minutes
Chill time: 1 hour

1 cup fresh, ripe strawberries
1 pint whipping cream alternative, Pastry Pride
1/4 cup sugar

Place a mixing bowl in the refrigerator and chill for at least an hour prior to using. Rinse and dry the strawberries. Crush, and place in the refrigerator to chill.

Remove the mixing bowl from the refrigerator and place the whipping cream alternative into it. With the whip attachment on a standing mixer, beat the cream on medium-high speed until it starts to become firm. While the mixer is beating, pour in the sugar, beating until very firm. Remove from the mixer and fold in the crushed strawberries.

Per Serving: Calories: 60 Cholesterol: 0mg Dietary Fiber: .1g Protein: 0g
Sodium: 15mg Carbohydrate: 5g Total Fat: 5g Saturated Fat: 4g
Calories from Fat: 67%, Calories from Carbohydrates: 33%, Calories from Protein: 0%

Ginger Cream

*F*inding the proper whipping cream alternative opens up all kinds of possibilities for you. Once you have conquered this problem, everything you use whip cream for can be at your fingertips. Just find the one that works for you and store extra containers in the freezer so you always have them on hand.

Makes 16 servings
Preparation time: 10 minutes
Chill time: 30 minutes

1/2 teaspoon vanilla extract
1/4 teaspoon freshly ground ginger
2 tablespoons confectioners' sugar
1 cup whipping cream alternative, Pastry Pride,
 very cold

First, place a medium mixing bowl in the refrigerator to chill for about 30 minutes.

Place all ingredients into the chilled mixing bowl and whip with an electric mixer until soft peaks develop. Serve. As with the other "creams," you can make this about 3 hours ahead, cover, and refrigerate until ready to use.

A great topping for pie, gingerbread, or fresh fruit.

Per Serving: Calories: 56 Cholesterol: 0mg Dietary Fiber: 0g Protein: 0g
Sodium: 15mg Carbohydrate: 4g Total Fat: 5g Saturated Fat: 4g
Calories from Fat: 72%, Calories from Carbohydrates: 28%, Calories from Protein: 0%

Homemade Chocolate Sauce

*F*or that chocolate craving, this thick, rich sauce meets the challenge! You can store any unused sauce in a covered container in the refrigerator until you're ready to use it. Just place the desired amount in the microwave and warm before serving.

Makes 16 servings
Preparation time: 15 minutes

**6 ounces semisweet chocolate chips, lactose free
  (see page 28)
1/2 cup light corn syrup
1/4 cup whipping cream alternative, Pastry Pride
1 tablespoon safflower oil margarine, Hollywood
1 teaspoon vanilla extract**

In a saucepan over low heat, melt the chocolate chips with the corn syrup. Stir constantly, blending well. Remove from the heat and stir in the whipping cream alternative, safflower margarine, and vanilla, blending completely. Serve the sauce warm.

Pour over homemade lactose-free ice cream, pound cake, cream puffs—any dessert!

Per Serving: Calories: 99 Cholesterol: 0mg Dietary Fiber: .6g Protein: .5g
Sodium: 25mg Carbohydrate: 15g Total Fat: 5g Saturated Fat: 3g
Calories from Fat: 42%, Calories from Carbohydrates: 56%, Calories from Protein: 2%

Chocolate Amaretto Sauce

Poured over lactose-free ice cream, angel food cake, or Pound Cake (page 207), this sauce spells heaven for the chocolate lover. It's a fun way to dress up the simplest dessert or fruit.

Makes 2¼ cups
Preparation time: 15 minutes

4 ounces bittersweet chocolate, chopped
1¼ cup whipping cream alternative, Pastry Pride
⅓ cup sugar
2 tablespoons safflower oil margarine, Hollywood
4 tablespoons amaretto liqueur

Place the chocolate, whipping cream alternative, sugar, and safflower margarine in a small saucepan over low heat. Constantly stir, blending until smooth and thick. Be careful not to burn the chocolate.

Remove from the heat and slowly stir in the amaretto. Serve while it is warm. You can reheat the sauce in the microwave, on a warming temperature, for 45 seconds.

Per Tablespoon: Calories: 61 Cholesterol: 0mg Dietary Fiber: 0g Protein: .1g
Sodium: 15mg Carbohydrate: 6g Total Fat: 4g Saturated Fat: 3g
Calories from Fat: 60%, Calories from Carbohydrates: 39%, Calories from Protein: 1%

Homemade Fresh Lemon Curd

Never use bottled lemon juice with this recipe. Only fresh lemons give it its strong, wonderful taste. Lemon curd is perfect served with

Lemon Cream Cake (page 203); place it on the side for dipping. You can also use this to fill a layer cake, cream puffs, or tarts.

Makes 20 servings
Preparation time: 30 minutes

10 large egg yolks
3/4 cup sugar
3/4 cup fresh lemon juice
1/2 cup safflower oil margarine, Hollywood

In a double boiler, bring the water to a simmer over medium heat. Whisk the egg yolks in the top portion of the double boiler, off the heat. Add the sugar by sprinkling it a little at a time, blending completely before adding more. Add the fresh lemon juice all at once.

Place the top pan over the bottom filled with simmering water. Stir the mixture constantly, cooking about 6 to 8 minutes. Do not allow the mixture to boil or burn. The mixture will become thick enough to coat a metal spoon.

Remove the mixture from the heat and, using a whisk, blend in the safflower margarine a little at a time until completely blended.

Cool, and when mixture is set (thick, creamy, and bright yellow), it is ready to use. You can store it in an airtight container in the refrigerator after it has cooled completely.

A perfect filling for cakes, cream puffs, or to serve on the side with cake.

Per Serving: Calories: 101 Cholesterol: 106mg Dietary Fiber: 0g Protein: 1g
Sodium: 50mg Carbohydrate: 8g Total Fat: 7g Saturated Fat: 2g
Calories from Fat: 63%, Calories from Carbohydrates: 32%, Calories from Protein: 5%

Lactose-Free Crème Fraîche Sauce

Using the proper substitutions, nothing is impossible. Even crème fraîche! This sauce adds a finishing touch to so many desserts. Its sweet, rich flavor accents the simplest food.

Makes 4 servings
Preparation time: 15 minutes
Chill time: at least 8 hours

2 tablespoons confectioners' sugar
1/3 cup sour cream alternative, Tofutti
1/3 cup whipping cream alternative, Pastry Pride, cold

Into a medium bowl, place all ingredients. With an electric mixer blend on low until smooth. Cover the sauce and refrigerate for a minimum of 8 hours. (Make it the night before and keep refrigerated until ready to use.)

Serve crème fraîche sauce over fresh fruit or Pound Cake (page 207).

Per Serving: Calories: 88 Cholesterol: 0mg Dietary Fiber: 0g Protein: .1g
Sodium: 27mg Carbohydrate: 8g Total Fat: 6g Saturated Fat: 5g
Calories from Fat: 64%, Calories from Carbohydrates: 36%, Calories from Protein: 0%

Old-Time Butterscotch Sauce

*U*sing alternatives lets you enjoy butterscotch flavor again. This sauce has a rich, old-fashioned "buttery" flavor.

Makes about 32 servings
Preparation time: 15 minutes

1/2 **cup safflower oil margarine, Hollywood**
1 **cup brown sugar, firmly packed**
3 **tablespoons light corn syrup**
1/2 **cup whipping cream alternative, Pastry Pride**

In a small heavy-gauge saucepan, melt the safflower margarine over medium-low heat. Stir in the brown sugar, corn syrup, and whipping cream alternative. Blend completely. Bring the mixture to a boil, and remove from the heat. Cool and serve.

Pour over homemade ice cream or cakes.

Per Serving: Calories: 61 Cholesterol: 0mg Dietary Fiber: 0g Protein: 0g
Sodium: 37mg Carbohydrate: 7g Total Fat: 4g Saturated Fat: 1g
Calories from Fat: 58%, Calories from Carbohydrates: 42%, Calories from Protein: 0%

Lactose-Free Cream Cheese Frosting

Craving those cream cheesy–topped cakes? This frosting brings back great memories and great taste.

Makes frosting for a three-layer 8-inch cake
Preparation time: 15 minutes

8 ounces cream cheese alternative, Tofutti
1/2 cup safflower oil margarine, Hollywood
16 ounces confectioners' sugar, sifted
1 teaspoon vanilla extract

In a large mixing bowl, beat with an electric mixer the cream cheese alternative and safflower margarine until creamy. On low speed, slowly add the confectioners' sugar. Once all the confectioners' sugar has been added, whip the mixture on high speed until light and fluffy. Blend in the vanilla.

Per Serving: Calories: 321 Cholesterol: 0mg Dietary Fiber: 0g Protein: .8g
Sodium: 201mg Carbohydrate: 46g Total Fat: 16g Saturated Fat: 3g
Calories from Fat: 44%, Calories from Carbohydrates: 55%, Calories from Protein: 1%

(**Note:** Nutritional values are based on per slice of cake.)

Creamy Fudge Frosting

A rich lactose-free frosting with a creamy texture can't be achieved without the substitution of lactose-free sour cream and whipping cream alternative. You can use this frosting to top any kind of cake, to create a special finale to a meal.

Frosts an 8-inch layer cake
Preparation time: 30 minutes

1/4 cup safflower oil margarine, Hollywood
1/4 cup whipping cream alternative, Pastry Pride
10 ounces bittersweet chocolate (see page 28), coarsely
    chopped
3/4 cup sour cream alternative, Tofutti
1 cup confectioners' sugar

Using a medium saucepan, over low heat, melt the safflower margarine with the whipping cream alternative. Stir to blend the margarine completely into the cream. Place all the chocolate into the saucepan, which remains over low heat. With a whisk, blend the chocolate into the mixture until it is smooth. This should take about 2 minutes; then remove the pan from the heat and allow it to cool for about 8 minutes.

Into the warm chocolate, whisk the sour cream alternative until completely blended and smooth. Slowly add the powdered sugar, a little at a time, whisking after each addition. Once all the sugar is added and blended, allow the mixture to set up, about 10 minutes. This will thicken it to frosting consistency. (Should your frosting stiffen too much, simply return it to low heat briefly, blending with a whisk.)

Decorate the cake with the frosting, using a damp knife or spatula to swirl it on.

Per Serving: Calories: 176 Cholesterol: 0mg Dietary Fiber: 1g Protein: 1g
Sodium: 44mg Carbohydrate: 22g Total Fat: 11g Saturated Fat: 5g
Calories from Fat: 51%, Calories from Carbohydrates: 47%, Calories from Protein: 2%

(**Note:** Nutritional values are based on per slice of cake.)

Orange Buttercream Frosting

This is the best orange frosting there is—creamy, rich, and orangey.

Makes enough to frost a layer cake, 24 cupcakes,
or a 9 × 13-inch cake
Preparation time: 15 minutes

16 ounces confectioners' sugar
6 tablespoons safflower oil margarine, Hollywood
2 large egg yolks, slightly beaten
2 tablespoons 100% lactose-free 2% lowfat milk
1 1/2 teaspoons vanilla extract
1 teaspoon grated orange zest
1/8 teaspoon salt

With an electric mixer, beat all the ingredients in a large mixing bowl. Beat until very smooth (add additional lactose-free milk if necessary), making a good spreading consistency.

Wonderful spread on an orange or white cake.

Per Serving: Calories: 209 Cholesterol: 36mg Dietary Fiber: 0g Protein: .5g
Sodium: 83mg Carbohydrate: 38g Total Fat: 7g Saturated Fat: 1g
Calories from Fat: 29%, Calories from Carbohydrates: 70%, Calories from Protein: 1%

(**Note:** Nutritional values are based on per slice of cake or per cupcake.)

Praline Cream

*T*he *whipping cream alternative gives this treat the creamy texture you need. The praline flavor is great. You can adjust the amount of flavoring according to your preference.*

Makes 8 servings
Preparation time: 15 minutes

1/2 cup whipping cream alternative, Pastry Pride, cold
1 tablespoon praline flavoring (I use gourmet praline
  flavoring available in specialty cook stores, but praline
  liqueur is good, too)
2 tablespoons confectioners' sugar

In a medium bowl, combine the whipping cream alternative and praline flavoring. Beat until foamy, then add the sugar, continuing to beat until soft peaks form. Serve immediately or cover and refrigerate.

A sweet treat for pound cake or angel food cake.

Per Serving: Calories: 60 Cholesterol: 0mg Dietary Fiber: 0g Protein: 0g
Sodium: 15mg Carbohydrate: 5g Total Fat: 5g Saturated Fat: 4g
Calories from Fat: 67%, Calories from Carbohydrates: 33%, Calories from Protein: 0%

Lactose-Free Pumpkin Whipped Cream

This simple, flavored whipping cream alternative turns everything into something "special."

Makes 24 servings
Preparation time: 15 minutes

1 cup whipping cream alternative, Pastry Pride, cold
3 tablespoons sugar
1/2 cup canned pumpkin
Dash ground cinnamon

In a chilled mixing bowl, beat the whipping cream alternative with the sugar. When stiff peaks form, fold in the pumpkin. Serve immediately, dusted with cinnamon.

Spice up a pumpkin pie, pound cake, or a holiday bread.

Per Serving: Calories: 42 Cholesterol: 0mg Dietary Fiber: 0g Protein: 0g
Sodium: 10mg Carbohydrate: 3.7g Total Fat: 3g Saturated Fat: 3g
Calories from Fat: 64%, Calories from Carbohydrates: 36%, Calories from Protein: 0%

Rum Sauce

*T*his wonderful sauce turns any plain dessert into a gourmet sensation.

Makes 12 servings
Preparation time: 15 minutes

1/8 teaspoon salt
2 tablespoons safflower oil margarine, Hollywood
1/3 cup light corn syrup
1/4 cup light brown sugar, firmly packed
1/3 cup water
1/2 teaspoon rum extract

In a saucepan over medium heat, cook the salt, safflower margarine, corn syrup, brown sugar, and water. Stir constantly until the sugar is completely dissolved. Reduce the heat to low, and continue to cook without stirring until the temperature on a candy thermometer reaches 230° F. Remove from the heat. Once the mixture cools slightly, stir in the rum extract, and serve immediately over ice cream or pound cake.

Per Serving: Calories: 54 Cholesterol: 0mg Dietary Fiber: 0g Protein: 0g
Sodium: 54mg Carbohydrate: 10g Total Fat: 2g Saturated Fat: .3g
Calories from Fat: 31%, Calories from Carbohydrates: 69%, Calories from Protein: 0%

Vanilla Cream Filling

*Y*ou can use this filling to stuff éclairs (page 242), cream puffs, a layer cake, or a cream pie.

Makes 24 servings
Preparation time: 20 minutes
Chill time: 2 to 3 hours

1¼ cups 100% lactose-free 2% lowfat milk
½ cup sugar
5 teaspoons cornstarch
⅛ teaspoon salt
1 large egg, slightly beaten
1 teaspoon vanilla extract

In a saucepan combine everything except the vanilla. With a wire whisk, blend the ingredients together. Place the saucepan over medium heat and bring to a boil while stirring constantly. After reaching a boil, cook for 1 more minute. Mixture should be thickening. Stir in the vanilla. Remove from the saucepan, place in a covered bowl, and put in the refrigerator. Chill for 2 to 3 hours until set and thick.

Per Serving: Calories: 28 Cholesterol: 10mg Dietary Fiber: 0g Protein: .7g
Sodium: 20mg Carbohydrate: 5g Total Fat: .5g Saturated Fat: .2g
Calories from Fat: 15%, Calories from Carbohydrates: 75%, Calories from Protein: 10%

Whipped Rum Cream

*T*his *is a simple, tasty cream topping. Make sure you choose a whipping cream alternative with the right consistency . . . it should be whip-able.*

Makes 32 servings
Preparation time: 10 minutes

2 tablespoons dark rum
2 cups whipping cream alternative, Pastry Pride, cold
1/4 cup confectioners' sugar

Prior to preparing the cream, place a mixing bowl into the refrigerator to chill. Then remove the bowl and place all ingredients into it. Whip on high speed with an electric mixer until soft peaks develop. This recipe can be made up to 3 hours ahead and kept covered in the refrigerator.

Add a dollop to pumpkin pie, mince pie,
even a cup of hot tea . . . it's wonderful!

Per Serving: Calories: 58 Cholesterol: 0mg Dietary Fiber: 0g Protein: 0g
Sodium: 15mg Carbohydrate: 4g Total Fat: 5g Saturated Fat: 4g
Calories from Fat: 72%, Calories from Carbohydrates: 28%, Calories from Protein: 0%

Cheese Sauce

This basic sauce can be used for a variety of dishes. It's good over vegetables such as broccoli, asparagus, cauliflower, or simply over noodles. Try it using other cheese alternatives.

Makes 12 servings
Preparation time: 15 minutes

1 tablespoon safflower oil margarine, Hollywood
1 tablespoon all-purpose flour
Dash freshly ground pepper
3/4 cup 100% lactose-free 2% lowfat milk
3/4 cup shredded cheddar cheese alternative, TofuRella

Over low heat in a small saucepan, melt the safflower margarine. Add the flour and pepper, stirring constantly. Continue stirring while adding the lactose-free milk. Cook the mixture until thick and bubbly. Avoid prolonged cooking; curdling could happen. If lumps form, use a whisk to break them up. Once the sauce is thickened, continue cooking for 1 more minute, then add the cheese alternative. Stir until the cheese is completely melted. Remove from the heat and serve.

Per Serving: Calories: 55 Cholesterol: 1mg Dietary Fiber: 0g Protein: 3g
Sodium: 163mg Carbohydrate: 2g Total Fat: 4g Saturated Fat: .6g
Calories from Fat: 62%, Calories from Carbohydrates: 16%, Calories from Protein: 22%

The Basic Cheese Fondue

*Y*ou won't be missing anything but discomfort as you dip into this rich, cheesy fondue. This is a lactose-free treat that will go unde-tected by everyone.

Makes 4 servings
Preparation time: 10 minutes

2/3 cup dry white wine
2 cups shredded cheddar cheese alternative, TofuRella
1/8 teaspoon dry mustard
3 ounces cream cheese alternative, Tofutti
Assortment of fruit or vegetable wedges, or lactose-free
   French bread (see page 25)

Using a medium saucepan over low heat, warm the wine until bubbly. Into the wine stir the cheddar cheese alternative and mustard. Continue to stir until the mixture is blended and returns to bubbly. Finally, add the cream cheese alternative, blending until smooth.

Once the mixture is well blended, pour into the fondue pot and serve with fruit, veggies, or rounds of French bread.

You can change the cheddar cheese to a Swiss alternative for a zippy difference.

Per Serving: Calories: 36 Cholesterol: 0mg Dietary Fiber: 0g Protein: 2g
Sodium: 121mg Carbohydrate: .9g Total Fat: 3g Saturated Fat: .3g
Calories from Fat: 66%, Calories from Carbohydrates: 10%, Calories from Protein: 24%

Creamy Buttermilk Dressing

You can find salad dressings that do not have lactose, but they usually are a vinegar- or oil-based dressing. This "creamy" dressing lets you enjoy more variety without the consequences.

Makes 8 servings
Preparation time: 15 minutes
Chill time: 15 to 20 minutes

1 1/2 teaspoons vinegar
1/2 cup 100% lactose-free 2% lowfat milk, approximately
1 cup mayonnaise, Best Foods or (Hellmann's)
1 tablespoon grated Parmesan cheese alternative, Soyco
1 tablespoon fresh chopped parsley
1/2 teaspoon celery salt
1/8 teaspoon seasoned pepper
1/4 teaspoon onion powder
1/4 teaspoon garlic powder

Place the vinegar in a glass measuring cup. Add enough of the lactose-free milk to measure 1/2 cup. Let stand a few minutes. This is your substitute for buttermilk.

Combine the vinegar-milk mixture with the remaining ingredients in a large bowl. Whisk or blend with a hand blender until smooth. Place in a covered container and put in the refrigerator to chill. You can store it, refrigerated, up to 2 weeks.

If the consistency is too thick, you can add 1 to 2 tablespoons lactose-free milk.

Makes great dip for fresh veggies.

Per Serving: Calories: 213 Cholesterol: 11mg Dietary Fiber: .1g Protein: 1g
Sodium: 304mg Carbohydrate: 1g Total Fat: 22g Saturated Fat: 3g
Calories from Fat: 96%, Calories from Carbohydrates: 2%, Calories from Protein: 2%

Caesar Salad Dressing

*S*alad dressings and dips without lactose are hard to find. You can enjoy this creamy, cheese dressing along with everyone else. The ingredients will be our secret.

Makes 1¼ cups
Preparation time: 10 minutes
Chill time: 20 minutes

3 tablespoons 100% lactose-free 2% lowfat milk
2 tablespoons cider vinegar
1 cup mayonnaise, Hellmann's (or Best Foods, west of the
  Rockies)
2 tablespoons grated Parmesan cheese alternative, Soyco
1 garlic clove, finely chopped
1/2 teaspoon sugar

Place all ingredients into a mixing bowl. Whisk together until well blended and smooth.

Cover the bowl and place in the refrigerator to chill.

Per Tablespoon: Calories: 84 Cholesterol: 4mg Dietary Fiber: 0g Protein: .4g
Sodium: 85mg Carbohydrate: 4g Total Fat: 9g Saturated Fat: 1g
Calories from Fat: 96%, Calories from Carbohydrates: 2%, Calories from Protein: 2%

White Sauce

Even most simple white sauces have become taboo for Lactose-Intolerant people. This recipe makes a rich, creamy sauce that's perfect for all your needs.

Makes 12 servings
Preparation time: 15 minutes

1 tablespoon safflower oil margarine, Hollywood
1 tablespoon all-purpose flour
1/8 teaspoon salt
Dash freshly ground pepper
3/4 cup 100% lactose-free 2% lowfat milk

Using a small saucepan, melt the safflower margarine. Slowly add the flour, salt, and pepper, stirring constantly. While stirring, add the lactose-free milk and cook over medium heat until the mixture becomes thick and bubbly. Continue to stir the mixture an additional minute. Remove from the heat and serve.

Per Serving: Calories: 14 Cholesterol: 1mg Dietary Fiber: 0g Protein: .4g
Sodium: 30mg Carbohydrate: .9g Total Fat: 1g Saturated Fat: .3g
Calories from Fat: 62%, Calories from Carbohydrates: 26%, Calories from Protein: 12%

General Index

A

Accent, 3, 117
Acidophilus Milk, 16, 16n
Almond butter, 30
Alternative Butters, 13–14
Alternative Cheeses, 8, 17–18
Alternative Chocolates, 28
Alternative Cottage Cheeses, 19–20
Alternative Creams, 14
Alternative Frozen Desserts, 20–21
Alternative Milks, 15–17
Alternative Sour Cream and Cream Cheeses, 18–19
Alternative Whipped Toppings, 14
Ambrosia Chocolate Chips, 28
Angel Food Cake, packaged, 27
Anticaking agent, 10
Appetizers, quickie, 31
Appetizers and Crackers, "safe" list, 23–24
Apple butter, 30
Armour products, 26
Aunt Jemima Pancake & Waffle Mixes, 24

B

Baker's Baking Chocolate Squares, 28
Ball Park Hot Dogs, 26
Banquet Beef Pot Pie, 26

Barbecue sauces, 27
Barilla Marinara, Tomato & Basil Sauces, 26
Baskin-Robbins Sorbets and Ices, 20, 28
Best Foods Fat Free French, Ranch, and
    Thousand Island dressings, 30
Betty Crocker "Golden" Pound Cake Mix, 28
Beverages, "safe" list, 29–30
Bisquick Baking Mix, 24
Blue Bonnet Diet Margarine, 13
Bohemian Hearth Breads, 25
Bon Appetit, 3
Brand Name Products, lactose-free
    "safe" list, 23–30
Bread machine, 65
Breads, Brand-Name "safe" list, 25
Breakfast foods, "safe" list, 24
Butter, 9
Butter alternatives, 30
Butterball turkeys, 26
Buttermilk, 17

C

Cakes, "safe" list, 27–28
Campbell's soups
    Golden Mushroom, 24, 121
    Manhattan Clam Chowder, 24
    New England Clam Chowder, 24
    Vegetable, 24
Canned foods, "safe" list, 25, 27

Carnation
    Coffee-mate Non-Dairy Creamer, 15
    Instant Breakfast, 24
    Sandwich spreads, 25
Carper, Steve, 6, 10
Casein, 9
Casseroles, frozen or packaged, 27
Cereals, Brand-Name "safe" list, 24
Cheddar, aged, 18
Cheese alternatives, 8, 17–18
Cheesecake, 8
Chinese Egg Rolls, 23
Chocolate substitutions, 28
Chun King products, 25–26
Cinnamon Teddy Grahams, 28
Clam sauce, 27
Cocoa, hot mixes, 29
Coconut milk, 29–30
Coffee-Rich Non-Dairy Creamer, 15
Coffees, "International," 29
Colosso Cake Ice Cream Cones, 29
Contraceptives, Oral, 10
Cookies, "safe" list, 28
Cool Whip, 14
Cottage cheese substitutions, 19–20
Cream, 9, 14
Cream cheese, 18–19
Cream Soda, 29
Creamy desserts, "safe" list, 29
Creme de Cacao, 29
Creme de Menthe, 29
Curds, 9, 17

D

Dairy Ease, 21
"Dairy free" label, 12
Dairy-free food, 3
Del Pastore fresh mozzarella, 42
Demulen, G. D. Searle, 10
Dessert alternatives, 20–21
DiCarlo Breads, 25
Diet Imperial Margarine, 13
Dole Fruit Sorbets, 20, 28
Drink mixes, frozen, 29
Dromedary Pound Cake, 28
Droste Cocoa, 28
Dry milk, 9
Duncan Hines
    Dark Chocolate Frosting, 28
    Mixes, 27

E

Eden Foods Soymilks, 16
EdenSoy Organic Soy Beverages, 15

F

Fermentation, 16, 16n
Fleischmann's
    Lower Fat Margarine (tub), 14
    Sweet Unsalted Margarine, 14
Foods
    caution with, 3, 10
    labeling of, 11–12, 21
Francisco Turkey Gravy, 26
French Connection bread, 37, 38
    See also Recipe Index
Frozen desserts, "safe" list, 28–29
Fruit
    butters, 30
    fresh, 325
    juices, 29
Fruit Bars, frozen, 29
Frying, with alternative butters, 14

G

Galaxy Lactose-Free cottage cheeses, 20
Geritol, 10
Ghirardelli
    chocolate products, 27–28
    cocoas, 29
Gravies, "safe" list, 27

H

Haagen-Dazs Sorbets, 20, 29
Hams, packaged, 30
Hawaiian Punch, 29
Health food stores, 7, 16, 30
Healthy Choice Chili Beef Soup, 24
Hershey's Reduced Fat Baking Chips, Cocoa
    for Baking, Dark Chocolate Bar, 28
Heublein Frozen Drink Mixes, 29
Hidden Valley Honey Bacon, Red Wine, and
    Herb dressings, 30
Hollywood Safflower Oil Margarine, 13

Honey Maid
  Graham Cracker Crumbs, 25
  Graham Crackers, 28
Hormel canned foods, 25
Horseradish, 27
Hot dogs, "safe" list, 26
Hungry Jack Pancake Mixes, 24
Hunt's Tomato Sauce, 26
Hydrox
  chocolate cookies, 12, 212
  Vienna Fingers, 28

I

Ice Bean, 20
Ice cream, 1, 3, 5
  alternatives, 14, 20
  See also Recipe Index

J

Jell-O
  Gelatin Pops, 20, 29
  Puddings, Gelatin, 29
JerseyMaid Lactose-Free and Reduced Milks,
    15, 16
Jiffy
  Baking Mix, 24
  Cornbread Mix, 25

K

Keebler
  Graham Crackers, 28
  Pecan and Almond Sandies, 28
  Town House Oval Crackers, 24
Kefir, 16
Kellogg's
  Corn Flake Crumbs, 25
  Pop Tarts, 24
Ketchup, 27
Knudsen Dairies Lactose-Free and Reduced
    Milks, 15, 16
Kool-Aid, 29
Kosher
  cakes, cookies, pastries, 27
  foods, 12
  margarines, 14

  meats, cold cuts, hot dogs, 23, 26
Kraft Barbecue Sauces, 27
Kumiss, 16

L

La Choy products, 26
Labels, 11–12, 21
Lactaid, 21
  100 2% lowfat milk, 12, 15, 16
  100 Lactose-Free Milk, 15
Lactalbumin, 9
Lactase enzyme
  broken down to lactid acid, 16
  list of products, 21
  pills, 8–9, 21
Lacteeze Drops, 21
Lactid acid, 9, 16
Lactobacillus acidophilus bacteria, 16, 16*n,* 19
Lactoglobulin, 9
Lactose, 9
  used as "filler," 10, 65
  where found, 3, 6
Lactose intolerance, explained, 2–6
Lactose-Free cottage cheeses, 20
Lactose-Free cream cheese, 20
"Lactose-Free" label, 11–12
Lactose-Free substitutions, 13–23
Lactrase, 21
Lady Fingers, packaged, 27
Lawry's Salt, 3, 117
Lean Cuisine products, 26
Libby Corned Beef, 25
Ling Ling Chicken Potstickers, 23
Lipton Noodle Soups, 24

M

Main meals, quickie, 32
Malibu Pie Festival, 5, 216, 223, 225, 227,
    240
MaMa's Italian Ices, 28
Margarines, 13–14
Marquez Supreme Taquitos, 26
Marv-Parv, 13
Mayonnaise, 27
Mazola Sweet Unsalted Margarine, 13
Medicines, 3
Melba Toast, 25

Milk, 1–3
alternatives, 15–17
protein, solids, 9
Milk Is Not for Everyone (Carper), 6, 10
Minute Tapioca, 29
Mocha Mix, 20, 29
Non-Dairy Creamer, 15
"Mommy Specials," 322
Moore's Breaded Mushrooms, 23
Mother's
Cookies, 28
Soft Margarine, 13
Mozzarella, fresh, 18, 42
Mrs. T's Potato and Onion Filled Pierogies, 23
MSG (monosodium glutamate), 3, 117
Musso's Croutons, 25
Mustard, 27

N

Nabisco
Cracker Meal, 25
Graham Crackers, 28
Saltines, 23
"Nancy's" Lowfat Cottage Cheese, 19
Nature's Plus Say Yes to Dairy, 21
Nature's Way Lactase Enzyme, 21
Newman's Own Balsamic Vinaigrette, 30
"No added" label, 11
"Nondairy" label, 11
Nucoa Smart Beat Super Light Margarine, 13

O

Old Country French Bread, 25
Ore Ida Snackin' Fries, 26
Oreos, 12
Oysterette Soup Crackers, 23

P

Pareve, 12, 14
Parkay Light Margarine, 13
Parmesan cheese, imported and aged, 38, 156–57
Pasta sauces, "safe" list, 26–27
Pastries, "safe" list, 28

Pastry Pride Nondairy Whipped Topping, 14
Peanut butter, 30
Penguino's frozen desserts, 20
Pepperidge Farms
Cookies, 28
Rolls, Pastry Sheets and Puffs, 25, 27
Perx Frozen Non-Dairy milk substitute, 16
Pills, lactase enzyme, 8–9
list of products, 21
Pillsbury
Boil-in-Bag entrees, 25
Creamy Chocolate Fudge Frosting, 28
Mixes, 28
Pioneer Rolls, Breads, Croutons, 25
Potato'n Sesame Snack Thins, 23
Prego Tomato Sauces, 26
Prescription drugs, 3
Price Costco, 8
Progresso Chicken Pasta Soup, 24
Promise Ultra Margarine, 13
Purity Margarine, 13

Q

Quaker Instant Oatmeal, Puffed Rice, and Puffed Wheat, 24

R

Relishes, 27
Restaurants, 3
Rice Dream, 20
beverages, 15
Rice milks, 16
Rich's Richwhip, 14
Ritz Crackers, 23
Royal Vanilla, Chocolate Puddings, 29
Ry-Krisp, plain, 24

S

Salad dressings, Brand-Name, 30
Salads, packaged, 27
Salsas, 27
Sandwich spreads, "safe" list, 25
Schiff Natural Milk Digest-Aid, 21
Scoopy's Cake Ice Cream Cones, 29
Seasoned Salt, 3

Seasonings, 3
Semi-sweet chocolate substitutions, 28
Shake 'n' Bake, 25
Shedd's
    Spread Country Crock Margarine (tub), 13
    Willow Run soybean margarine, 13
Simplesse, 9
Smart N Final, 8, 14
SnackWell Chocolate Fudge Frosting, 28
Sociables Crackers, 23
Sodium caseinate, 9
Solait Beverage Powder, 16
Solgar Lactase, 21
Sorbet alternatives, 20
Soups, "safe" list, 24
Sour cream, 18–19
Sour milk, 16, 17
Soy milks, 16
Soy Moo by Health Valley, 16
Soy Sauce, 27
Soya Kaas
    Cheeses, 17
    Cream Cheese Style, 19
Soyamel, 16
Soyco cheeses, 20
Soymage cheese alternative, 17
Spectrum Naturals and Spread, 14
Squeeze Pro Nondairy Whipped Topping, 14
Stella D'Oro
    Breadsticks, 25
    Swiss Fudge, Anisette Sponge, Anginetti, Margherite Combinations, 28
Substitutions, 12
    "safe" list, 13–21
Sunbeam White Bread, 25
Supermarkets, 30
Swanson products, 26
Swiss cheese, aged, 18

T

Tang Breakfast Beverage, 29
Tartar sauce, 27
Time-saver recipes, 31–32
Tofu, 20

Tofulicious, 20
TofuRella Cheeses, 17, 36
Tofutti
    Better Than Cream Cheese, 19
    frozen desserts, 20
    Sour Supreme Better Than Sour Cream, 18
Tone's Poultry Gravy Mix, 27, 129
Top Hat Whipped Topping, 14
Treats, quickie, 32
Triscuit Whole Wheat Wafers, 23
Tuna, canned, 25, 27
Turkeys, prebasted, 30
Tuscan Tofu Bars, 20

V

Vanilla ice cream, 5
Vegetables, canned, 27
Veggie Cheese, 17
Vinegar, 17
Vitamite Non-Dairy Milk Substitute, 15
Vitasoy, 15

W

Weight Watchers light margarine, 13
Western Bagels, 25
WestSoy Organic Beverages, 15
Wheatsworth Stone Ground Wheat Crackers, 24
Whey, 9, 11, 17–18
Whipped topping alternatives, 14
White Wave alternative cheeses, 17
Worcestershire Sauce, 27

Y

Yogurt, 16

Z

Zesta Saltines, 23

Recipe Index

A

All-American Whipped Mashed Potatoes, 90–91
ALMOND
  Bar, Lactose-Free, 298
  Cookies, Special Occasion, 280–82
  Spritzer Cookies, 258–59
Amaretto Chocolate Sauce, 338
APPETIZERS, 35–43
  Garlic, Roasted on French Bread, 38–39
  Herb-Garlic Bread, 37–38
  Mushrooms, Stuffed, 42–43
  Parmesan Eggplant Slices, 40
  Potato Skins, Baked, 36–37
  Spinach Triangles, 41–42
APPLE
  Bread, 66
  Caramel Pound Cake, 197–98
  Crumb Pie, 225–27
  Pie, Award-Winning French, 227–28
  -Raisin Pork Chops, 144–45
Applesauce Cinnamon Coffee Cake, 200–201
Asparagus Pasta, Creamy, 177–78
Award-Winning French Apple Pie, 227–28

B

Baked Cheesy Egg Casseroles, 160
Baked Garlic Tomatoes, 91–92
Baked Macaroni and Cheese, 161–62
Baked Potato Skins, 36–37, 54–55
Baked Tomato-Zucchini Dish, 92–93
Baked Ziti, 174–75
BANANA
  Milk Shake, 332
  -Nut Bread, 67–68
Barbecued Baby Back Ribs, 46, 145
Basic Cheese Fondue, 351
Basic White Bread, 84–85
BEEF, 117–26
  Creamed Dried, 119
  Meat Loaf, Savory, 122–23
  Porterhouse Broiled Steaks, 120–21
  Stew, Easy, 121–22
  Stroganoff, 118
  Stuffed Pepper Cups, 123–24
  Ultimate Cheesesteak Sandwich, 168–69
  Veal Parmigiana, 125–26
Berry Vanilla Cheesecake, 220–22
Black Forest Tower, 192–93
  whipped toppings for, 14
BLT Comeback, Grilled, 166–67
BLUEBERRY(ies)
  Berry Vanilla Cheesecake, 220–22
  Coffee Cake, 196–97
  Muffins, 68–69
  Scones, 235–36
  Streusel Pie, 228–30
Brandy Alexander, 329

Brandy Chicken, 128–29
BREADS, 65–88
　Apple, 66
　Banana-Nut, 67–68
　Biscuits, Sweet, 70
　Blueberry Muffins, 68–69
　Corn, Quick, 78
　Egg Bread, Ultimate, 86
　French, with Roasted Garlic, 38–39
　French Connection, 81–82
　Glazed Cinnamon Rolls, 71–72
　Granna's Date-Nut, 73
　Herb-Garlic, 37–38
　Oatmeal Buttermilk, 77
　Potato Scones, 87–88
　Raisin Sticky Buns, 79–80
　Rye, Light, 74
　Wheat, 75–76
　White, Basic, 84–85
　White, Plain, 83
BREAKFAST recipes, 53–63
　Blueberry Scones, 235–36
　Dad's Famous Pancakes, 55–56
　Old Country French Toast, 58
　Scrambled Eggs, 60
　Updike Nut Roll, 254–55
　Waffles, 62–63
BROCCOLI
　Casserole, Swiss, 112–13
　Cheddar Casserole, 94
　Soufflé, 109–10
BROWNIES
　Caramel-Drizzled, 259–60
　The Express, 322–23
　Raspberry, 261–62
Brunch Baked Potato Skins, 54–55
BRUNCH recipes
　Baked Potato Skins, 54–55
　Blueberry Scones, 235–36
　Eggs in a Mushroom Cup, 61–62
　Omelet, Lactose-Free, 56–57
　Peach Cobbler, 246–47
　Poached Eggs, 59
Butter Cookie, 282–84
Buttermilk Dressing, Creamy, 352
BUTTERSCOTCH
　Cookies, 279–80
　Sauce, Old-Time, 341

C

Caesar Salad Dressing, 353
CAKES, 191–209
　Black Forest Tower, 192–93
　Blueberry Coffee Cake, 196–97
　Caramel Apple Pound Cake, 197–98
　Cherry Surprise, 199
　Cinnamon, 205–6
　Cinnamon Applesauce Coffee Cake,
　　200–201
　Creme-Filled Cupcakes, 201–3
　Lemon Cream, 203–4
　Pound, 207–8
　Strawberry Angel Cloud, 321
　Updike's Famous Fruitcake, 208–9
　White Layers Under Clouds of Icing,
　　193–95
CANDIES, 295–303
　Almond Bar, Lactose-Free, 298
　Caramels, 296
　Chocolate Lollipops, 302–3
　Chunky, The Lactose-Free, 299
　Fudge, Granna Hadley's Famous, 297
　Peanut Butter Cup Frenzy, 300–301
　Turtle Truffle Tart, 252–53
Cannoli, Lactose-Free, 244–45
CARAMEL
　Apple Pound Cake, 197–98
　-Drizzled Brownies, 259–60
Caramels, 296
Carrot Soufflé, 97–98
CASSEROLES, 159–69
　Baked Macaroni and Cheese, 161–62
　Broccoli Cheddar, 94
　Cheesy Egg, Baked, 160
　Swiss Broccoli, 112–13
Celery Soup, Creamy, 47–48
Champagne, Strawberry, 328–29
Cheddar Broccoli Casserole, 94
Cheddar Pasta Bake, 176–77
CHEESE
　Broccoli Cheddar Casserole, 94
　Cheddar Pasta Bake, 176–77
　Egg Casseroles, Baked, 160
　Fondue, Basic, 351
　Macaroni Casserole, Baked, 161–62
　Sauce, 350
　-Steak Sandwich, Ultimate, 168–69
　Stuffed Potatoes, 165–66

O

Oatmeal Buttermilk Bread, 77
Oatmeal Raisin Cookies, 273–74
Old Country French Toast, 58
Old-Time Butterscotch Sauce, 341
OMELETS
  Lactose-Free, 56–57
  Sweet Surprise, 234–35
ONION(s)
  Creamed, 96
  French-Fried Rings, 100–101
  Fry Pan, 114
  Soup, French, 51–52
ORANGE
  Buttercream Frosting, 344
  Cookies, 274–75
  Sherbert, Spiked, 313
  Sorbet, 311
  Squares, No-Bake, 271–72

P

ncakes, Dad's Famous, 55–56
rika Chicken, 140–41
RMESAN
Eggplant, 179–80
Eggplant Slices, 40
STA, 171–89
Baked Macaroni and Cheese Casserole,
  161–62
Cheddar Bake, 176–77
Creamy Asparagus, 177–78
ettuccine Alfredo, Lactose-Free, 180–81
usilli Chicken in Cream Sauce, 136–37
inguine with Garlic and Olive Oil
  184–85
ostaccioli with Basil Sauce, 185–86
g in a Haystack, 188–89
uffed Shells, 187–88
ti, Baked, 174–75
Cobbler, 246–47
Drink, 326
NUT BUTTER
ocolate Cups, Frozen, 319–20
p Frenzy (candy), 300–301
anna Hadley's Famous Fudge, 297
sion Cookies, 276
wheels, 277–79

PIE CRUST
  for Chicken Potpie, 138–39
  for Chocolate Raspberry Tart, 240–41
  Homemade, 224–25
  for Pizza, 172–73
PIES, 223–31
  Apple Crumb, 225–27
  Blueberry Streusel, 228–30
  Chocolate Raspberry Tart, 240–41
  French Apple, Award-Winning, 227–28
  Pumpkin, 230–31
Pig in a Haystack, 188–89
Pizza, Real, 172–74
Plain Coffee Cookie, 284–85
Plain White Bread, 83
Poached Eggs, 59
PORK, 143–46
  Barbecued Baby Back Ribs, 145–46
  Chops, Apple-Raisin, 144–45
Porterhouse Broiled Steaks, 120–21
POTATO(es)
  Gratin, Lactose-Free, 103–4
  Mashed and Whipped, All-American,
    90–91
  Scalloped French, 107–8
  Scones, 87–88
  Skins, Baked, 36–37
  Skins, Brunch Baked, 54–55
  Stuffed, 165
Poultry. See CHICKEN; TURKEY
Poultry Stuffing, 127–42
POUND CAKE, 207–8
  Caramel Apple, 197–98
Praline Cream, 345
PUDDINGS
  Quick Surprise, 317
  Rice, Homemade, 315
  Tapioca, Lactose-Free, 318
PUMPKIN
  Cheesecake, 216–17
  Pie, 230–31
  Pie Ice Cream, Lactose-Free, 307–8
  Whipped Cream, Lactose-Free, 346

Q

QUICHES
  Crab, Lactose-Free, 150–51
  Mushroom, Lactose-Free, 163–65
Quick Flounder au Gratin, 151–52

CHEESECAKES, 211–22
  Berry Vanilla, 220–22
  Hydrox Cookie, 212–13
  Lemon Cheesecake, The Ultimate, 218–19
  Lemon Swirl, 214–16
  Pumpkin, 216–17
Cheesesteak Sandwich, The Ultimate, 168–69
Cheesy Chicken Dinner, 128–29
Cherry Surprise, 199
CHERRY TOMATO(es)
  Sauté, 95
  Seasoned, 110–11
CHICKEN
  Brandied, 128–29
  Cheesy Dinner, 129–30
  Creamy Soup, 48–49
  with Fusilli, in Cream Sauce, 136–37
  Homemade Potpie, 138–39
  à la King, 131–32
  Lasagna, 132–34
  Paprika, 140–41
  -Veggie Stew, 134–36
Chilled Strawberry Soup, 46
CHOCOLATE
  Amaretto Sauce, 338
  Chip Cookies, 263
  Coffee Spritzer Cookie, 286–87
  cookie dough, for Peanut Butter Pinwheels,
    277–78
  Cookie Express, 288–89
  Dessert Crepes, 237–39
  -Dipped Fingers, 264–65
  Éclairs, 242–43
  Lemon à la Raspberry Parfait, Frozen,
    309–10
  Milk Shake, 332
  Mountains (cookies), 290–91
  Peanut Butter Cups, Frozen, 319–20
  Quick Pudding Surprise, 317
  Raspberry Tart, 240–41
  Sauce, Homemade, 337
  Turtle Truffle Tart, 252–53
  Velvet Glaze, 261–62
  See also CHOCOLATE CANDIES
CHOCOLATE CANDIES
  Almond Bar, Lactose-Free, 298
  Chunky, Lactose-Free, 299
  Fudge, Granna Hadley's Famous, 297
  Lollipops, 302–3
  Peanut Butter Cup Frenzy, 300–301

CINNAMON
  Applesauce Coffee Cake, 200–201
  Cake, 205–6
  Rolls, Glazed, 71–72
  Sugar Cookies, 266–67
COFFEE CAKES
  Blueberry, 196–97
  Cinnamon Applesauce, 200–201
Coffee Cookie, Plain, 284–85
Coffee Liqueur Chocolate Spritzer Cookie,
  286–87
Confection Sugar Glaze, 334
COOKIES, 257–93
  Almond, Special Occasion, 280–82
  Almond Spritzer, 258–59
  Butter, 282–84
  Butterscotch, 279–80
  Chocolate Chip, 263
  Chocolate Coffee Spritzer, 286–87
  Chocolate Express, 288–89
  Chocolate Mountains, 290–91
  Chocolate-Dipped Fingers, 264–65
  Cinnamon Sugar, 266–67
  Karen's Jam Crescents, 267–68
  Molasses Mountains, 268–69
  Mom's Icebox, 270–71
  Oatmeal Raisin, 273–74
  Orange, 274–75
  Peanut Butter Passion, 276
  Peanut Butter Pinwheels, 277–79
  Plain Coffee, 284–85
  Raspberry Linzer Heart, 291–93
Cool Peach Drink, 326
Corn Bread, Quick, 78
Crab Quiche, Lactose-Free, 150–51
Cream Cheese Frosting, Lactose-Free, 342
Cream Puff Extravaganza, 248–49
Creamed Dried Beef, 119
Creamed Onions, 96
Creamy Asparagus Pasta, 177–78
Creamy Buttermilk Dressing, 352
Creamy Celery Soup, 47–48
Creamy Chicken Soup, 48–49
Creamy Fudge Frosting, 342–43
Creamy Mushroom Soup, 49–50
Crème Fraîche Sauce, Lactose-Free, 340
Creme-Filled Cupcakes, 201–3
Crepes, Chocolate Dessert, 237–39
Cupcakes, Creme-Filled, 201–3

D

Dad's Famous Pancakes, 55–56
Date-Nut Bread, Granna's, 73
DESSERTS. *See also* CAKES; CHEESE-
    CAKES; CHOCOLATE; ICE CREAM;
    names of fruits
    Cannoli, Lactose-Free, 244–45
    Chocolate Crepes, 237–39
    Cream Puff Extravaganza, 248–49
    Éclairs, 242–43
    Frozen Chocolate Peanut Butter Cups,
        319–20
    Orange Sherbet, Spiked, 313
    Orange Sorbet, 311
    Orange Squares, No-Bake, 271–72
    Peach Cobbler, 246–47
    Pudding Surprise, Quick, 317
    Rice Pudding, Homemade, 315–16
    Sweet Omelet Surprise, 234–35
    Tapioca Pudding, Lactose-Free, 318
    Tiramisù, Lactose-Free, 250–51
    Turtle Truffle Tart, 252–53
    Updike Nut Roll, 254–55
    Waffles, 62–63
    Wine-ing Raspberry Sherbet, 314–15
Deviled Eggs, 99
DRESSINGS. *See* SALAD DRESSINGS
DRINKS
    Banana Milk Shake, 332
    Brandy Alexander, 329
    Chocolate Milk Shake, 332
    Eggnog, 326–27
    Float, The, 330–31
    Milk Shake, The Ultimate, 331–32
    Peach, 326
    Strawberry Champagne, Frozen, 328–29
    Strawberry Milk Shake, 332
    Strawberry Smoothie, 330

E

Easy Beef Stew, 121–22
Éclairs, 242–43
Eggnog, 326–27
EGGPLANT
    Parmesan, 179–80
    Parmesan Slices, 40

EGG(s)

    Baked Cheesy Casseroles, 160
    Bread, The Ultimate, 86
    Deviled, 99
    Eggnog, 326–27
    in a Mushroom Cup, 61–62
    Poached, 59
    Salad, 162–63
    Scrambled, 60

F

FETTUCINE
    Alfredo, 180–81
    Pig in Haystack, 188–89
FILLINGS
    Fresh Lemon Curd, Homemade, 338–39
    Vanilla Cream, 348
The Float, 330–31
Flounder au Gratin, Quick, 151–52
Fondue, Basic Cheese, 351
The French Connection, 81–82
French Onion Soup, 51–52
French Toast, Old Country, 58
French-Fried Onion Rings, 100–101
Fresh Strawberry Cream, 335
FROSTINGS
    Cream Cheese, Lactose-Free, 342
    Creamy Fudge, 342–43
    Fresh Strawberry Cream, 335
    Ginger Cream, 336
    Orange Buttercream, 344
    Praline Cream, 345
    Pumpkin Whipped Cream, Lactose-Free,
        346
Frozen Chocolate Peanut Butter Cups, 319–20
Frozen Lemon à la Parfait, 309–10
Frozen Strawberry Champagne, 328–29
Fruitcake, Updike's Famous, 208–9
Fry Pan Onions, 114
FUDGE
    Frosting, Creamy, 342–43
    Granna Hadley's Famous, 297
Fusilli Chicken in Cream Sauce, 136–37

G

GARLIC
    -Herb Bread, 37–38
    and Linguine with Olive Oil, 184–85
    Mushrooms, Sautéed, 106–7

    Roasted, on French Bread, 38–39
    Tomatoes, Baked, 91–92
Ginger Cream, 336
Glazed Cinnamon Rolls, 71–72
GLAZES
    Chocolate, 201–3
    Confection Sugar, 334
    Velvet Chocolate, 261–62
Granna Hadley's Famous Fudge, 297
Granna's Date-Nut Bread, 73
Green Bean Walnut Salad, 115–16
Green Pepper Cups, Stuffed, 123–24, 124
Grilled BLT Comeback, 166–67
Grilled Shrimp-Mushroom Kabobs, 148–49
Grilled Stuffed Mushrooms, 101–2

H

Herb-Garlic Bread, 37–38
Homemade Chicken Potpie, 138–39
Homemade Chocolate Sauce, 337
Homemade Fresh Lemon Curd, 338–39
Homemade Italian Sauce, 181–82
Homemade Pie Crust, 224–25
Homemade Rice Pudding, 315–16
Hydrox Cookie Cheesecake, 212–13

I

ICE CREAM, 305–23
    Frozen Lemon à la Raspberry Parfait,
        309–10
    Pumpkin Pie, Lactose-Free, 307–8
    Rich Vanilla Lactose-Free, 306–7
Icebox Cookies, Mom's, 270–71
ITALIAN DISHES, 171–89. *See also* PASTA
    Homemade Sauce, 181–82
    Meatballs, 183–84
    Real Pizza, 172–74

K

Karen's Jam Crescents, 267–68

L

Lactose-Free Almond Bar, 298
Lactose-Free Cannoli, 244–45
Lactose-Free Chunky (candy), 299

Lactose-Free Crab Quiche, 1
Lactose-Free Cream Cheese
Lactose-Free Crème Fraîche
Lactose-Free Fettuccine Alfr
Lactose-Free Mushroom Q
Lactose-Free Omelet, 56–5
Lactose-Free Potato Gratin
Lactose-Free Pumpkin Pie
Lactose-Free Pumpkin Wh
Lactose-Free Rich Vanilla
Lactose-Free Tapioca Pud
Lactose-Free Tiramisù, 25
Lasagna, Chicken, 132–3
LEMON(s)
    Cheesecake, The Ulti
    Cream Cake, 203–4
    Curd, Fresh Homem
    à la Raspberry Parfai
    Swirl Cheesecake, 2
Light Rye Bread, 74
Linguine with Garlic a
Lollipops, Chocolate,

Macaroni and Chees
    161–62
Meat Loaf, Savory,
Meatballs, Italian, 1
MILKSHAKES
    Banana, 332
    Chocolate, 332
    Strawberry, 332
    Ultimate, 331–
Molasses Mounta
Mom's Icebox Co
Mostaccioli with
Muffins, Blueber
MUSHROOM(
    Garlic, Sauté
    Grilled Stuff
    Quiche, Lac
    -Shrimp Ka
    Soup, Crea
    Stuffed, 42–

No-Bake Or

CHEESECAKES, 211–22
  Berry Vanilla, 220–22
  Hydrox Cookie, 212–13
  Lemon Cheesecake, The Ultimate, 218–19
  Lemon Swirl, 214–16
  Pumpkin, 216–17
Cheesesteak Sandwich, The Ultimate, 168–69
Cheesy Chicken Dinner, 128–29
Cherry Surprise, 199
CHERRY TOMATO(es)
  Sauté, 95
  Seasoned, 110–11
CHICKEN
  Brandied, 128–29
  Cheesy Dinner, 129–30
  Creamy Soup, 48–49
  with Fusilli, in Cream Sauce, 136–37
  Homemade Potpie, 138–39
  à la King, 131–32
  Lasagna, 132–34
  Paprika, 140–41
  -Veggie Stew, 134–36
Chilled Strawberry Soup, 46
CHOCOLATE
  Amaretto Sauce, 338
  Chip Cookies, 263
  Coffee Spritzer Cookie, 286–87
  cookie dough, for Peanut Butter Pinwheels,
    277–78
  Cookie Express, 288–89
  Dessert Crepes, 237–39
  -Dipped Fingers, 264–65
  Éclairs, 242–43
  Lemon à la Raspberry Parfait, Frozen,
    309–10
  Milk Shake, 332
  Mountains (cookies), 290–91
  Peanut Butter Cups, Frozen, 319–20
  Quick Pudding Surprise, 317
  Raspberry Tart, 240–41
  Sauce, Homemade, 337
  Turtle Truffle Tart, 252–53
  Velvet Glaze, 261–62
  See also CHOCOLATE CANDIES
CHOCOLATE CANDIES
  Almond Bar, Lactose-Free, 298
  Chunky, Lactose-Free, 299
  Fudge, Granna Hadley's Famous, 297
  Lollipops, 302–3
  Peanut Butter Cup Frenzy, 300–301

CINNAMON
  Applesauce Coffee Cake, 200–201
  Cake, 205–6
  Rolls, Glazed, 71–72
  Sugar Cookies, 266–67
COFFEE CAKES
  Blueberry, 196–97
  Cinnamon Applesauce, 200–201
Coffee Cookie, Plain, 284–85
Coffee Liqueur Chocolate Spritzer Cookie,
    286–87
Confection Sugar Glaze, 334
COOKIES, 257–93
  Almond, Special Occasion, 280–82
  Almond Spritzer, 258–59
  Butter, 282–84
  Butterscotch, 279–80
  Chocolate Chip, 263
  Chocolate Coffee Spritzer, 286–87
  Chocolate Express, 288–89
  Chocolate Mountains, 290–91
  Chocolate-Dipped Fingers, 264–65
  Cinnamon Sugar, 266–67
  Karen's Jam Crescents, 267–68
  Molasses Mountains, 268–69
  Mom's Icebox, 270–71
  Oatmeal Raisin, 273–74
  Orange, 274–75
  Peanut Butter Passion, 276
  Peanut Butter Pinwheels, 277–79
  Plain Coffee, 284–85
  Raspberry Linzer Heart, 291–93
Cool Peach Drink, 326
Corn Bread, Quick, 78
Crab Quiche, Lactose-Free, 150–51
Cream Cheese Frosting, Lactose-Free, 342
Cream Puff Extravaganza, 248–49
Creamed Dried Beef, 119
Creamed Onions, 96
Creamy Asparagus Pasta, 177–78
Creamy Buttermilk Dressing, 352
Creamy Celery Soup, 47–48
Creamy Chicken Soup, 48–49
Creamy Fudge Frosting, 342–43
Creamy Mushroom Soup, 49–50
Crème Fraîche Sauce, Lactose-Free, 340
Creme-Filled Cupcakes, 201–3
Crepes, Chocolate Dessert, 237–39
Cupcakes, Creme-Filled, 201–3

D

Dad's Famous Pancakes, 55–56
Date-Nut Bread, Granna's, 73
DESSERTS. *See also* CAKES; CHEESE-
    CAKES; CHOCOLATE; ICE CREAM;
    names of fruits
    Cannoli, Lactose-Free, 244–45
    Chocolate Crepes, 237–39
    Cream Puff Extravaganza, 248–49
    Éclairs, 242–43
    Frozen Chocolate Peanut Butter Cups,
        319–20
    Orange Sherbet, Spiked, 313
    Orange Sorbet, 311
    Orange Squares, No-Bake, 271–72
    Peach Cobbler, 246–47
    Pudding Surprise, Quick, 317
    Rice Pudding, Homemade, 315–16
    Sweet Omelet Surprise, 234–35
    Tapioca Pudding, Lactose-Free, 318
    Tiramisù, Lactose-Free, 250–51
    Turtle Truffle Tart, 252–53
    Updike Nut Roll, 254–55
    Waffles, 62–63
    Wine-ing Raspberry Sherbet, 314–15
Deviled Eggs, 99
DRESSINGS. *See* SALAD DRESSINGS
DRINKS
    Banana Milk Shake, 332
    Brandy Alexander, 329
    Chocolate Milk Shake, 332
    Eggnog, 326–27
    Float, The, 330–31
    Milk Shake, The Ultimate, 331–32
    Peach, 326
    Strawberry Champagne, Frozen, 328–29
    Strawberry Milk Shake, 332
    Strawberry Smoothie, 330

E

Easy Beef Stew, 121–22
Éclairs, 242–43
Eggnog, 326–27
EGGPLANT
    Parmesan, 179–80
    Parmesan Slices, 40

EGG(s)

EGG(s)
    Baked Cheesy Casseroles, 160
    Bread, The Ultimate, 86
    Deviled, 99
    Eggnog, 326–27
    in a Mushroom Cup, 61–62
    Poached, 59
    Salad, 162–63
    Scrambled, 60

F

FETTUCINE
    Alfredo, 180–81
    Pig in Haystack, 188–89
FILLINGS
    Fresh Lemon Curd, Homemade, 338–39
    Vanilla Cream, 348
The Float, 330–31
Flounder au Gratin, Quick, 151–52
Fondue, Basic Cheese, 351
The French Connection, 81–82
French Onion Soup, 51–52
French Toast, Old Country, 58
French-Fried Onion Rings, 100–101
Fresh Strawberry Cream, 335
FROSTINGS
    Cream Cheese, Lactose-Free, 342
    Creamy Fudge, 342–43
    Fresh Strawberry Cream, 335
    Ginger Cream, 336
    Orange Buttercream, 344
    Praline Cream, 345
    Pumpkin Whipped Cream, Lactose-Free,
        346
Frozen Chocolate Peanut Butter Cups, 319–20
Frozen Lemon à la Parfait, 309–10
Frozen Strawberry Champagne, 328–29
Fruitcake, Updike's Famous, 208–9
Fry Pan Onions, 114
FUDGE
    Frosting, Creamy, 342–43
    Granna Hadley's Famous, 297
Fusilli Chicken in Cream Sauce, 136–37

G

GARLIC
    -Herb Bread, 37–38
    and Linguine with Olive Oil, 184–85
    Mushrooms, Sautéed, 106–7

Roasted, on French Bread, 38–39
Tomatoes, Baked, 91–92
Ginger Cream, 336
Glazed Cinnamon Rolls, 71–72
GLAZES
Chocolate, 201–3
Confection Sugar, 334
Velvet Chocolate, 261–62
Granna Hadley's Famous Fudge, 297
Granna's Date-Nut Bread, 73
Green Bean Walnut Salad, 115–16
Green Pepper Cups, Stuffed, 123–24, 124
Grilled BLT Comeback, 166–67
Grilled Shrimp-Mushroom Kabobs, 148–49
Grilled Stuffed Mushrooms, 101–2

H

Herb-Garlic Bread, 37–38
Homemade Chicken Potpie, 138–39
Homemade Chocolate Sauce, 337
Homemade Fresh Lemon Curd, 338–39
Homemade Italian Sauce, 181–82
Homemade Pie Crust, 224–25
Homemade Rice Pudding, 315–16
Hydrox Cookie Cheesecake, 212–13

I

ICE CREAM, 305–23
Frozen Lemon à la Raspberry Parfait, 309–10
Pumpkin Pie, Lactose-Free, 307–8
Rich Vanilla Lactose-Free, 306–7
Icebox Cookies, Mom's, 270–71
ITALIAN DISHES, 171–89. See also PASTA
Homemade Sauce, 181–82
Meatballs, 183–84
Real Pizza, 172–74

K

Karen's Jam Crescents, 267–68

L

Lactose-Free Almond Bar, 298
Lactose-Free Cannoli, 244–45
Lactose-Free Chunky (candy), 299

Lactose-Free Crab Quiche, 150–51
Lactose-Free Cream Cheese Frosting, 342
Lactose-Free Crème Fraîche Sauce, 340
Lactose-Free Fettuccine Alfredo, 180–81
Lactose-Free Mushroom Quiche, 163–65
Lactose-Free Omelet, 56–57
Lactose-Free Potato Gratin, 103–4
Lactose-Free Pumpkin Pie Ice Cream, 307–8
Lactose-Free Pumpkin Whipped Cream, 346
Lactose-Free Rich Vanilla Ice Cream, 306–7
Lactose-Free Tapioca Pudding, 318
Lactose-Free Tiramisù, 250–51
Lasagna, Chicken, 132–34
LEMON(s)
Cheesecake, The Ultimate, 218–19
Cream Cake, 203–4
Curd, Fresh Homemade, 338–39
à la Raspberry Parfait, Frozen, 309–10
Swirl Cheesecake, 214–16
Light Rye Bread, 74
Linguine with Garlic and Olive Oil, 184–85
Lollipops, Chocolate, 302–3

M

Macaroni and Cheese Casserole, Baked, 161–62
Meat Loaf, Savory, 122–23
Meatballs, Italian, 183–84
MILKSHAKES
Banana, 332
Chocolate, 332
Strawberry, 332
Ultimate, 331–32
Molasses Mountains, 268–69
Mom's Icebox Cookies, 270–71
Mostaccioli with Basil Sauce, 185–86
Muffins, Blueberry, 68–69
MUSHROOM(s)
Garlic, Sautéed, 106–7
Grilled Stuffed, 101–2
Quiche, Lactose-Free, 163–65
-Shrimp Kabobs, Grilled, 148–49
Soup, Creamy, 49–50
Stuffed, 42–43

N

No-Bake Orange Squares, 271–72

O

Oatmeal Buttermilk Bread, 77
Oatmeal Raisin Cookies, 273–74
Old Country French Toast, 58
Old-Time Butterscotch Sauce, 341
OMELETS
    Lactose-Free, 56–57
    Sweet Surprise, 234–35
ONION(s)
    Creamed, 96
    French-Fried Rings, 100–101
    Fry Pan, 114
    Soup, French, 51–52
ORANGE
    Buttercream Frosting, 344
    Cookies, 274–75
    Sherbert, Spiked, 313
    Sorbet, 311
    Squares, No-Bake, 271–72

P

Pancakes, Dad's Famous, 55–56
Paprika Chicken, 140–41
PARMESAN
    Eggplant, 179–80
    Eggplant Slices, 40
PASTA, 171–89
    Baked Macaroni and Cheese Casserole,
        161–62
    Cheddar Bake, 176–77
    Creamy Asparagus, 177–78
    Fettuccine Alfredo, Lactose-Free, 180–81
    Fusilli Chicken in Cream Sauce, 136–37
    Linguine with Garlic and Olive Oil
        184–85
    Mostaccioli with Basil Sauce, 185–86
    Pig in a Haystack, 188–89
    Stuffed Shells, 187–88
    Ziti, Baked, 174–75
Peach Cobbler, 246–47
Peach Drink, 326
PEANUT BUTTER
    Chocolate Cups, Frozen, 319–20
    Cup Frenzy (candy), 300–301
    Granna Hadley's Famous Fudge, 297
    Passion Cookies, 276
    Pinwheels, 277–79

PIE CRUST
    for Chicken Potpie, 138–39
    for Chocolate Raspberry Tart, 240–41
    Homemade, 224–25
    for Pizza, 172–73
PIES, 223–31
    Apple Crumb, 225–27
    Blueberry Streusel, 228–30
    Chocolate Raspberry Tart, 240–41
    French Apple, Award-Winning, 227–28
    Pumpkin, 230–31
Pig in a Haystack, 188–89
Pizza, Real, 172–74
Plain Coffee Cookie, 284–85
Plain White Bread, 83
Poached Eggs, 59
PORK, 143–46
    Barbecued Baby Back Ribs, 145–46
    Chops, Apple-Raisin, 144–45
Porterhouse Broiled Steaks, 120–21
POTATO(es)
    Gratin, Lactose-Free, 103–4
    Mashed and Whipped, All-American,
        90–91
    Scalloped French, 107–8
    Scones, 87–88
    Skins, Baked, 36–37
    Skins, Brunch Baked, 54–55
    Stuffed, 165
Poultry. See CHICKEN; TURKEY
Poultry Stuffing, 127–42
POUND CAKE, 207–8
    Caramel Apple, 197–98
Praline Cream, 345
PUDDINGS
    Quick Surprise, 317
    Rice, Homemade, 315
    Tapioca, Lactose-Free, 318
PUMPKIN
    Cheesecake, 216–17
    Pie, 230–31
    Pie Ice Cream, Lactose-Free, 307–8
    Whipped Cream, Lactose-Free, 346

Q

QUICHES
    Crab, Lactose-Free, 150–51
    Mushroom, Lactose-Free, 163–65
Quick Flounder au Gratin, 151–52

Quick Pudding Surprise, 317
Quick-Bake Veggies, 104–5

R

RAISIN
  Oatmeal Cookies 273–74
  Sticky Buns, 79–83
RASPBERRY(ies)
  Berry Vanilla Cheesecake, 220–22
  Brownies, 261–62
  Chocolate Tart, 240–41
  with Frozen Lemon Parfait, 309–10
  Linzer Heart (cookies), 291–93
  Sorbet, 312
  Wine-ing Sherbet, 314–15
Real Pizza, A, 172–74
Ribs, Barbecued Baby Back, 145–46
Rice Pudding, Homemade, 315–16
Rich Vanilla Lactose-Free Ice Cream, 306–7
Roasted Garlic on French Bread, 38–39
ROLL(s)
  Cinnamon, Glazed, 71–72
  Turkey, Stuffed, 141–42
  Updike Nut, 254–55
Rum Cream, Whipped, 349
Rum Sauce, 347
Rye Bread, Light, 74

S

SALAD DRESSINGS
  Caesar, 353
  Creamy Buttermilk, 352
SALADS
  Egg, 162–63
  Walnut Green Bean, 115–16
SANDWICHES
  BLT Comeback, Grilled, 166–67
  Ultimate Cheesesteak, 168–69
SAUCES
  Basil, with Mostaccioli, 186
  Butterscotch, Old-Time, 341
  Cheese, 350
  Chocolate, Homemade, 337
  Chocolate Amaretto, 338
  Crème Fraîche, Lactose-Free, 340
  Italian, Homemade, 181–82
  Rum, 347

Vanilla, for Chocolate Dessert Crepes, 237–38
  White, 354
Sautéed Garlic Mushrooms, 106–7
Sautéed Scallops, 152–53
Savory Meat Loaf, 122–23
Scalloped French Potatoes, 107–8
SCALLOP(s)
  Bundles, 154–55
  Sautéed, 152–53
SCONES
  Blueberry, 235–36
  Potato, 87–88
Scrambled Eggs, 60
SEAFOOD, 147–57
  Crab Quiche, Lactose-Free, 150–51
  Flounder au Gratin, Quick, 151–52
  See also SCALLOP(s); SHRIMP
Seasoned Cherry Tomatoes, 110–11
SHRIMP
  Marinara, 156–57
  -Mushroom Kabobs, Grilled, 148–49
SIDE DISHES, 89–116. See EGGS(s); names
  of vegetables; SALADS; VEGETABLES
Simply Butterscotch Cookies, 279–80
SORBETS
  Orange, 311
  Raspberry, 312
SOUFFLÉS
  Broccoli, 109–10
  Carrot, 97–98
SOUPS, 45–52
  Creamy Celery, 47–48
  Creamy Chicken, 48–49
  Creamy Mushroom, 49–50
  French Onion, 51–52
  Strawberry, Chilled, 46
Spiked Orange Sherbet, 313
Spinach Triangles, 41–42
STEAK(s)
  Cheese Sandwich, 168–69
  Porterhouse, Broiled, 120–21
STEWS
  Beef, Easy, 121–22
  Chicken-Veggie, 134–36
STRAWBERRY(ies)
  Angel Cloud (shortcake), 321
  Champagne, Frozen, 328–29
  Cream, Fresh, 335
  Cream Puff Extravaganza, 248–49

(*STRAWBERRY[ies]* continued)
Milk Shake, 332
Smoothie, 330
Soup, Chilled, 46
Stuffed Mushrooms, 42–43, 101–2
Stuffed Pasta Shells, 187–88
Stuffed Pepper Cups, 123–24
Stuffed Potatoes, 165–66
Stuffed Turkey Rolls, 141–42
Stuffing, for Poultry, 111–12
Sweet Biscuits, 70
Sweet Omelet Surprise, 234–35
Swiss Broccoli Casserole, 112–13

T

Tapioca Pudding, Lactose-Free, 318
Tiramisù, Lactose-Free, 250–51
TOMATO(es)
BLT Comeback, Grilled, 166–67
Garlic, Baked, 91–92
-Zucchini Dish, Baked, 92–93
See also CHERRY TOMATO(es)
TOPPINGS
Ginger Cream, 336
Strawberry Cream, Fresh, 335
Whipped Rum Cream, 349
TURKEY
Stuffed Pepper Cups, 123–24
Stuffed Rolls, 141–42
Turtle Truffle Tart, 252–53

U

Ultimate Cheesesteak Sandwich, 168–69
Ultimate Egg Bread, 86

Ultimate Lemon Cheesecake, The, 218–19
Ultimate Milk shake, The, 331–32
Updike Nut Roll, 254–55
Updike's Famous Fruitcake, 208–9

V

Vanilla Cream Filling, 348
Vanilla Ice Cream, Lactose-Free, 306–7
Veal Parmigiana, 125–26
VEGETABLES
Cheddar Pasta Bake, 176–77
-Chicken Stew, 134–36
Quick-Bake, 104–5
See also names of vegetables

W

Waffles, 62–63
WALNUT(s)
Chocolate Mountains (cookies), 290–91
and Green Bean Salad, 115–16
Updike Nut Roll, 254–55
Wheat Bread, 75–76
Whipped Rum Cream, 349
White Bread, Basic, 84–85
White Bread, Plain, 83
White Layers Under Clouds of Icing, 193–95
White Sauce, 354
Wine-ing Raspberry Sherbet, 314–15

Z

Ziti, Baked, 174–75
Zucchini-Tomato Dish, Baked, 92–93

About the Author

A New Yorker at heart, life has taken Sheri Updike to the shores of Malibu, California, where she spends her days with her husband of twenty-eight years, Harold "Zip" Updike, and her two grown children, Chrissy, a gifted artist and aspiring actress, and David, a Santa Monica Mountains park ranger. Her passion is cooking every chance she gets. She is always playing in her kitchen and has a wall decorated with ribbons from local baking contests. She also has a huge fan club of taste-testers.

Sheri grew up with very artistic parents, Eileen Duffy and Hugh Rawdon, who encouraged her to express her creative ability in many forms. Today, she focuses that creativity on her passion for cooking and baking lactose free. When Sheri's husband discovered he was severely Lactose Intolerant in 1986, she started experimenting with substitutions for dairy products containing lactose. The frustration she encountered when trying to find help with amending standard recipes led her to start collecting her own recipes. Over the years she met many other frustrated Lactose-Intolerant people who wanted to enjoy "real food" without feeling restricted. The lack of available materials, such as a special cookbook designed specifically for the Lactose Intolerant, prompted her to want to share her perfected recipes with everyone. This cookbook is the result.